Seiðr
Magic

Seiðr
Magic

THE NORSE TRADITION OF DIVINATION AND TRANCE

Dean Kirkland, Ph.D.

Destiny Books
Rochester, Vermont

Destiny Books
One Park Street
Rochester, Vermont 05767
www.DestinyBooks.com

Destiny Books is a division of Inner Traditions International

Cataloging-in-Publication Data for this title is available from the Library of Congress

ISBN 978-1-64411-944-0 (print)
ISBN 978-1-64411-945-7 (ebook)

Printed and bound in the United States by Lake Book Manufacturing, LLC

10 9 8 7 6 5 4 3 2 1

Text design and layout by Debbie Glogover
This book was typeset in Garamond Premier Pro with Gill Sans MT Pro,
Mrs Eaves and Swear Display used as display typefaces

To send correspondence to the author of this book, mail a first-class letter to the
author c/o Inner Traditions • Bear & Company, One Park Street, Rochester, VT
05767, and we will forward the communication.

Scan the QR code and save 25% at InnerTraditions.com.
Browse over 2,000 titles on spirituality, the occult, ancient
mysteries, new science, holistic health, and natural medicine.

❦

I would like to dedicate this work to the old man, Grímnir—the original student of seiðr who inspires the quest for knowledge and wisdom at any cost.

❦

Contents

Acknowledgments

I would like thank Dr. Neil Price, whose work has provided confirmation that there is sufficient archaeological evidence from Scandinavia for us to begin piecing together and reconstructing the practice of seiðr as described in historical and literary sources.

As always, I am grateful for the forbearance of all my teachers—but especially Simon Buxton and Jörgen Eriksson, who opened my eyes first to the practice of shamanism and then to the possibility that my ancestors may have had their own Indigenous shamanic modalities. My eternal affection goes out to the Clan of the Alder Moon for steady support when things got dark, so that I might bring these findings back to the light.

Thanks to my wife and long-suffering children, who understood the call to produce this work and kept me going. I am also grateful to Destiny Books for taking a chance on a new author.

Foreign Terms
and Pronunciation

This book contains many specialized terms from the medieval Old Norse language, most of which (including divine names such as Óðinn, Freyja, etc.) have been kept in their original form. In some cases, anglicized forms have been used, such as for the cosmological place-names of Midgard (Miðgarðr) and Asgard (Ásgarðr).

SIMPLIFIED PRONUNCIATION GUIDE
FOR OLD NORSE

The guide below is not meant to be definitive but should help the reader to approximate a basic pronunciation of the Old Norse terms found in this book.

Consonants

b, *d*, *f*, *h*, *k*, *l*, *m*, *n*, *s*, *t*, and *v* are generally pronounced as in modern English.

g   always hard as in *get*

j   as English *y* in *yes*

p   as in English *pin*, except when preceding *t*, then pronounced as *ft*

r   trilled *r*

þ   as *th* in *thing*
ð   as *th* in *rather*

Vowels and Diphthongs

a   as in *art*
á   as in *father*
e   as in *bet*
é   as *a* in *date*
i   as in *it*
í   as *ee* in *seed*
o   as in *ore*
ó   as *oa* in *boat*
ø   as *e* in *bet* with rounded lips
ö   as in *not*
u   as *oo* in *book*
ú   as *oo* in *boon*
y   *ee* with rounded lips
ý   *ee* with rounded lips, but longer
æ   as *ai* in *air*
œ   as *u* in *urn*
au   as *ou* in *oust*
ei   as *ay* in *say*
ey   diphthong of Old Norse *e* + *y*

An Introduction to Seiðr

The historical development of seiðr (pron. SAY-ther), a shamanic modality attested from medieval Scandinavia, is closely tied to an ancient northern European pagan religion (or set of related localized religions) that we refer to as *Germanic heathenry.** Heathenry is a modern name for these beliefs and customs, because when they were originally being practiced, people felt no need to give them a name—it was just what they *did*. To understand seiðr, which is the subject of this book, it is important to have at least a basic understanding of heathenry.

Heathenry, or heathenism, is the modern practice of following the old pantheon of pagan gods that were historically worshipped throughout much of northern Europe, including England and Scandinavia, before these cultures converted to Christianity.† All of the Germanic peoples seem to have shared a core group of primary deities, for example, the high god called Odin (Old Norse Óðinn) by the Scandinavians

---

*A note on the term *Germanic*: When we speak about the Germanic gods, Germanic peoples, and/or about ancient Germanic religion and culture, we are *not* referring to a modern national group, the German people. Instead, we are talking about a broader and older *linguistic* classification, referring to those who spoke the various Germanic dialects. Germanic is, in turn, a distinct branch of the Indo-European language family, which also includes Italic, Celtic, Balto-Slavic, the Indo-Iranian languages of Sanskrit and Avestan, and many others.

†Other terms that are sometimes used to refer to modern heathenry include *Ásatrú* ("faith in the Æsir") and *troth* (likewise referring to "trust or faith in the old gods"). In recent decades a plethora of more regionally focused or historically specific branches of heathenry have also sprung up, often with their own self-designations.

1

has a counterpart in the Anglo-Saxon Woden (Old English), the continental Wodan (Old Saxon) or Wuotan (Old High German), and so forth. While these divine names share a common root, their divergent forms are also reflective of the fact that ancient Germanic religion was never codified or uniform in expression. Religious practices varied from tribe to tribe and place to place, and certain local gods might be worshipped in one area but not another. Nevertheless, common patterns can be seen and thus we employ *heathenry* as a broad term that encompasses a wide range of practices and beliefs.

Iceland is of special importance for both the history of heathenry and its modern revival. The first migrants from Norway arrived on the island in the latter half of the ninth century, having fled from oppression or simply to seek their own land. These original settlers were pagans. Christianity would not be adopted in Iceland until the year 1000, in a relatively peaceful and tolerant manner. Alongside the new faith, the old pagan practices could still be conducted privately, at least for an initial period, though they were eventually outlawed once the Church gained full control.

In contrast to the situation in much of mainland Europe at the time, the medieval Icelanders were able to cultivate a high rate of literacy and develop a robust vernacular literary tradition of both poetry and prose. This is most famously preserved in the eddas and sagas, which vividly recount the cosmology and mythology of the heathen gods and the lives of human figures both historical and legendary. Popular literature of this sort, which also often refers to heathen religious practices, seems to have been less suppressed by the Christian Church in Iceland than it was in other countries and therefore offers an invaluable window into pre-Christian beliefs.

Early medieval literature, and particularly what was preserved in Iceland, has been a vital resource for the revival of heathenry in modern times. In heathen circles today, the greater corpus of Old Icelandic literary material, together with a small amount of related but often fragmentary texts from continental northern Europe and Anglo-Saxon England, has come to be known as the "heathen lore," or simply "the lore." Unlike the Abrahamic religions, heathenry has no single holy book or sacred scripture. Heathenry has no orthodox dogma nor any ten commandments like the Bible. Instead, our myths and practices are referred to in several different ancient sources, and it is up to each practicing heathen to interpret those sources—the lore—in his or her own way. There is no orthopraxy or dogma within heathenry, no concept of heresy, no right or wrong way of interpreting the literature.

It is beyond the scope of the present work to present a full description of contemporary heathen practice. If you are not already a heathen and feel that this path may be for you, there are various introductory books you might explore, although the quality of these works can be very inconsistent. What will quickly become apparent to you as a budding heathen, though, is that your most important resource is the lore itself—the original sources such as the *Poetic Edda,* the *Prose Edda,* and the many Icelandic sagas.*

So, what is *seiðr*? This is not necessarily a straightforward question to answer, and some controversy surrounds it. In most books you will see seiðr described as ancient Norse or Germanic witchcraft. While it is quite clear from the surviving literature that it was indeed some form of Germanic esoteric practice, "witchcraft" is probably not the right term. Some of this confusion has likely arisen from questionable nineteenth- and early twentieth-century translations of the word when it appears in medieval Old Norse literature.

A seiðr-worker (practitioner), particularly a female seiðr-worker, was referred to by various names: *völva, spákona, seiðkona,* and *myrkriða* among them. All of these names have different connotations, and as some people specialized in prophecy, second sight, healing, or even

---

*Several translated editions of the Eddic material can be found in the bibliography. An excellent introduction to the saga genre is the Penguin Classics anthology *The Sagas of Icelanders,* edited by Jane Smiley (2005).

battle magic, the particular name probably gave a clue as to the magical speciality of the person involved. Such subtleties were glossed over when the Icelandic sagas first began to be translated into English at the end of the nineteenth century. To avoid having to explain the subtleties of early Norse occultism to a largely conservative Victorian Christian audience, it was easier for the translator to simply render *all* these terms with the only widely recognized English term for a magic worker of the female persuasion: witch.

It is very unlikely that seiðr resembled anything we would recognize today as witchcraft. For example—and despite the many claims of many modern "Norse witches"—none of the following were historically part of the practice of seiðr: tarot cards; casting spells; casting circles; or calling to the four quarters, directions, or the elements. Some of these Norse witches might come back with the argument: *Well, how do you know? The literature isn't clear, there isn't a lot of it, and what it says is often vague—so can't we use any practice at all and call it seiðr, because nobody can prove otherwise?*

It is true that even the prominent accounts regarding seiðr in Old Norse literature *are* often vague. However, there are over sixty surviving references to seiðr in the sagas, and some of the more obscure passages contain very interesting details. But perhaps even more compelling is the archaeological record, which contrary to popular belief is quite extensive, although it is not (yet) well known. There is sufficient evidence for us to begin reconstructing seiðr from historical records, but these new interpretations of the surviving literature alongside the relevant archaeological evidence provide no support for claims that popular techniques of modern witchcraft have anything in common with traditional seiðr practices.

In fact, the interpretation of the literary and material sources points in a surprising direction. Although we still lack any final or definitive proof, there is compelling evidence to suggest that seiðr was a type of *shamanism*. This in itself would indicate that it had an entirely different basis and praxis from any sort of modern witchcraft.

In New Age circles today, "shamanism" is the flavor of the month. There is an unfortunate tendency to lump all sorts of things under the shamanic umbrella—from books to oracle cards, cheap pagan ornaments, crystals, and even plastic "fairy doors"—none of which have any real connection to shamanism. This leads to confusion in many people's minds about what shamanism is. It also adds fuel to the fire for the "Norse witches" who want to call their favorite practices "seiðr" simply because they are good at them, but not because they have any historical authenticity.

Although shamanism is still poorly understood by most people coming from a Western culture, there are some very clear definitions that have been developed by cultural anthropologists concerning what shamanism is and—perhaps as importantly—what it is not. Shamanism revolves around the practitioner using a state of ecstatic trance to enter a shamanic *non-ordinary reality* (NOR) in which the vast majority of the work will take place. This requires a completely different mindset to the traditional witch, because in witchcraft the practitioner remains in the "middle world," in *ordinary* or *consensual reality* (OR), and the vast majority of techniques designed to work in OR simply do not work in the same way in NOR. In certain circumstances, it can even be dangerous to use techniques designed for OR in NOR.

A careful reading of Mircea Eliade's classic work *Shamanism: Archaic Techniques of Ecstasy* (1964) will reveal that there are seven functions that can be seen as having developed as part of the historical practice of shamanism:

1. Finding food and other resources
2. Divination
3. Healing
4. Harming and battle magic

5. Dealing with the surrounding environment/nature and the spirits of nature
6. Dealing with the ancestors and the dead
7. Dealing with the gods

Over the course of the present book, we will see how seiðr can be associated with nearly all of these functions.

In taking the approach that seiðr is much closer to classical shamanism than witchcraft, it is important to acknowledge that we are not being strict "reconstructionists" who would claim that we can replicate exactly how seiðr was practiced in ancient Norse culture. We need to have some flexibility to weave wider shamanic knowledge into our attempts to re-create these practices. This is because the literature is vague in many cases and does not provide exact instructions as to how things were done. And while some additional hints may be gleaned from the archaeological record, these are often misunderstood by academic cultural specialists who have no background in shamanic theory.

For example, as we will see in chapter 3, there is a certain structural feature on many seiðr-staffs (*seiðstafir*, sg. *seiðstafr*) found in the archaeological record that has puzzled archaeologists as to its function. They admit that it probably does have a function, otherwise why does it appear on so many different staffs? Spirit workers are often inherently conservative and generally don't include things on their tools without a reason—everything usually has a purpose above and beyond mere decoration. But there are no known parallels to this feature in any surviving European culture.

However, the Chukchi, a Siberian people who until recently had an unbroken shamanic tradition, also use a lot of staff work in their practices. They are known to have a remarkably similar feature on their shamanic staffs that is used in a very particular way for divination. But scholars as well as modern heathens tend to dismiss this similarity out of hand because the Chukchi are a completely distinct culture from the

Norse, located at the other side of the world, and historically the two groups could not possibly have had any contact. A cross-cultural knowledge of shamanism will also reveal that there are many similarities between the magical chants (*varðlokur*, sg. *varðloka*) of the Norse völva and the *icaros* or sacred songs taught by spirits to modern Indigenous Amazonian shamans and curanderos.

Could three different cultures so separated by time and space possibly influence each other? The answer is clearly no, they couldn't have *directly* influenced each other. But we know that shamanism is an extremely ancient practice, and some people would go so far as to claim it is the precursor of all religion. While there isn't sufficient evidence to fully support that particular statement, it is true that the earliest artifacts linked to shamanic practice are at least 40,000 years old and distinctly paleolithic. If a "single origin of man" theory is correct, then it seems likely that knowledge of shamanic techniques and practices would have accompanied various groups of humans as they dispersed from a single place. Initially, these practices would have been very similar, but soon they would have begun to vary as the groups spread out and developed into distinct cultures. Such variations would not have occurred in a uniform way—they would have affected different parts of the knowledge at different times, so that some cultures might still remember and use an older version of techniques of healing with a staff, for example, while others might focus on healing songs to attract the spirits. (And some might continue to do both.) The result is the situation we find today, with four or five distinct cultures in very different parts of the world utilizing a particular shamanic technique that is essentially quite similar, while the rest of their respective shamanic traditions may vary widely.

Norse seiðr is culturally unique, which means that no single external culture, even a neighboring one,* can serve as a complete and

---

*A case in point would be the Sámi, a neighboring culture to the Norse that may be the closest geographically, but whose shamanic modality is spiritually one of the furthest removed from what we know about how seiðr was practiced.

wholistic model upon which we might base the full reconstruction of seiðr practices. However, we might be able incorporate elements from several different cultures—elements that represent the closest fit even if this is solely due to historical accident. And although these elements may not precisely match what was historically done in seiðr, with a little "cultural tweaking" they can help us to forge viable and more complete methods of seiðr practice in the modern world.

The fact that seiðr is a Norse form of shamanism does not mean that it can be re-created by simply taking what is now known as "core shamanism" as a model and dressing it up in Old Norse terms. The techniques of core shamanism were initially taught by Michael Harner (notably in his book *The Way of the Shaman*) and further developed by his students and followers specifically to appeal to a modern Western audience. Historical seiðr, however, is a variation of tribal or cultural shamanism, often raw and perhaps sometimes even unpalatable to our modern Western sensibilities. As such, it is a far cry from the sanitized, safe techniques presented as core shamanism.

In the reconstruction of seiðr, then, we must walk a very thin tight-rope and finding the balancing point is not easy. As a form of tribal shamanism, seiðr bears no relation to modern witchcraft, but in trying to make it a living tradition once more we are hardly following strict reconstructionist principles. A reconstructional purist would argue that any details that are unattested in the extant Norse literature should not be included as part of the practice. But if we held to this line, we could not even attempt the reconstruction of seiðr, because although the literature clearly says that our ancestors used seiðr to achieve certain effects, it is very light on the details of how they did this and which specific techniques were used. However, by looking at the archaeological evidence—the tools that seiðr-workers left behind—and the similarities between the Norse artifacts and the tools still used in other shamanic cultures today, and considering how Indigenous shamans use those tools, we begin to get an idea of how seiðr may have been done.

Last but not least, I should mention a source of experiential information that is very important to shamans and practitioners in all cultures around the world: *unverified personal gnosis* (UPG). This type of knowledge is not recognized or understood by the majority of reconstructionists, who prefer to follow strict rules that simply cannot accommodate the concept of UPG. In my view, however, if the practice of seiðr is to have relevance to our lives today, it must be a living, growing practice with its roots in the past but flexible enough to incorporate changes inspired by UPG *where appropriate*. What I present in this book will therefore contain some aspects of my own UPG, and I will endeavor to point these out to the reader whenever possible. And I am perfectly happy if those of you who come after me take this forward and incorporate your own UPG—as long as those insights arise in the spirit of the heathen lore, rather than perhaps in strict accordance with it—so that the practices change and evolve to remain relevant to whatever time they find themselves in.

1

Seiðr Practice
Historically and Today

SEIÐR IN THE GENERAL HEATHEN COMMUNITY

Historically, seiðr was never a core element of heathenry, nor was it practiced as an aspect of the general worship of the gods, led by a priest or ritual specialist called a *goði*,* in which most heathens would have taken part. Instead, seiðr would have been considered a form of magic. All types of Germanic "magic" were viewed with some suspicion by the general populace, but this did not stop people from making use of magic when they considered it necessary. Each community would have a few known magical specialists, runemasters, and spirit workers who mediated with the unseen on everyone else's behalf. However, it is clear from the saga literature that these specialists themselves weren't exactly trusted in Germanic societies—they would have been forced to live at the edge of the village or community, or even out in the forest slightly removed from everyone else. This relative isolation also had some advantages, as it provided the quietude and stillness away from a busy village center that are often required for esoteric work. The spirit worker may have been closer to sources of

---

*In pre-Christian Norse society, the *goði* (pl. *goðar*; the equivalent female figure was the *gyðja*, pl. *gyðjur*) ran the temples and large public ceremonies and taught the people how to have a relationship with the gods. Unlike a Christian priest, the goði/gyðja could not mediate or interfere with that relationship, which existed solely between the individual person and a particular god or gods.

certain herbs and plants needed in their healing practices, and for the clients who visited the specialist, the remote location may have provided a certain level of discretion and confidentiality in seeking answers to perhaps some of their most intimate problems without the rest of the village knowing about it. Privately, people would probably be grateful for a healing or other such services that they received, but the spirit worker would be largely ignored in public as a necessary but uncomfortable—perhaps even embarrassing—presence.

This ambivalence regarding the use of magic is important to understand as it has affected how seiðr was practiced both historically and in the present day. For a start, it means that in heathenry it is relatively uncommon for people to become directly involved with magic. This is quite a different a situation from other modern neo-pagan paths such as Wicca, where everybody is expected to take part in magic to one degree or another, and the main rites such as esbats and sabbats are themselves essentially considered "magical." The two primary heathen rites, the *blót* and the *sumbl*,* are considered more spiritual or religious than magical in nature, and most average heathens will have little to do with magical practices. There may be other reasons for this as well. In heathenry the belief seems to exist that only a few people—those chosen for special attention by the gods—are capable of practicing magic. Magical ability is therefore seen as both a blessing and a curse, and the average heathen would prefer not to be the recipient of this level of attention from the sometimes harsh Germanic gods, even going so far as to avoid it wherever possible.

There also appears to be some sort of genetic component that influences the ability to be a spirit worker. In the sagas, for example, there are several descriptions of magical abilities being passed down along family lines. Unlike so many people in the recent past, however, we

---

*The main ceremony in heathenism for making an offering to the gods is known as a *blót*. The word is related to the Old Norse verb *blóta*, "to sacrifice, worship," as well as to the word for "blood," *blóð*. The *sumbl* ("feast") is a community-building ceremony that consists of a ritualized drinking circle in which the participants make toasts, boasts, and oaths.

should avoid the mistake of confusing genetic and racial factors, as this has nothing to do with ethnicity or racial background.*

It is evident from the medieval saga literature that there was a certain mistrust of the magical specialists who performed seiðr, and this seems to influence present-day attitudes. As a modern seiðr-worker, therefore, you should not assume that you will always be welcomed with open arms. You may well encounter some animosity and mistrust in the heathen community—until they need your help, of course.

Some modern heathens veil their mistrust toward seiðr with cynicism. For example, they may deny that seiðr was really a "thing" at all, or claim that Germanic magical specialists did not exist and the stories about them were nothing more than a load of fairy tales to frighten children. Such claims are easily dismissed. Besides the fact that seiðr and seiðr-workers are mentioned numerous times throughout the lore, archaeologists have now identified the graves of a number of seiðr-workers. They clearly existed just as the sagas describe.

It should be kept in mind that seiðr-workers are no better or worse than those in the heathen community who choose not to involve themselves with magic; they are simply different. The gods always required some people to be warriors, some to be farmers, some to be craftsmen, and a few to be spirit workers. But given the lingering attitudes of distrust toward magic and seiðr, I would recommend that you be somewhat circumspect when discussing your interest in the esoteric arts, as you could potentially garner some hostility from the wider heathen community—even though we dedicate our work to that community, and it is supposed to provide us with support!

It also needs to be said that Germanic magic, and seiðr in particular, is not for everyone. In ancient times, only a certain proportion of people were thought to be capable of using magic. But it also takes a

---

*Interestingly, there is considerable evidence that the ancient Norse recognized the ability of *other* races to perform magic. Certain Finns (Sámi), for example, were seen as magical workers par excellence.

combination of raw ability, talent, and training to master the necessary skills to perform seiðr successfully.

I reiterate that magical ability does not appear to have any basis in race, and we should not exclude people based on their ethnicity. There are times, however, when we must exclude people from the practice to ensure their own safety and that of others. If I am accused of gatekeeping for saying this, so be it. The lore makes it clear that seiðr is dangerous. Seiðr-workers often deal with very powerful and sometimes even hostile (though not "evil") wights or spirits.* Even for experienced practitioners, things can go wrong. I have known practitioners who have died in the course of their work, or even worse—yes, there are some things in the spirit worlds that could be considered worse than death. Imagine what could go wrong in the hands of those who can have absolutely no influence and no control over the powers with which they are working. Inept practitioners are not only a danger to themselves, but to everyone around them.

There is a school of thought that says perhaps we should encourage anyone who has an interest in seiðr to pursue it regardless of ability, as the process should be self-selecting. In other words, those who lack the necessary ability will soon be weeded out through their own mistakes in a kind of Darwinian selection. This would be fine, except for the fact that the people who would be weeded out can do a significant amount of collateral damage before they get to this point. A responsible teacher in any shamanic modality has a duty to ensure that a prospective student possesses certain basic capabilities before they start to give that student serious training. And it is not solely down to the teacher to determine whether or not a student is capable; a teacher should always consult the wights, or spirits, to see if the student has the necessary abilities before taking him or her on. Seiðr-workers are

---

*The term *wight* derives from the Old English *wiht,* which is related to Old Norse *vættr* (pl. *vættir*). The Old Norse word also appears in compounds like *landvættr,* "land-wight, guardian spirit of a country."

chosen by Wyrd, which is to say fate or destiny,* and made by the gods.

This is a roundabout way of reiterating that seiðr will not be for everyone, and not everyone will be able to deal with the material in this book. The same is true of all serious esoteric pursuits, although this is often glossed over by many people in this field as it is generally unconducive to book sales. That being said, this book is intended to be an introduction to seiðr, so the exercises I will present are as safe as they possibly can be, especially in the opening chapters. But if you find your-self struggling with a fundamental skill like journeying or basic protec-tion, for example, then you should seriously consider whether you want to go forward with the rest.

And if you ultimately decide that seiðr is not for you, there is no reason to panic. You are still free to pursue other forms of esoteric work, and there are many methodologies you could try. Since seiðr is a sha-manic modality, however, this could be an indication that other forms of shamanism are unsuitable for you as well.

SEIÐR AS COMMUNITY SERVICE

It is important to ask yourself: *Why* do you want to learn seiðr—and is it for the right reasons?

Many people in modern Western societies come to shamanic modalities because they have read about them in New Age books or have been involved in internet groups that claim to present informa-tion about shamanism. As a result, unfortunately, they may have gotten some misleading ideas.

Shamanism in general and seiðr in particular have little to do with

---

*Wyrd effectively refers to the Germanic version of fate or destiny. In Norse heathen cos-mology, it is controlled by three female spirits called the Norns (whose names are Urðr, Verðandi, and Skuld) who have a similar function to that of the Greek Fates. The name Urðr, which means "that which has become," is directly cognate with Old English *wyrd*, "destiny." Wyrd will be discussed in detail in chapter 6.

"self-development" or "spiritual development." While spiritual develop-ment inevitably does occur, it is a secondary side effect of practicing seiðr with the right intention. The effect of shamanic work must be shared with others—if you focus solely on yourself and your own spiritual devel-opment, you are coming at this from an ego-based approach, and ego is the implacable enemy of all shamans. While it is acceptable and even necessary to do the occasional healing for yourself (if you are able to), many shamans struggle to do work on themselves and their close family, and must seek the help of other shamans. You will struggle to give help to others if you are suffering yourself. But focusing all your effort solely on yourself is a waste of time and energy and will only take you so far.

A prime illustration of these issues is the rise in "plant-spirit tour-ism." Untrained and unprepared Westerners fly down to South America to ingest ayahuasca, thinking that taking the entheogen a few times will solve all their problems and instantly make them into a "shaman." In effect, however, all they are doing is disrespecting the plant spirit. Moreover, plant-spirit tourism has a negative impact on the environ-ment: it requires flying huge distances and encourages the overharvest-ing of wild plants from the Amazonian forest. It leads to the exploitation of deprived Indigenous communities, which receive very little benefit from putting on these ceremonies. The plant-spirit tourist industry has also provided the incentive for local criminal gangs to get involved in the organization of these ceremonies as a way of extorting money from rich "gringos." How can anything "spiritual" result from all this?

Indigenous shamans, on the other hand, train for years, working with the plant spirits and with the much wider community, treating both with respect. They learn about the plant and its ecology so that they are able to gather it without damaging the species or its habitat; they live and work locally and do not expend huge amounts of carbon in walking into the forest; and the local villagers who benefit from this work are poor, so there is little if any money exchanged and nothing to attract the more nefarious elements.

All shamanic modalities, including seiðr, rely on the wights or spirits. Shamans can achieve nothing without their wights to support them. Wights—at least the ones open to working with people—are not so interested in the fate of a single individual, but rather in the development of all living beings. They will help you, but only insofar as it helps others and brings them to the wights. Shamans have a singular natural advantage in this, as they are able to both sense and interact with the wights, whereas other people in the general community may not be able to do so. Therefore, the wights demand that the shaman becomes the bridge between spirit and the community. You are not unique in this capacity; if you refuse, there are others out there who have the same abilities and will willingly do as the wights ask.

At their "heart core," then, shamanism and seiðr are all about service—first to the wights and then to the community. As a shaman, you will be expected to drop everything else with very little notice, and use all resources at your disposal, including your life savings, to help the wights do what they need to do. You may have visitors show up on your doorstep at 3:00 a.m. expecting you to do a healing, because the wights have sent them to you and you must deal with it there and then—no matter whom else in the house it disturbs. You may well be asked by the wights to buy a very expensive piece of equipment—such as a new powwow drum, which can literally cost thousands—because the wights expect you to lead a specific public ceremony. The wights know little about money and will not care if this wipes out all your savings and means your family will not be able to go on holiday this year—but you can bet your family will not be as understanding. So, what do you do: upset your family or upset the wights? You still have free will and personal choice; you can refuse to do as the wights ask and they cannot force you to do anything. But this generally just makes them angry, and angry wights have lots of ingenious little and not-so-little ways of making their anger known!

Seeking to learn seiðr under the delusion that it will give you personal power over the wights and over others, and will further your own spiritual development, is a sure way of showing disrespect to the wights. In fact, some of the most powerful practitioners were forced to learn seiðr to get some relief from being bothered by the wights, because they had been chosen by them for one reason or another to do this sort of work. Once the wights have made their mind up about something, they can be very persistent and persuasive until they get what they want. In many Indigenous cultures there is a phenomenon known as "shamanic illness": once the wights have decided that someone is to become a shaman, but the person refuses the call, the wights visit the prospective shaman with a certain illness. The illness starts off at a chronic and low level, as an annoyance rather than anything life-threatening. Yet no matter how many different doctors are consulted, modern Western medicine cannot seem to identify the cause. Gradually, the illness begins to worsen, and nobody can get the bottom of what is wrong. If the prospective shaman continues to resist the calling, then the illness will eventually kill them, although it may take years before it does so. In the meantime, if the person gives in and starts to learn shamanism, all symptoms promptly disappear, and the trainee shaman becomes healthy and whole again.

So, if you are drawn to seiðr because you believe you have a genuine call from the wights to serve the community, that is fine. If you are learning seiðr to heal in response to the onset of shamanic illness, that is also fine—though relatively rare as most people hear and accept the call from the wights long before it gets to that point. But if you are learning seiðr because you believe it will bring you personal power and spiritual development, that is almost a surefire way to anger the wights. Be very honest with yourself: What are your motives? Magician, know thyself!

Similar arguments surround the use of titles. When is it acceptable to call yourself a völva, or seiðkona, or seiðmaðr, for example? The answer: it *never* is! Titles should not be taken for oneself, but only bestowed by others. This will happen when you have been genuinely called by the spirits; when that call has been acknowledged by a respected teacher; and when you have completed a long apprenticeship, and during that apprenticeship you have not only worked on yourself but have done significant work in the wider community and the community has seen and understood that you are capable of performing certain procedures safely and effectively a number of times. It is at this point that the community, in conjunction with your teachers, might consider you to have reached the level where you are respected enough to be called a völva.

There are plenty of self-proclaimed völvas and *tauframenn* ("charms-men" or enchanters) in the world, but relatively few true seiðr-workers. How do you tell the difference? Since there are no government regulations that concern shamanism and no overseeing body like the medical profession, the only way to really tell is through wide community support of that person. This should consist of more than a lone recommendation: it is relatively easy to pull the wool over the eyes of a single person, but less so the whole community. Feel free to ask about a practitioner's experience, about their teachers and their lineage, about their insurance. A genuine seiðr-worker will not mind answering any questions you might have.

MISCONCEPTIONS ABOUT SEIÐR

Having established that seiðr is a form of Norse shamanic magic, we must consider how it was practiced. Perhaps the first thing to do is to dispel some common misconceptions. The first of these concerns the claim a drum was used in seiðr performance; the second concerns the gender of seiðr-workers.

Was a Shamanic Drum Used in Seiðr?
The references to seiðr in the lore contain no clear indications that drums or drumming were used in the practice. There is one very obscure reference to some sort of seiðr tool or object in stanza 24 of the Eddic

poem "Lokasenna" (The Flyting of Loki), and certain translations refer to this as a drum. It appears in the following stanza, in which Loki taunts Óðinn:

En þik síða kóðu Sámseyu í,
ok draptu á vétt sem völur;
vitka líki fórtu verþjóð yfir,
ok hugða ek þat args aðal.

But you, they say, practised seid [seiðr] on Samsey,
and you beat on the drum [*vétt*] as seeresses do,
in the likeness of a wizard you journeyed over mankind,
and that I thought the hallmark of a pervert.
(Larrington 2014, 85)

The problematic phrase is the second line, "*draptu á vétt sem völur*," which Larrington has rendered as "you beat on the drum as seeresses do." However, no one really knows what a *vétt* is. This is the sole instance in the whole of the literature where this word appears, and it is unrelated to any other Norse word for a drum. It could just as easily mean the platform that we know a völva used based on saga accounts. The exact sense of the verb *drepa* (conjugated here as *draptu*) is also somewhat unclear, as it can variously mean "to strike," "to beat," "to knock," but also "to slay."

The suggestion that the vétt might refer to a drum that was used in Norse "sorcery" or seiðr is largely due to scholars drawing a comparative conclusion from the shamanic practices of the Sámi, a neighboring Indigenous group. The Sámi are a Finno-Ugric people whose traditional homeland (Sápmi) lies in northern regions of Norway, Sweden, Finland, and the Kola Peninsula of Russia. They are recognized as having a shamanic culture, though in the last few centuries this has been heavily suppressed to the point of near extinction by the local authorities. The Sámi *noaidis*, the shamans, are well known for using drums in their work, and many of these objects have been preserved in ethnographical collections.

Arguably, the archaeological record provides the most compelling evidence *against* the idea that drums were used in Norse seiðr: in ancient Norse graves, we have never found the remains of a single drum (Price 2019, 129–30). What has been found in the graves of what appear to be *völur*, or seeresses, are staffs. Indeed, the staff is one of the defining features of such graves. This is fitting, as the name völva seems to mean "staff-bearer" (it derives from the word *völr*, "staff").

If seiðr-workers did not use a drum, then how did they induce trance? An answer can be found in what is probably the most famous description of a seiðr-worker that we have: the story of Thorbjorg the seeress from *Eirik the Red's Saga* (*Eiríks saga rauða*), where she uses the staff and a kind of magical song or chant called a varðloka to create the same effects as one would get from beating a shamanic drum.

Is Seiðr "Women's Work"?

There is a very serious misconception, prevalent in a lot of modern heathen groups, that seiðr can only be practiced by women, or perhaps in some cases by gay men as well, but never by straight men. According to this belief, straight men somehow do not have the capacity to perform seiðr. Now, there is nothing wrong at all with both women and gay men practicing seiðr—both are perfectly capable of doing so—but the fact is, so is everybody else, including straight men.

In terms of sheer numbers, the archaeological record would suggest that female practitioners were probably in the majority, because we have found more graves of female practitioners than male, although this disparity could be the result of the random nature of what has been found. Graves of male practitioners certainly exist, and often when males are found they are buried in the same graves as female practitioners, suggesting that as well as working together, the couple may have been married.

In contrast to the archeological record, the literary lore contains more references to male practitioners than female, and many of these *seiðmenn* were also married and went on to father children. While this cannot be taken as proof of heterosexuality, especially in times where homosexuality was strongly frowned on, it is highly unlikely that these were all closeted gay people, either. Just like today, it seems that practitioners were a mixture of women and men, gay and straight. Gender and sexual orientation probably did not matter; raw talent and the potential ability to perform were more important. However, the way in which male practitioners were perceived in the surrounding culture may well have differed from how female seiðr-workers were viewed, and these ancient perceptions were certainly not the same as those we hold today.

This modern misconception about the gender of seiðr-workers arose from the ancient descriptions of men performing seiðr and being referred to as *argr* (which had the connotations of "unmanly, effeminate, cowardly") and being involved with *ergi* ("lewdness, perversity"). To understand why this was so, we need to consider the prevailing attitudes in ancient Norse culture.

In ninth-century Scandinavia, although there were many roles available to men—such as farmer, smith, craftsman, trader, and so forth—the society was distinctly dominated by a warrior elite. In battle, the warrior was supposed to stand face to face with the enemy. As skilled as any warrior might be, there was still a significant risk that he could be injured or killed, even by a less-skilled opponent. A momentary loss of concentration, a single slip, or quite literally an accident of nature like uneven or slippery ground could mean the difference between life and death. For men in battle, the question of who would emerge victorious was down to sheer fate, Wyrd, or even the will of the gods. As a result of one's greater training and skill, it might be possible to nudge Wyrd slightly in your favor, but you can never have control over it.

But seiðr could also be used in battle—much to an opponent's vexation. Instead of the seiðr-worker being within reach of your sword arm, he might be at the other end of the battlefield or even completely out of sight, hidden somewhere off the field where you had no chance of locating him—yet through seiðr he could deal as much damage as someone standing right in front of you. What is worse, if you did not understand magic yourself—and very few did—you could not use a shield or other weapon to parry their blow. You would have no defense, nor any chance of dealing damage back. The odds therefore seemed to be weighted much more heavily toward the seiðr-worker, and so seiðr was often seen as an unfair, dishonorable, or unmanly way of fighting. As a result, seiðr-workers had a poor reputation as cowards.

There is also something relevant to point out here about the way trance work functions. To be effective, the practitioner empties his or her ego in order to become like a "hollow bone" and allow the wights to enter their body. Essentially, this entails being "penetrated" by the wights in a way that is completely intimate and very close to sexual. While it was fine for a woman to be penetrated in this way, for a man to allow himself to be penetrated was seen as a major sign of weakness in Norse culture.

It was acceptable for a man to do the penetrating, taking the active role—so much so that successful male raiders were occasionally known to openly rape other males they had beaten as a sign of their dominance and scorn for a defeated enemy. The dominant male suffered no social stigma from this act; to the contrary, it might even enhance his reputation. However, for the man who allowed himself to be sexually penetrated in this way, it was a sign of defeat and ultimately weakness, and many would rather die than live with the shame. So, for a man not only to accept, but to consciously seek out opportunities to be penetrated by the wights, to live in this close intimacy with them, to accept their dominance and take a very inferior position, was seen as very strange and deviant behavior indeed.

Of course, this perception of weakness on the part of the seiðr-worker is very far from the truth. A practitioner is not subservient to their spirits and never gives up control, even while in the deepest trance. A practitioner works in partnership with their wights, and is not dominated by them, although to outside observers the situation may seem as if it is the other way around.

Cultural attitudes in the modern West are very different from what they were in early medieval Scandinavia. As long as it is consensual, for a man to allow himself to be penetrated is more likely to be an act of love than of defeat and shame. And whether this concerns physical penetration by a human partner or spiritual penetration by a wight does not really matter. This brings up another important point, however: no one should ever feel compelled to submit themselves sexually to anyone else, against their own will. Maintaining your personal sovereignty and control is vitally important to a magical practitioner. Having unwanted sex with anyone will in no way enhance your abilities as a shaman or seiðr-worker. If anything, because of the loss of sovereignty, it will probably only reduce your ability to work with the wights, despite what other people may claim.

I only mention this here because certain unscrupulous individuals have made use of these past misconceptions about seiðr to assert that it is essential for straight men to have sex with other men—usually themselves!—in order to be able to practice the art. They will even try to include this as part of a "master-student initiation." This is patently misleading. To reiterate: there is nothing wrong with same-gender sex if it is consensual and loving. But anyone who forces you to have sex against your will is never working in your best interest, only theirs—and it should be considered rape regardless of whether it occurs in a mundane or a supposedly "ritual" context.

AN ARRAY OF NAMES

As identified in Neil Price's book *The Viking Way: Magic and Mind in Late Iron Age Scandinavia* (2019, 72–83), seiðr-workers, both male and female, could be referred to with a variety of names in Old Norse literature. These names probably reflected the type of work in which the practitioner was specialized.

Names for female practitioners:

Völva (pl. *völur*)—"staff-bearer," the general female term for a seiðr-worker, but one who may also specialize in divination with the dead or divinities. The völva may also have some associations with the Norns and thus be able to influence Wyrd and ensure that their prophecies are more likely to come to pass. In one Old Norse story, the *Nornagestsþáttr* (Tale of Nornagestr), they are are even referred to as "norns" (see Flowers and Chisholm 2015, 15). Unlike the spákona, the völva generally must use ceremony and ritual to enter a state of ecstatic trance.

Seiðkona (pl. *seiðkonur*)—"seiðr woman/wife," a term for a female seiðr-worker who may be more of a generalist. This designation is often used interchangeably with völva, perhaps indicating someone who had a much wider range of abilities than those restricted to divination.

Spákona (pl. *spákonur*)—"prophecy woman/wife," essentially someone who possesses second sight. Two related terms are *spámeyja*, "prophecy maiden," and *spákerling*, "old prophecy woman," which refer more specifically to the age of the spákona. In contrast to the more formal trance work of a völva, the prophetic second sight, or *spá*, seems to arise spontaneously. A ceremony or ritual is not required to induce spá, which also means it is uncontrolled and may manifest at random and sometimes inconvenient times. Spákonur also seem to lack the ability to influence Wyrd: their prophecies are generally accurate, but the spákona lacks the ability to change or influence them, so events turn out exactly as dictated by the wights and cannot be changed. Spá is often felt to be as much a curse as it is a blessing. The term also appears as a tenth-century kenning, or poetic circumlocution, for arrows in flight (Price 2019, 76)—once loosed, its direction cannot be changed.

Vísendakona (pl. *vísendakonur*)—"wise woman/wife," a general term for a "cunning woman."

Galdrakona (pl. *galdrakonur*)—*galdr* is literally translated as the "cawing of crows" or "crowing of cockerels," so this is a "woman that crows." A sorceress who specializes in galdr is one who uses chants and magical sounds in her work.

Vitka (pl. *vitkur*)—a general sorceress, possibly one who specialized more in physical rune work than seiðr.*

Heiðr—as both a noun and a personal name, this term has quite interesting connotations. In the Eddic poem "Völuspá" (The Prophecy of the Völva), Heiðr is mentioned in stanza 22. It is unclear whether Heiðr is a mortal, a wight, or a goddess (tied to both Gullveig and Freyja as the originator of seiðr), but she is spoken of as equivalent to the ancestral first shaman in the Norse tradition. The name Heiðr is linked to the English word "heath" and denotes a high, unenclosed, and treeless land. But heiðr is also the general name used for a seiðr-worker and may indicate something like "one who belongs to the old settlements of the land."

Fjölkyngiskona (pl. *fjölkyngiskonur*)—"folk-magic woman/wife," someone who deals with physical charms, herbs, and potions. There would usually be one in each village. As someone specialized in what is considered lower folk magic, a fjölkyngiskona may not know or understand the high magic of seiðr.

Myrkriða, kveldriða, trollriða—"murk/dark-rider," "evening-rider," "troll-rider/binder," respectively. These terms refer to those who generally deal in the darker arts, including shapeshifting and the ability to bind wights and send them out to work against others. There is some overlap between the wights and the person

---

*This type of rune work involves empowering the runes by physically carving and coloring them into wood, stone, metal, or skin, instead of only speaking or chanting them (as in galdr). Although slower to take effect than galdr, the results of these workings are permanent until the runes are physically destroyed.

who sent them, for example the term myrkriða can be used to describe both the nightmare (the horse-like wight sent to haunt and exhaust a victim in his or her dreams) and the sorceress who sent it. This is a stark reminder that seiðr could be used to bring both weal and woe alike.

Fordæða, flagðkona, fála, hála, gýgr, and skass are all derogatory terms for a sorceress. They carry a range of negative connotations: sexually licentious, ugly, stupid, and evil—in other words, they describe a figure more like a storybook wicked witch.

There are significantly fewer names for male practitioners in the lore, but they include:

Seiðmaðr (pl. seiðmenn)—"seiðr man," by far the most common description of a male seiðr-worker, this refers to a generalist.

Spámaðr (pl. spámenn)—"prophecy man" or "man with second sight." Although spontaneous prophecy did sometimes occur in men, this designation appears much less frequently than the female equivalent spákona, because the gift is said to pass down along the female line. A spámaðr is most likely to be a specialist in divination.

Falsspámaðr (pl. falsspámenn), villuspámaðr (pl. villusspámenn)—both meaning "false prophecy man." These terms appear much more commonly than spámaðr and refer to a man who lies about having the gift of second sight in order to dupe others.

Galdrmaðr (pl. galdrmenn)—"man who crows," a specialist in the use of chants and sounds in magic.

Seiðskratti (pl. seiðskrattar)—a male seiðr-worker who specializes in the dark arts, and thus would be even more dubious than the seiðmaðr in the minds of most Norse people.

Seiðberendr (pl.; not attested in the singular)—"seiðr-carriers," a term that could potentially be applied to both sexes but was more often applied to men. It seems to have had even greater connotations of argr and ergi than seiðmaðr, so perhaps the term described a specialist in sexual magic.

Vitki (pl. *vitkar*)—a male sorcerer, but one likely to specialize in physical rune work rather than seiðr.

Fjölkyngismaðr (pl. *fjölkyngismenn*)—"folk-magic man," like the female *fjölkyngiskona*, this refers to a worker of lower magic involving charms, herbs, and potions rather than someone who uses seiðr.

Vísendamaðr (pl. *vísendamenn*)—"wise man," "cunning man," "one who knows"; not necessarily a magician.

Tauframaðr (pl. *tauframenn*)—"charms-man," enchanter, a snake-oil merchant, a traveling peddler of cheap amulets, false elixirs, and cures.

GENERAL HEATHEN CONCEPTS

There are several heathen concepts that will be useful to understand while working with seiðr, so we will consider these briefly now. They concern the special significance of certain numbers in heathen cosmology, and the important but often misunderstood concepts of *hamingja* and *megin*.

Heathen Numerology

There is no evidence that ancient heathens knew of any complete numerological system, but there were certainly a few individual numbers that can be seen as having a special significance in the lore. The numbers 1–3 and the number 9 are particularly important.

The numbers 1–3 are each seen as essential in the creation myth:

• The number 1 represents Ginnungagap, the undifferentiated potential and original source of all things in Norse cosmogony.

The third stanza of the Eddic poem "Völuspá" describes the primordial conditions thus:

> Sea nor cool waves nor sand there were;
> Earth had not been, nor heaven above,
> But a yawning gap (Ginnungagap), and grass nowhere.
>   (Bellows 1923, 4)

- The number 2 represents the emergence of duality as the first step necessary for creation. For the northern Germanic peoples, the primordial duality was that of fire and ice, the coming into being of which was a necessary precursor for every other thing in the universe. The duality of fire and ice is later reflected in the worlds of Muspelheim and Niflheim, two of the nine worlds or realms that collectively make up the universe (perhaps better described as the multiverse).*
- The number 3 represents both Wyrd and the midwives of Wyrd, the greater Norns. Wyrd provides the framework around which creation can occur. The number 3 also represents the act of creation itself, alongside the creator gods: Óðinn, Vili, and Vé. The number 3 is therefore one of the most important numbers in Norse cosmogony and mythology, as stanza 4 of "Völuspá" suggests:

> Then Bur's sons [Óðinn, Vili, and Vé] lifted the level land,
> Mithgarth the mighty there they made;
> The sun from the south warmed the stones of earth,
> And green was the ground with growing leeks.
>   (Bellows 1923, 4)

---

*A detailed discussion of these realms will be found in chapter 5.

Three is perhaps even the most important number because multiples of 3 are also seen as highly significant. This is true of the number 6 to a certain extent, as 3 doubled gives twice the power. But it is especially the case with the number 9, or 3 × 3, or 3 to the power of 3, which can be interpreted as "Wyrd times the power of Wyrd" or "creation times the power of creation." Nine is the only number that may potentially rival 3 in terms of its importance in the lore.

In Norse mythology, things are often given or done in triads. Therefore, the efficacy of a magical working can often be increased through the incorporation of the number 3 or its multiples. Calendrical days of 3 and 9, for example, are particularly auspicious times for doing magic. If an element of a working—such as chanting or galdr—needs repeating or reinforcement, it should be repeated 3 or 9 times. In the creation of amulets, talismans, and sigils, if the amulet has to be stored away for a while to enable its power to grow to maturity, it should be left for multiples of 3 or 9 hours, days, weeks, or even months. There are many ways that the number 3 can be incorporated into your magical workings, and the more you are able include it, the stronger the effects will be. Also, the more obscure and hidden the 3 or the 9 is in the working, the better. For example, carrying out a working on the 27th day of the month might not at first glance seem to add any additional power. But it is a number full of both threefold and ninefold significance: $27 = 3 \times 9$ (or $3 \times 3 \times 3$, or 3^3). Moreover, in numerology the practice is to add digits together until you reach a single number, thus $2 + 7 = 9$. The ways in which the numbers 3 and 9 can be incorporated into magical workings are limited only by your imagination.

Although there is no evidence from the lore that any other numbers (from 4–8) had particular significance to our ancestors, this has not stopped some modern practitioners from extending the system of Norse numerology to include them as well. So, if you discover your own meanings for one or more of these numbers—whether from traditional numerology or from your own UPG—by all means incorporate them into your work if you find this increases the efficacy. I do this myself occasionally, as one further number I have found useful is 4. In traditional numerology the number 4 represents the power of creation (= 3) embedded in the physical world (+ 1). If I want to ensure that the changes I am effecting in the spirit worlds will take place and grow in the physical world, incorporating 4s into my ritual really helps with that process.

Hamingja and Megin

Hamingja and megin and are two concepts that are prominent in heathenry and which need to be discussed in terms of what they mean and how they relate to shamanism in general and to seiðr in particular. Hamingja is very difficult to translate directly into modern English. Most people equate hamingja with "luck," but it is not quite the same thing. Hamingja is an innate spiritual force that may be part of our individual soul complex. Megin, by contrast, is a non-innate but acquirable force.

It often helps to think of hamingja and megin as different types of money: hamingja would be inherited money passed down from our ancestors, while megin is more like a salary—money earned as a reward for work that is accomplished. People can "spend" hamingja to influence their own destiny or ørlög.* Hamingja can be used to bring you into alignment with "the flow"—when you use hamingja, your life gets better and you come closer to your individual ideal. You are more likely to win games of chance and succeed at gambling, random positive events tend to happen, your chances increase of winning the lottery or receiving unexpected money from previously unknown sources, or

---

*The Old Norse term ørlög essentially means "that which has been laid down" and refers to the fate or destiny of things. It works on both a universal level and an individual level. On a universal level, it describes the underlying rules that govern the whole of Wyrd. But as this also determines your individual path and existence, one could also say that ørlög forms your own unique thread in the tapestry of Wyrd. Your ørlög is therefore your individual fate as a person. Ørlög will be discussed in greater detail in chapter 6.

your ideal career may just fall into your lap. In battle, a warrior who "spends" hamingja is likely to have their opponent randomly slip at the most inopportune moment or have their assailant's weapon break just when they are at their most vulnerable. People with substantial hamingja tend not to get sick, do not seem to come down with cancer, and so on—or if they do become ill, the treatments are remarkably effective and they recover quickly. Hamingja can be used to make things just "go your way" in life. But most people who rely on hamingja do so unconsciously and naturally—they do not make a deliberate decision to spend hamingja, it just happens.

There is one noticeable issue with hamingja, however: it has limits. Our hamingja appears to be given to us at birth by our individual Norns, and it seems to be finite. We are each given a certain amount of hamingja, which varies from person to person. Just like inherited money, some receive a lot while others hardly receive a thing. But unlike the case with inherited funds that get deposited in your bank account, where you can just log onto a website and find out your bank account balance, with hamingja we simply do not know how much of it we possess at any one time. You can make a guess, of course. Someone who appears to be constantly "lucky," who is always winning things, and who—as a local saying goes—"if he fell in a bucket of horseshit, would come out smelling of roses" probably has significant hamingja. By contrast, someone who is suddenly down on their luck, having just lost all their savings in a stock-market crash, and whose divorced wife has taken the kids to the other side of the world, has probably just run out of hamingja. The problem with hamingja is that it is very easy to spend but takes a long time to rebuild—and unless you take definite measures to invest and protect it effectively, once it's gone, it's gone. Furthermore, how do you invest and protect it when you don't know exactly how much you have in the first place?

This seems patently unfair: Why do the Norns make sure that some people are born with more hamingja than they can possibly get through in a single lifetime, while others hardly receive any at all? One theory is that it all has to do with spiritual evolution. In religions such as Hinduism or Buddhism it is said that people with lots of luck have an easy ride through life; they never have to struggle for anything. But, by the same token, they also cannot develop spiritually. Spirituality depends on struggle; we learn most from what we perceive as negative experiences. If we were only ever to meet with positive experiences, our opportunities for learning would severely limited. When we struggle, we are much more likely to turn to those outside of ourselves for help. Struggle forces us to work in closer relationships with other beings—such as the wights or even the gods—and to make compromises.

However, most religions that uphold this belief would also claim that the evolutionary spiritual pathway—whichever form it may take in that religion—is too long to complete in a single lifetime. In other words, there is a corresponding belief in reincarnation. According to these religions, this is the difference between a "new" or an "old" soul. A new soul is one that has just graduated up to being human and has just incarnated in the middle realms (the material world) for the first time. It has enough to cope with just trying to get used to living in a physical world, which works in very different ways to the spirit realms that it had formerly inhabited. So, to help, spirit ensures that the soul has a relatively easy life in the physical world by giving it lots of luck. And the new soul does not have to worry about spirituality at this stage—it has many more lifetimes ahead of it, in which it can try to come to grips with the concept of spirituality. As a result of this situation, new souls tend to be highly materialistic and not spiritual at all.

An old soul, on the other hand, has probably been through the physical world several times at least and should be used to it by now. Therefore, it is time that these people began to pay a bit more attention to the reason they incarnated in the first place, which is to start developing spiritually. So, with each lifetime that comes around, they get less and less luck, and life becomes more and more difficult, with greater struggles—forcing that person to forget materiality and to rely more heavily on their external relationships with spirit.

We might wonder, then, what all of this may mean for a religion such as heathenry. Heathenry does not deny the possibility of reincarnation, and even preserves several prominent examples of it in the lore. But reincarnation is also seen as the exception rather than the rule, and it is not the usual fate of the human soul. I will leave it up to you to come to your own conclusions, because it is areas such as this, where there appears to be some contradiction in the lore, that often lead us to our first glimpse of the deeper mysteries, which one has to discover for oneself.

Let us now return to the matter of hamingja and consider some different scenarios. From a practical standpoint, we know that people with a lot of hamingja do not necessarily make the best esoteric workers. Life hands them everything they need on a plate, they have never known need or struggle, and they do not have to work hard for what they desire. So, they have no inclination to try to change their path in life with magic—because their life is easy enough anyway—nor the discipline to learn the necessary techniques even if they were interested. And so it goes, until their hamingja suddenly runs out—a situation for which these people will not have developed any coping mechanisms at all.

Some people with an average amount of hamingja will, instead of spending all of it, unconsciously learn how to get conscious control over it; they begin to expend it consciously. In most situations they have enough hamingja to see them through life, but in certain situations they may not have enough, and in some very specific situations they lack what they need and begin to face want and suffering. Therefore, they learn to consciously focus their hamingja onto certain things. This is the beginning of magic. For example, a magician will realize that she does not have enough hamingja on her own to achieve everything she wants, so she must call on other external powers such as the runes. But when doing so she focuses her hamingja, her own internal spiritual power, to guide and control these external powers, giving them specific barriers and a remit in which to operate. Viewed from a heathen perspective, the vitka/vitki or rune master—or even the modern Wiccan or witch— who raises and calls on external energies to achieve a desire is aware of his or her own limited internal power and rations that power to marshal and control the external powers. Similarly, a ceremonial magician uses hamingja to create the circle in which an external power arises, is concentrated, and is focused before being sent out into the world. The demonologist uses hamingja to create the circle to contain the hostile spirit and prevent it from doing damage to the magician before he can get the information he requires.

So how does the application of hamingja affect the shaman? This is an important question, and the answer is that hamingja is not great for trance workers. Broadly speaking, hamingja feeds the ego, and the ego is the explicit enemy of the shaman. But it is also important to have a balanced ego to be able to form barriers, so you can establish where the "self" ends and the "other" (everything that is not part of the self) begins. An unbalanced ego is not beneficial for the shaman. If you are full of the great "I am," with your mind overly focused on your own power and potential, then there is little room for spirit. And if you are not able to become hollow, to serve as the "hollow bone," then a spirit cannot enter and merge with you.* Since a shaman relies on their spirits for everything they do, without them you cannot function. So, while the possession of hamingja may be vaunted as an innately positive attribute in the heathen community, it is a double-edged sword and cultivating hamingja is not particularly useful in the context of seiðr.

Fortunately, however, the Norse also believed that there is a second spiritual force that affects the lives of people. This force was called

---

*The shamanic technique of merging is explained in the "Protection in Seiðr" section of chapter 4.

megin.* Among modern heathens, megin is certainly not as well known as hamingja and is perhaps even more poorly understood. But similar concepts can be found in shamanic cultures worldwide.

Megin in its literal sense means "power, might," but I would suggest it can also be understood more figuratively as "honor." It forms a distinct but complementary force to hamingja. We are not born with any megin, and it is not presented by the Norns. Unlike hamingja, megin is also practically limitless, and if treated in the right way it can be built up and increased very quickly. We gain megin every time we carry out a specific deed or act in a certain way that is considered to be honorable: if we help a person in need; if we stand up for someone against enormous pressure; if we keep appointments, keep a promise, or maintain an oath; if we are in balance with the universe; or if we deliver on what we have agreed upon with someone, be they a human or a spirit. Megin is also increased through blót and sumbl by showing correct gratitude and respect to the wights. We lose megin through doing exactly the opposite: if we treat our friends with disrespect; if we miss appointments, break promises or oaths; if we fail to deliver what was agreed upon; and if we are generally unreliable.

I am not referring here to being "good"—good and evil are matters of perspective. An oath you make to the gods to seek revenge on your enemies would probably not be viewed as a positive thing by most people; in fact, it could be seen as distinctly evil. But if you kept your word and fulfilled that oath, then it would still earn you megin: you delivered what was agreed upon; therefore, you can be relied on to deliver in future. Lying is another gray area. Most religions insist on absolute truth in all things, but you will find that in most cases "truth" is very subjective, and there is nothing absolute about it. If by way of a gentle lie you can make someone feel better about themselves or are able to

---

*The Old Norse word *megin* has an essentially identical parallel in the Old English word *mægen*, which is the source of our modern word "main" (for example, in the phrase "might and main").

stop them grieving about something, and that lie does not harm anyone else, then it may still earn you megin, especially with the other person involved. This is yet another reason why absolute codes of ethics that espouse truth as one of those virtues are not particularly helpful.

Megin does not feed the ego like hamingja. The more megin you have, the more trustworthy you are to the wights and the more likely they are to engage with you, be influenced by you, and to do as you ask. Generally, the more powerful the wight, the more megin it will take to convince it to work with you. Or to put it another way: the more megin you have, the more powerful a seiðr-worker you become.

In conclusion we can say that hamingja is vital for the vitki/vitka, but it can become a blockage for seiðr. Megin, on the other hand, may not necessarily be important for the vitki/vitka, but it is essential for the seiðr-worker. So, now, even before you begin undertaking any of the basic exercises in this book, it is important to consider pursuing some ways in which you can build your own megin.

2
Seiðr Trance

STATES OF CONSCIOUSNESS

The human mind is remarkably complex. Scientists studying the brain have demonstrated that the mind can operate in up to five states of consciousness. These states are defined by their patterns of electrical activity in the brain, which scientists can monitor using an electroencephalogram (EEG). The frequency of the brainwaves is measured in cycles per second, notated as hertz (Hz). From highest to lowest activity, the five states of consciousness are:

Gamma (35 Hz and up)—a state of highly active, focused concentration
Beta (12–35 Hz)—aroused, active state of engagement
Alpha (8–12 Hz)—relaxed, passive state of attention
Theta (4–8 Hz)—deeply relaxed, inward-focused state
Delta (0.5–4 Hz)—sleep

The mind is preprogrammed to fall quite naturally into a trance state when it enters the theta state of consciousness. This is a completely natural process and one that is not at all scary. Most people already do this at least twice a day, if only quite briefly, without even realizing it: at the point for the few minutes just before they fall asleep, and when they wake up but have not yet become completely alert.

What many people may not realize is that a trance state of this type can be deliberately induced and maintained over a period of time. In the context of shamanism, the ability to enter a trance state is one of the primary tools of an effective shaman. The trance state (also called a "shamanic state of consciousness") enables the shaman to travel in the spirit realms and directly engage with the spirits that reside there.

SEIÐR JOURNEYING

An essential skill of the seiðr-worker is the ability to enter into a trance state that allows the practitioner to journey in the spirit realms and obtain the assistance of wights (spirits). This ability can be learned and developed through regular practice. Here I will present some basic guidelines and instructions for these first journeys.

A 7 Hz frequency will automatically induce the brain to create brainwaves of the same length. The rate of 7 Hz equates to a rhythm of approximately 4–7 beats per second, and thus a repetitive rhythm in that tempo range will bring the brain into the theta state of consciousness—in other words, a trance state. Any sound with a repetitive beat of 4–7 beats per second can work for this purpose, such as clapping your hands, chanting, or using a rattle, but in most shamanic cultures a drum is used to create the beat. Seiðr, which is culturally specific to the Norse, does not traditionally use a drum to induce trance; instead, it employs both the seiðstafr and the varðloka, a type of repetitive chant, to create the same rhythm.*

❖ Your Initial Journeys

You will want to find a location where you can practice this exercise undisturbed. Unless you have prior experience with a shamanic drum

---

*The seiðstafr and varðloka are explored in detail in chapters 3 and 4, respectively.

(and own such a drum yourself), it is probably best to use a prerecorded shamanic drumming track for your initial journeys.* In addition to the drumming track, you will need something to cover your eyes that will gently seal out as much light as possible. If you do not already have your own seiðr hood (see chapter 3), you can use a scarf or bandana, or some other suitable piece of natural cloth.

While seated in a comfortable position with your your eyes covered, listen to the drumming track. Silently repeat your intention, "To begin to journey and experience the spirit realms," three times in your head. The beat of the drum will soon allow your body to relax and bring your mind into a light trance. You do not need to force anything; just let yourself slip into this state of consciousness.

You should begin to feel like your spirit is free and in some form of landscape. I say "feel" because those who have read books on shamanism may expect to have a very strong visual experience and to "see" the landscape. This is not necessarily the case, however. When people first begin to enter trance, what they experience will very much depend upon their dominant sense in ordinary reality. Thus, whereas "visual" people might indeed see a landscape, more aurally focused people may experience a "soundscape" full of birdsong, natural sounds, speaking, and even music (this is what I got when I first started to journey); kinesthetic people may "feel" the breeze, the uneven ground beneath their feet, the plants brushing against their legs, and the feathers of the birds, and so on; and "nasal" people may be met by a barrage of different smells that evoke images and memories, which they then interpret. You will sensually perceive whatever is right for you. Eventually, with more experience, you will develop *all* your senses in non-ordinary reality, just as you use them in ordinary reality, and you will experience the visuals alongside the sounds, feelings, and smells.

When you first experience yourself in this landscape, try to make

---

*Various prerecorded examples can be found (on CD or on YouTube) and you can experiment to find one that works most effectively for you.

it one that exists in ordinary reality and with which you are relatively familiar. Navigation—and perhaps more importantly, returning to your place of origin—is relatively easy if you follow a few simple rules. The most important rule is that *you both depart from and return to a place that exists in physical reality*. This place becomes your axis mundi (world axis), around which the rest of the spirit realms orbit. It is your cosmic tree or pillar—your personal avatar of the World Ash tree Yggdrasil, which the god Óðinn uses to navigate through the nine realms.

The nine realms or worlds of the Norse multiverse exist spatially across three levels, which can be distinguished vertically as upper, middle, and lower. The middle realms (including the human realm of Midgard) are located at the center of the cosmic axis. To reach the upper realms, one must travel *upward* on the axis; to reach the lower realms, one must travel *downward*. Therefore, it is important for you to choose a personal axis mundi *that allows you to go in both directions, up and down*. Apart from that, your axis mundi can be anything—a mountain with a cave at its base, a tree with roots you can follow downward and branches you can follow upward, a staircase with both upper and lower landings from a central ground level, or even a sewer pipe with an aboveground ladder nearby.

To reiterate: it is crucial is that the place you choose as your axis mundi *actually exists on Earth*, in the physical world of Midgard. Why is this so important? Consider the following. Every place you see in your imagination does exist *somewhere* in the infinite spirit realms, but it may not necessarily be in the middle world (Midgard) of Earth. Places you might envision that have no clear reference point in Midgard are more likely to exist somewhere in the upper or lower spirit realms. So, if you use a purely imagined location as your starting point from which to journey, this will make it likely that at least part of your traveling spirit (soul complex) will have difficulty returning to Earth and finding your physical body at the end of the journey, which can cause a host of problems.* You will also be unable to integrate anything you learn on that particular journey, so the whole thing will have been a waste of time. So, to avoid this: *always travel from and return to somewhere that exists physically on Earth.* You will find that your spirit automatically remembers the way to this axis mundi wherever you are in the spirit realms, and from the axis mundi to your body in the physical realms.

Having entered a trance state, you will begin to experience a "landscape" different to the one in which your physical body normally rests. You can begin to "imagine" yourself moving about it just as you would in the physical realm. You will find that you can walk or run around.† Some people with a strong natural affinity for shamanic work may even find their spiritual body equipped with wings, which allow them to fly in the spirit worlds.‡ Once you are in a trance state, you can then walk/run/fly toward your axis mundi, and go up or down as appropriate. For your initial journey, you will be going down to the lower realms.

Having reached your axis mundi, you should find yourself at the

---

*This is the equivalent of soul loss and disassociation, which will be discussed in chapter 8. It leads to energetic weakness, fatigue, loss of mental clarity, potentially chronic disease, and vulnerability to external spiritual attack such as soul theft. It will also require someone with more experience in shamanism to go in search of the lost soul parts and return them to the physical body.

†Those with physical disabilities may find that their spiritual body shares the same disability, at least initially. In the spirit realms we create our own reality, so we tend to shape our spiritual body according to prior experience—in this case, that of having lived with the disability in the physical world. Ultimately, however, the spiritual body is extremely plastic; its shape is simply a matter of choice and can be willfully altered. With practice, for example, someone with a missing limb will find that their spiritual body has the full set of limbs, and someone who is blind will find that their spiritual eyes are fully functional and they can "see" as well as any sighted person (in the spirit realms visual perceptions are not the result of photons hitting the optic centers, but rather energetic projections that influence the subject's chemical and mental balance and affect different parts of the brain).

‡Though it is quite rare to have this occur on your first journey, it is not impossible. With experience, most people can develop this ability.

opening to a passageway or tunnel. You may also come across a physical barrier blocking the tunnel—a wall, hedge, fence, rockfall, or the like. This is the result of your mind becoming unsettled by a new experience that lies beyond its comfort zone, so it erects mental barriers. It is perfectly safe to continue—in fact, you must train your mind that there is nothing to fear. So, if you do come across a barrier, try to keep pushing through it. The barrier will eventually disappear and you can begin to travel down the tunnel.*

At the end of the tunnel, you will eventually reach another "landscape." Congratulations, you have entered the spirit realms! This landscape can be experienced as extremely different to the one you have just left, or it may not be. The physical world is consensual and operates according to certain rules, whereas the spirit worlds are non-consensual and the rules are very different—if they exist at all. Each realm has its own rules, distinct from all the others, and there are an infinite number of realms. You may find that you perceive this realm as similar to the one you have just left and as being composed of relatively normal plants, animals, rocks, and air, or you may come to a realm that you perceive as pure "umami" (until you experience it yourself, no one can describe it for you). Try to avoid having any expectations and be open to whatever you find; it will be right for you.

Travel across this new landscape as you normally would any landscape in the physical world. You may encounter various wights inhabiting the landscape. This is perfectly fine. For the most part, they are likely "the locals" and belong there. They may have the appearance of an animal, plant, or human—or they may have a form like nothing else on Earth. The vast majority of wights you come across will have never incarnated. Their entire existence has been in the spirit realms, so they

---

*Depending on how stubborn (or afraid) your mind is, you may not achieve this in a single journey. It may take several journeys for the barriers to disappear. This becomes a matter of sheer will—your will to get through the barrier has to be greater than your mind's fear of the unknown. The key is not to give up.

have no idea what beings from Earth normally look like (and there-fore cannot assume such appearances). Form is simply a matter of will, and the form they choose to display is entirely to give you information about themselves—or to scare you half to death if they want to avoid any interaction with you. The wight we know as Óðinn, for example, does not have a physical body or even an assigned gender, being com-posed of both masculine and feminine attributes.* It does not have a body unless it decides to visit Midgard, the only place where a physical body can exist. However, it will still usually appear as a long-haired, one-eyed, elderly man brandishing a spear; in this way we are generally preprogrammed for our subconscious to instantly make the connection that "this must be Óðinn" (thus, the wight does not have to announce, "I am Óðinn!" every time it appears to anyone). Though as we have said, form is usually just a matter of choice and a wight can appear in any form it wants. For a wight to reveal its original true form to anyone is a great honor—it shows a deep level of trust. A true form is like a true name, and to understand a true form gives you power over that wight and anything it has created.

As you travel across the landscape, you are free to interact with any wights you come across. Introduce yourself and talk to them, but don't force it. If the wights do not want to interact with you, leave them alone. Always be respectful.

Now, when talking about wights, do I mean individual spirits? From a traditional perspective, shamans all around the world know these as individual consciousnesses, each with their own separate exis-tence, which are just as real or individual as you or me. I deliberately chose to use the phrase *know*, rather than *believe in*, because this isn't a matter of belief but of *gnosis*. The shaman engages with these spirits on a day-to-day basis, just as you might engage with the clerk at your local grocery store. (Once you have done so several times, it would be

---

*The masculine is perhaps more dominant, however, so we generally refer to it as a "he" because this is a familiar categorization in human terms.

very hard to claim that you only "believe" the clerk behind the counter exists, and that he might be a figment of your imagination, a mental archetype—yet one solid enough to be able to ring up your groceries every day!)

Does it matter if you don't believe in the existence of spirits? That depends. In shamanism the basic idea is that all power comes from spirits, and without spirits there can be no power. If you reject the idea that *any* forms of spirits exist, you cannot practice shamanism. There is no such thing as a completely atheistic shaman. However, there are some modern Western shamans who do not accept the existence of spirits as separate *individual* beings but who are at least open-minded enough to see the spirits as psychological archetypes, as constructs of their own mental processes. This is at least initially sufficient to enable you to begin to engage with the spirits—even if you think you are only engaging with your own subconscious mind. Hopefully, over time, a prospective shaman who feels this way will gain enough of their own experience of the spirits to conclude that they *are* indeed separate individual beings. Shamans can function to a certain extent by believing in spirits as archetypes, but it does limit them. There are certain advanced techniques that will only work if you understand spirits as individual beings, and psychological shamans will never reach their full potential. But it is also the case that no one can have these experiences on your behalf. You will never truly *know* what someone else tells you, so you must find it out for yourself—and the only way to do that is through direct experience.

Once you have completed what you need to do in the spirit realms, or you hear the callback signal (if you are using a drumming track, the callback will be a different, faster beat than the regular trance drumming), thank any spirit with which you have been talking, and begin to retrace your steps back to the axis mundi. You will find that you remember the way, which allows you to automatically follow the path back. Go through the tunnel at the axis mundi and travel back to your resting body. Take your time and don't panic; you have all the time in the world.* With experience you will find you do not have to wait for the callback signal and can return at any time.

As you continue to practice journeying and further explore the realms of the Norse multiverse (see chapter 5), you can begin to engage more directly with the wights you encounter and enlist their aid for the seiðr skills that we will explore in the rest of this book (starting with chapter 4). Not all of this occurs on the spiritual level, however. Your practice will also be greatly enhanced as you obtain and empower the traditional physical tools of seiðr, which we will address in the next chapter.

---

*Even if the callback signal finishes, you still have time to return to your body; the function of the callback is to indicate the start of the return journey.

3

The Tools of Seiðr

It was a custom of Thorbjorg, in the winter time, to make a circuit, and people invited her to their houses, especially those who had any curiosity about the season, or desired to know their fate; and inasmuch as Thorkell was chief franklin thereabouts, he considered that it concerned him to know when the scarcity which overhung the settlement should cease. He invited, therefore, the spae-queen to his house, and prepared for her a hearty welcome, as was the custom where-ever a reception was accorded a woman of this kind. A high seat was prepared for her, and a cushion laid thereon in which were poultry-feathers.

Now, when she came in the evening, accompanied by the man who had been sent to meet her, she was dressed in such wise that she had a blue mantle over her, with strings for the neck, and it was inlaid with gems quite down to the skirt. On her neck she had glass beads. On her head she had a black hood of lambskin, lined with ermine. A staff she had in her hand, with a knob thereon; it was ornamented with brass and inlaid with gems round about the knob. Around her she wore a girdle of soft hair, and therein was a large skin-bag, in which she kept the talismans needful to her in her wisdom. She wore hairy calf-skin shoes on her feet, with long and strong-looking thongs to them, and great knobs of latten at the ends. On

her hands she had gloves of ermine-skin, and they were
white and hairy within.

—*Eirik the Red's Saga*, chap. 3
(Sephton 1880, 12–13)

There are only a few tools that are necessary for the practice of seiðr. Some of these, such as the staff and the "armor," are material objects and will be discussed in detail in this chapter. A further spiritual tool, which is not of a material nature, comes in the form of varðlokur, or "magical songs." While it will be necessary to refer to these songs in the present chapter, they will receive a more detailed treatment in chapter 4. We will begin with what is perhaps the most important tool of all: the seiðr-worker's staff.

THE SEIÐR STAFF

The defining characteristic of the ancient grave of a völva or seiðr-worker is the presence of a staff, the *seiðstafr*. Many of them were wooden, although a few from high-status graves were forged from solid iron. These staffs share a similar basic design, with some unique features that would not be found on a general stick used for walking or the like.

What was the staff specifically used for? To be honest, we do not know for certain because there are no surviving literary descriptions of how the staff was employed. However, the unique features that are found on the staff provide us with some important clues. By comparing the features on the Norse staffs to those found in other surviving shamanic cultures around the world, we can get some ideas about their functionality.

It appears that the staff may have been used in several specific ways: as a divinatory tool and as an instrument used in healing (for carrying out an extraction). But overall, the staff may have served a similar role to a shamanic drum, as a means to create a rhythm for inducing ecstatic trance.

In the mid-twentieth century, there was an anthropological expedition to document the lives of the Native American Pomo tribe of California. Film footage was recorded of healing ceremonies led by the spiritual leader of the Kashaya (Kashia) Pomo, a woman named Essie Pinola Parrish (1902/3–1979), known in her native language as Piwóya. The film, which has since become relatively famous in shamanic circles under the title *Sucking Doctor* (1963),* shows an evening healing ceremony that took place inside a *kiva*, a subterranean chamber or temple used for religious rites by Indigenous Puebloan tribes such as the Pomo, Hopi, and Zuni in the Southwest. Now, many people might ask: How can a tribe from the southwestern desert of the United States teach us anything about the practices of a people who were living in medieval Scandinavia, at the edge of the arctic circle?

In the film, Essie Parrish, acting as healer and ceremony leader, enters the dimly lit kiva where others from the tribe have already gathered and are seated around the periphery. She is carrying two staffs—one in each hand. She circles around the person in need of healing, who is lying on a fur-covered platform in the center of the kiva. She starts to beat the staffs on the floor as she walks, creating a distinct rhythm at the same time as she chants a sacred song, which the rest of the tribe begin to take up, and she uses these sounds to induce a light trance and call in the spirits for the healing ceremony.

In reality, this film was a reenactment rather than a field recording of an actual ceremony. The man "requiring healing" is Essie's husband, acting the part, and the whole event was staged specifically for the cameras, because it was thought that the spirits would be offended and would cause problems for the tribe if they tried to film a real ceremony. Nevertheless, the film shows all the basic processes that were involved in a healing conducted by the Pomo.

Although we tend to associate Native American shamanism with

---

*A shorter excerpt of the footage was also released under the title *Pomo Shaman* (1963).

the use of drums, it is interesting to note that in the ceremony depicted on film there are no drums anywhere in sight, nor can any be heard. In fact, the whole thing is strongly reminiscent of the description of the völva in *Eirik the Red's Saga*, with her staff and magic songs called varðlokur, which are sung by both the seeress and a chorus of people watching the ceremony.

✤ Finding a Seiðstafr

The first thing we are going to do is gather our tools in a sacred way, starting with the most important of them: the seiðstafr. This is going to require several walks in the outdoors. The best time of the year to do this is in the autumn or winter when the plants are dormant and sleeping, so you will cause as little disruption to them as possible. You can do this in one or two sessions. I would suggest two trips, as it makes the logistics a bit easier. It may take some time to find the staff at this time of year, so you can mark some potential locations on the initial trip. If or when you begin to run out of daylight, you can return another day to collect the one you have finally decided upon.

In any shamanic process it is vital to set your intention for the exercise before you begin. Energy flows where intention goes, so by setting an intention you are almost laying down a railway track for the energy of the venture to follow. This makes it much harder for the energy to be diverted or sidetracked, and success becomes even more likely. Your intention in this endeavor is "To undertake a sacred walk to find a piece of wood that will act as my seiðstafr." Repeat this statement of intention to yourself three times, either silently or aloud, before you begin.

Once you have set your intention, you can start your walk. Head out to an area where there are trees. This is a sacred walk of intention, not an idle stroll in the country, so approach it as you generally would a meditation, for example. You can bring along the dog if they are quiet and well behaved, but if they are likely to disturb your concentration, it would be preferable to go alone. It is also better if you remain silent or at least keep talking to a minimum. Try to always retain your intention in the mind, and be open to any perceptions and sensations that may come to you.

While you are walking, it helps if you hold your hands in a position that you normally would not—for example, down by your sides and open with the palms facing out, but the thumb and first finger touching—and try to gaze with the "shaman's vision," in which you do not look at the ground but keep your eyes approximately level with the horizon. Do not focus your vision on anything in particular; just relax and try to take in as much visual information as possible. This gaze gives you the widest field of vision, so you can see things at your sides that you would otherwise miss.

If you are ready to receive and work with a seiðr staff, the right one will make itself known to you. The manner in which it does so will also probably reveal something about the relationship between you and your future staff. You may perceive a tingling sensation somewhere in your body, notice an unusual smell, experience an interesting visual effect like a glow, hear a strange noise, or just sense that you are somehow approaching the "right staff." Such signs will get stronger as you get nearer to your staff. Or you may experience some other sort of sensation than the ones I have mentioned—be open to what comes along and trust your own instincts. You will know it when you feel it.

As we are all unique individuals, the staff that wants to work with you will also be unique. Therefore, you should not set out with any expectations regarding which type of tree will call to you. In theory, any kind of wood could be used, but it is worth keeping in mind that some trees have a better growth pattern for producing a staff than others (you should look for something relatively straight).

From a mythological perspective, certain trees also have specific resonances and properties, as well as associated divinities:

Ash—the World Tree Yggdrasil, magic, and journeying; the ultimate shaman's staff; Óðinn.

Hazel—wisdom, domesticity; Frigg.

Willow—feminine power, the moon; Freyja.

Blackthorn—the crone, protection, the shadow, death; Hela.

Sweet chestnut—prosperity, luck, and abundance. Since it is nonnative to northern Europe, sweet chestnut has no obvious connections with a Germanic god, but you might find one that you associate with it.

Holly—darkness, winter, Yule, survival; Skaði.

Yew—winter, hunting, death, resurrection; Ullr.

Oak—warrior, masculinity, strength; Thor.

These are probably the best types of trees for use as a staff, although oak can sometimes be quite difficult to work with.* They are generally native to northern Europe (sweet chestnut is not, but it has been naturalized); tend to be relatively straight when young; and have durable wood, which will hold some of the modifications you will want to add later. The staff that calls to you can also sometimes give you a good indication of which area of shamanic and magical work you might want to specialize in.

Other types of trees beyond these can certainly be used as well, but they tend to have some practical disadvantages. For example, elder is a very powerful tree magically, and also grows quite straight when young, but it tends to have hollow branches and very light, thin wood, which does not allow for much shaping, nor can it support a lot of weight. Similarly, sycamore produces strong straight staves, but being nonnative it has few spiritual and magical associations. But if you find a piece that specifically calls to you, use it!

---

*Despite oak's mythological and divine resonances, it is generally not an ideal wood from which to make a staff. Even when young, it never seems to grow straight enough, which can make it difficult to handle when used in healing and divination. However, if you do find a rare straight branch—or are willing to spend some time to straighten one—oak can serve as a very durable staff. And a branch of lightning-struck oak would arguably be the most powerful wood you could use!

In terms of length, the branch or sapling of wood you select needs to extend from the ground to at least chest-height. Some people prefer something around 4 feet long, so that it reaches the center of their chest, as this produces a staff that is relatively light and easier to handle. Others prefer something longer, perhaps equivalent to their own standing height, as it can make an impressive impact—theater is an important element in shamanic work!—but this can be more difficult to maneuver in delicate operations. For some, a length like that of a typical hiking staff (about 5'6") may feel best. This is up to you.

Once you have located the suitable branch or sapling, you should decide whether to gather it then and there, or come back later to collect it (in which case you will need to mark the particular limb in some way).

The wood should be harvested in sacred ceremony, so you will need to gather a few things:

- Cutting tools: loppers are generally the easiest to use for a decent-sized sapling, but you may want to bring along a small sharp saw and knife. It is generally best to cut from a living tree rather than to collect dead wood. If this is done properly, you will not harm the tree.
- A naked flame that is protected from the elements (and therefore cannot start a wildfire); for example, a tea light in a small lantern.
- Some incense* or a smudge stick made from native herbs (mugwort is good; avoid nonnative sage if you can). This is optional but nice to have. If you are going to burn loose incense on a charcoal block, be sure to have a proper heatproof receptacle for it. As with the candle, this should be handled with great caution to avoid starting a wildfire.
- Something to use to induce trance. Preferably, this would be one of your varðlokur if you have any,† but if you are just starting out

---

*The Old Norse word for incense is *reykelsi*, a borrowing from Old English *rēcels*.
†For instructions on how to gather and work with varðlokur, including the shamanic technique of merging with a wight, see chapter 4: "Varðlokur and Protection."

in seiðr you might not have gathered them yet. So, although we try to avoid drumming in seiðr, in this case a small drum (if you have experience with using it for shamanic trance) or even a shamanic drumming track played on an audio device (such as an MP3 player) is acceptable.

- Something to cover your eyes. This could be your shamanic mask or hood (see the section "The Seiðr Hood" below), or, failing that, a scarf or bandanna.
- An offering. Mead is generally the offering of choice in seiðr, but whatever you think is appropriate.

The procedure you will carry out can be summarized as follows:

1. First you need to light the candle and walk around the area to create an enclosure of sacred space. If you have brought incense and feel it is necessary, burn it in the area to disperse any negativity.
2. Sit before the branch or sapling in a comfortable position, cover your eyes, and induce a light trance using the method you have chosen. Set your intention "To harvest the right piece of wood that will act as my seiðstafr." Journey into the spirit realms and find a wight that will guide you to the spirit of the tree. Ask the spirit of the tree for confirmation it is happy that you would take the wood. If you sense any negativity at all from the spirit of the tree, do not take that piece of wood. (In this case, you will need to start the process over and look for another branch or sapling.)
3. If the tree is happy, make an offering of mead (or whatever you have brought) to thank it.
4. You can again offer incense smoke around the branch itself if you feel the need to dispel any negativity.
5. Cut the branch or sapling. Try to make this a clean cut, doing as little damage to the tree as possible. If you cut during the autumn or winter, the limb should be dormant and the sap will

remain in the tree roots, which minimizes damage. If you can, cut just above another bud as this will allow the tree to regrow from that bud. Angle the cut so that it is not flat but slopes slightly; this will allow any water to flow away so that it does not get trapped in the wood, which can cause rot.

If you are harvesting a sapling, you will want to cut it at a point on the trunk that is several inches above where it emerges from the soil. This will effectively coppice the tree, which will stimulate it to regrow stronger than before.

The branch or sapling that you have cut will have to be seasoned to avoid it warping or splitting as you work it. So, it will need to be stored for a while and allowed to dry out slowly. Generally, a cool location with good air circulation is best, but most importantly the area must be dry. The wood should not be allowed to get wet, or it may rot. The seasoning process can take several months, but you can still work with the staff shamanically during this time, provided that you only take it out of its seasoning storage for short periods, and then put it straight back. You should not try to decorate your staff until it is fully seasoned.

❊ Making the Seiðstafr

Historically, many of the staffs found in the archaeological records had a very similar design. They share several distinctive features that at first seemed slightly odd to the archaeologists who found them. Each of these features, which will be discussed below, was designed to be used in a specific way in certain techniques involved in seiðr. It is your staff, so you can of course choose to decorate it exactly as you like, and you do not necessarily have to incorporate all of these features. Without some of them, however, it may make it much more difficult to carry out certain more advanced techniques later.

Staffs could be made from either wood or iron. But for our ancestors, as today, iron is much more expensive than wood, and the cost of having a craftsman make an iron staff would have been high. The iron staffs were very high-quality items that only the richest could afford. Iron also tends to be very heavy, which makes the staff unwieldy to work with. Wood is a perfectly acceptable alternative.

My own staff is based on a design that is very common in the archaeological record, but for convenience I have had to incorporate some modern materials and fasteners. As it was beyond my means to commission an iron staff to be forged by a professional blacksmith, the modern elements were the closest I could source to the original historical parts. I think this is a reasonable approach. After all, our ancestors were also adaptive and would have used whatever materials they had at hand. I have, however, tried to stick to natural materials and metals, avoiding plastics, as I find plastic to be spiritually dead.

I was specifically directed by the wights to make the main shaft of my staff from seasoned ash. I like how ash looks, but moreover this tree has strong mythological connections to Yggdrasil, the World Tree, which is referred to as an *askr* (ash) in the Eddic lore. I also do a lot of work with the ash tree as a plant spirit ally of mine.

The top of the staff always had some sort of finial, for example, the knob (*knappr*) mentioned at the end of Thorbjorg's staff in *Eirik the Red's Saga*. In the highest-quality examples found by archeologists, these finials could be very detailed and intricate, for example, a carving of an animal's head or, in one case, a detailed miniature model of a Viking longhouse. Both of these finials likely served as a kind of spirit house—a place for spirits to reside or be temporarily contained in the staff, similar to an *ongon* in Mongolian shamanism.

When seeking a suitable finial to use on the head of my own seiðstafr, as hard as I tried, I could not find anything I liked for a price that I could afford. Since my taste tends toward the simple, in the end I opted for a cubic quartz crystal.

Contrary to popular belief, Indigenous shamans the world over do not generally make great use of crystals in their work. "Shamanic crystals"

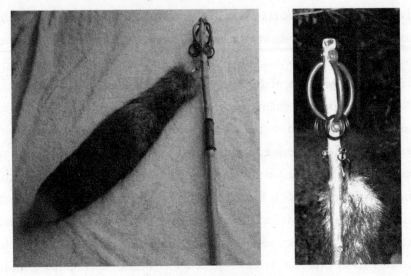

Head of the author's seiðstafr
(photos by Dean Kirkland)

tend to be an accoutrement of Western New Age "shamans" and are not traditional at all. There is one simple reason for this: crystals depend on having a fixed structure or matrix that gives them their properties, but this matrix can only exist in the physical realm. Once you take them out of the physical realm, say into the spirit realm, this matrix becomes mutable: their structure, form, and function changes—and in many cases, they stop working altogether. So, for most shamans, whose work takes place outside the physical realm, crystals are almost completely useless.

The one exception to this is clear quartz. For some reason—which is not greatly understood—it is the only crystal that maintains its form, and therefore its function, in all of the spirit realms. In addition to its energetic properties, clear quartz serves another function for the shaman: it can be used both temporarily and permanently to safely hold and store spirits without doing them any harm. This makes it helpful for healings—for example, in a soul retrieval it serves as a safe vessel for transporting the lost soul parts back to the individual so they can be reintegrated—and it can also be used as a type of ongon or spirit house. Thus, clear quartz is a suitable and relatively inexpensive alternative to the elaborate carved finials such as one might find on a historic seiðstafr.

Just below the finial on the seiðstafr there are often four metal bridge-shaped or D-shaped structures, equally spaced around the top of the staff, that form a kind of basketwork "handle." This structure puzzled archaeologists for a very long time—so much so that the first staffs to be found were classified as roasting spits, with this basketwork assumed to be the handle by which the spit was turned. (Notwithstanding the fact that the rest of the staff was too blunt, and the other structures on the shaft would have made it almost impossible to effectively pierce a hunk of meat for cooking!) Nor is the location of this structure, at the top of the staff, a particularly suitable place to form a handle for a walking stick.

The structure of this "handle" began to yield certain clues, however, regarding its real purpose. Other archaeologists pointed out that its appearance was very similar to that of a distaff, often used in spinning to wrap the spun thread around once it had been worked on a drop spindle. A distaff tended to be shorter, though, and a 5-foot-long iron distaff would be far to heavy and cumbersome to be of practical use in spinning. These D-shaped structures were also often heavily decorated, with the two ends of each D often carved into the faces of animals or people and the bridge between coming out of the animals' mouths so that they a shared joint tongue, reminiscent of some of the stories from Norse mythology of the rainbow bridge Bifröst being created by different wights and connecting different realms. This suggested that the basketwork hilt had some symbolic and spiritual significance. In fact, the basketwork has a quite practical function in shamanic healing, which we will explore later in chapter 8.

For the purposes of fashioning a seiðstafr today, it would be very difficult to find a highly decorated equivalent to the historical basketwork fixture without commissioning something to be custom made by an artist-metalsmith. But four cast-iron D-shaped drawer handles, arranged at an equal distance around the top of the staff, can serve the same purpose. And because they have holes for screws at either end, they are also easy to attach to the staff. On my staff I have adapted these slightly and added iron O-rings to each of the handles. There is no historical evidence that such rings were found on the original staffs, but in my experience when I am using the staff it creates an interesting rattle that not only boosts the sound, making it louder and easier to hear in a crowded room, but it is also pleasing to the wights.

A few inches below the basketwork there was usually a triangular piece of metal, placed horizontally so that the shaft of the staff passed through it. One of the corners of the triangle was extended so it stuck out a half inch or so beyond the shaft of the staff. This corner was always pierced with a circular hole that passed right through it, as though something was supposed to be tied to it. Again, I struggled to find a modern equivalent for this feature, but if your woodworking skills are sufficient, you could probably make something similar out of a flat, triangular piece of wood. I am no woodworker myself, so I settled for a metal hook and eye with a screw at one end that I could secure into the wood of the shaft. Usually there would only be a single one, but personally, being very fond of symmetry, I chose to put four equally spaced around my staff to give it balance, as well as something to tie an object to. This feature is very important in how the staff can be used for divination, which we will explore in chapter 6.

When I am in deep concentration during a ceremony, I have found that the hands can become sweaty and the staff slippery, and it is easy to lose one's hold and end up knocking someone else with the staff. So, I added a handle made from thick organic cotton cord, wrapped tightly around the shaft to provide some extra grip. Leather would work just as well for this purpose (as with the other components, it is best to stick to natural material if you can). No evidence for a grip has been found on any ancient seiðstafr, but thin organic material of this sort would have rotted away quickly anyway, so we cannot definitively say that it did not exist either.

The staff should be finished by adding a metal ferrule at the bottom. This is obviously unnecessary on an iron staff, but on a wooden staff it will stop the bottom from splitting or fraying and help to extend the life of the object. It also helps to make a louder noise as you beat it against the floor (or against the seiðr platform [seiðhjallr] in more advanced rites), adding to the impact of the ceremony.

In the end it is your staff, so you might also choose to decorate it further, for example by carving or burning runes into it. If you do this, it is also a good opportunity to "blood" the staff and bond it to you before it goes into the final stages of awakening (further instructions on how to do this will be found below).

❄ Awakening the Staff

This requires undertaking a shamanic journey to find and awaken the wight of the staff. As we are trying to learn seiðr, this is probably best done by using a varðloka to help induce the trance for the journey. However, at this early stage of their training, some people may still be nervous about finding and using a varðloka. If that is the case, you can use another method of journeying for this exercise, such as a drum (if you have experience using one) or prerecorded drumming track.

That being said, if you are serious about learning the practice of seiðr, *I would recommend that this be the last time you journey using the drum.* Working with varðlokur can require some time to get used to, and it will take longer to pick up the technique if you are mixing varðlokur with drumming.

Using the methods below, you will effectively create a conscious wight in your staff, a living spirit ally to help you in your seiðr work. Thus, your staff will need to be accorded a certain amount of respect—it should be treated like a friend and periodically you should spend some time working directly with the spirit of your staff. As you do this, you can also ask your staff if there is anything it wants or needs. If it makes any requests of you, make sure you satisfy them if you possibly can. In this way, the power of your staff will increase over time, which will make your own seiðr work easier and enable you to master more advanced techniques.

⚸ Finding a Varðloka

In order to find a varðloka for awakening your staff, you will first need to read the appropriate sections in chapter 4 before beginning to work. This is the standard method for finding a varðloka, regardless of what purpose the latter will be used for. Since you will be using this technique many times in your seiðr work, you will want to practice until the process becomes very familiar and you are able to accomplish it naturally.

Set your intention "To journey to the lower realms to receive a varðloka to awaken and empower my staff." As you travel through the lower realms, keep an eye out for anything unusual that might catch your attention. In all likelihood you will be approached by a wight that will offer you to teach you a varðloka, but you may just hear it on the wind or see it written down somewhere. Be open and accept that whichever way it makes itself known will be right for you. Once you have your varðloka, return in the normal way, but make sure to note your varðloka in your journal so that you can remember it in future.

❄ Empowering Your Staff

For this work you should find a location where you will not be disturbed for at least thirty minutes. I would recommend that you do this journey indoors, in your own home, as this is potentially the safest location. The journey should take place in the middle realms, in Midgard. However, this is a potentially dangerous place and at this stage your protection will be limited, so be aware of this and take sensible precautions of the sort I will suggest below. In chapter 4 we will be looking specifically at ways of protecting yourself in seiðr, but generally speaking, in order to do so you need to have access to a varðloka and an active and empowered staff. Traditionally, a teacher probably would have done this step with the student, extending their own protection to the student as they worked. However, these days it is very rare to be in such a situation, and you often must accomplish this next stage on your own. This is fine as long as you are sensible in how you proceed.

Wherever you plan to do this next step, it is important to first use your intuition and try to feel if there are local wights present in the immediate area. If you do come across any with a negative intent, avoid doing this work until you are sure that they have gone and everything is clear. I would strongly recommend first clearing the room—both physically, by tidying up the space (sweeping, vacuuming, dusting, etc.), which will help to shift negative energies, and then with a spiritual cleansing using whichever means you find effective. One method would be to burn some incense (*reykelsi*), particularly mugwort if you can get it.* Sound can also be effective in clearing an area. This could be a specific varðloka or a chanted galdr of runes (I would recommend *algiz* and *laguz*, but you should go with what you feel is most appropriate).† When using either incense or sound it is important that you not only start in the center of the room, but also make sure the smoke and sound is directed to all of the corners, and particularly anywhere a wight could get in—windows, doors, and don't forget the fireplace if there is one.

Methods of protection that are commonly used in esoteric spiritual work, such as casting a circle in Wicca or ceremonial magic, tend to be ineffective when undertaking trance work. This is because those methods are fixed in time and space, whereas in journeying work the spirit is

---

*Although white sage is commonly sold as a purifying incense in the form of "smudge sticks," I would recommend against it for several reasons. As a New World plant native to California, it was never used by our Germanic ancestors. It is also threatened in the wild due to overharvesting.

†The practice of galdr and runic chanting is a whole art unto itself and beyond the scope of the present work. For a very concise and practical primer, I can recommend Edred Thorsson's *Rune-Song* (2021).

highly mobile and may travel great distances very quickly. Even simple, slightly more mobile methods, such as visualizing a cloak of protection around oneself, generally cannot keep pace with the spirit. Shamans around the world use other methods to protect themselves.

However, for this exercise we are going to try to minimize the movement of your spirit, therefore you won't lose anything by using some of the more common methods of protection. If you are accustomed to "casting a circle," then feel free to try it in this situation. It cannot do any harm—but remember that the circle is on the room and not on yourself.

Before you begin, you should sing or chant your varðloka to your staff three times.* Set your intention "To journey to the middle realms to meet the wight of my seiðstafr and awaken and empower it." Journey as normal, but hopefully you will not have to go far, as the wight should already be near or even in the staff. Once you have found the wight, introduce yourself and sing the varðloka to it three times. While you are singing, notice how the essence of the wight changes. Ask the wight if it has anything it needs to tell you, or something it needs you to do. If it makes a request, be sure to fulfill this to the best of your ability. Ask the wight if it needs to you to complete any specific ritual in the future to feed the staff. Thank the wight and ask it to merge with the physical staff and witness as it does this. Return from the journeying and sing the varðloka to your staff another three times (this makes nine times throughout the ritual). Remember to make any notes in your journal.

❖ Allowing the Power to Grow

You can use the staff with full functionality at this point. However, there is another optional step that you can take to boost the power of your staff. This is based on modern UPG from several sources and is not necessarily something our ancestors would have practiced. If

---

*For instructions on gathering the appropriate varðloka, see the first part of chapter 4, "Varðlokur and Protection."

you are going to do this, you will need a large piece of black cloth, of sufficient size in which to wrap the staff completely, and some red cord. Both should preferably be made from natural material.

Take the staff and wrap it in the cloth so that no light can reach any part of the staff. Use the cord to tie the cloth around the staff, wrapping the cord around the bundled staff nine times. Using suitable words, explain to the staff that it is being cast into the darkness of Ginnungagap to develop and grow. Ideally, this should be done in alliterative verse, so you may want to spend some time composing something suitable.*

The bundled staff is then put away in a dark location, such as a cupboard or wardrobe, where no light will get to it. It can be kept there for a period of nine hours, days, weeks, or even months. The longer you store it, the more powerful the staff can become, but there is obviously a balance to be struck because while it is stored away it cannot be used. From my experience, nine days is a good length of time that will allow the power to mature but also let you retrieve the staff relatively soon in order to resume your journey work.

When the time has elapsed, the staff can be removed from its store and the bundle carefully unwrapped. At this stage it is also customary to welcome the staff back into the world as you would welcome a new child at birth. Again, alliterative verse can be used for this purpose. It is also customary to give the new staff wight a name, something that is reflective of its purpose.

When the wight has been acknowledged with a name and welcomed,

---

*Alliterative verse is a poetic style that is not based on end-rhyme but rather the reoccurrence of similar sounds at the beginnings of words within a set line or phrase. The oldest Germanic poetry was alliterative and followed a specific metrical pattern, and the tradition persisted well into the Middles Ages in various parts of northwestern Europe. The Old Icelandic Eddic poems are marked by this style, as is the Old English epic "Beowulf." In Scandinavia, alliterative verse was used extensively by the Norse poets known as *skalds* (similar in some respects to the Celtic bards) in their elaborate praise poems to the kings and gods, and was thought to have magico-religious properties. For examples of traditional-style alliterative verse in English, Lee M. Hollander's translation of the *Poetic Edda* (2011) is a useful resource.

you can "blood" the staff if you wish. This is in no way obligatory, but—as seen in several of the sagas—it is traditional and helps to create an energetic bond between you and the staff.* The bond enables the staff to better understand you and your needs, and to react more quickly and precisely to what you want to do.

Using a sterile needle or diabetic lancet, prick the end of your thumb and squeeze it to release a small amount of blood. You do not need much—a few drops are sufficient to carry your energetic signature. You can either smear the blood directly onto the body of the staff itself, or you can mix it with a small amount of red ochre powder and raw linseed oil until it is the consistency of a thin paste. This is called a *tiver* and is used for coloring runes. So, for example, if you have chosen to decorate you staff by carving runes into it, the tiver can be used to color and empower them, while at the same time binding the staff to you.

The new staff wight can be likened to a thought-form or what in esoteric discourse is sometimes called a *tulpa*. It takes the original wight from the tree and adds some energy from both the runes (if carved into the staff) and some energy and consciousness from the practitioner, melding them all together to form what is effectively a new gestalt. Thus, it is a new wight: an "upgrade" built around the original framework but now differentiated from it, and at the same time more closely aligned with the practitioner.

THE ARMOR

The account of the seeress Thorbjorg from *Eirik the Red's Saga* is very descriptive concerning the costume she wears while she is working seiðr. This costume is based on standard clothes of the day, but in this case

---

*This is essentially the same process as when a runemaster "activates" a carved inscription by coloring the runes with blood and/or tiver. An example from the sagas can be found in chapter 44 of *Egil's Saga* (Smiley 2005, 68).

they are of extremely high quality, probably her best clothes—fur-lined and inlaid with gems. It is unusual for an Icelandic saga writer to describe someone's clothing in such detail, so there must be a reason for doing so here. It becomes clear that this is the standard costume of the völva. It does not represent an ostentatious display of Thorbjorg's wealth, but rather is a way of reinforcing her spiritual power in the minds of those watching.

Shaman's "armor," such as Thorbjorg's costume, is essentially ritual dress. There are two main reasons why you might choose to wear such clothing during a ceremony. From the shaman's perspective, the theory is that if you wear the same clothing for each ritual, the wights come into contact with your clothing as you are working and they leave some of their power and blessing behind. This accumulates over time, giving you extra layers of protection that will then help you during future ceremonial work.

There is also a practical reason why you might choose to wear ritual costume, and this has to do with theater. Every good shamanic performance should include a bit of theater and drama, as it can help to put anyone who is watching in the right frame of mind. It signals that something different and out of the ordinary is happening and draws attention to the person in the funny hat who is directing things.

If you are working alone it is usually unnecessary to don your ritual costume unless you are engaged with some very deep-level work. You will be relying on other forms of protection anyway. By the same token, however, if you think your solo work could benefit from a little boost of extra power—by all means, wear your armor.

Circumstances can also arise that prevent the use of your ritual costume. For example, in the event of an unexpected emergency—and yes, spiritual emergencies do crop up occasionally!—you may not have time to run home to grab your costume. You will have to carry out your work wherever you happen to be, in whatever clothes you happen to be wearing. So, if you discover that you are simply unable to conduct seiðr work in jeans and a t-shirt—or, worst case scenario, in your pajamas—then you probably should not be working shamanically in the first place.

It should be kept in mind, of course, that outside of Halloween, modern people are not used to seeing anyone in a full costume of any kind. So, depending on the situation, you must try to determine beforehand whether it is appropriate to wear your armor. Ritual clothing can really add to the impact of a seiðr working in cases where other people are present, but even here you should know your audience.

If you are going to be working with someone alone, on a one-to-one basis—for example, to conduct a healing—and you suddenly appear in full shaman's armor, it could be very intimidating for the client. In this case, it is often preferable to adopt a more professional look. This is why I keep two sets of shaman's armor, one of which is very understated. When dealing with a single client or a small group, particularly if meeting them for the first time, I generally wear a white shirt, a tie, and a specific waistcoat as my armor. This outfit is not so outlandish as to violate any modern dress codes, but it is nevertheless something slightly out of the ordinary, which impresses upon the client that I know what I'm doing and that something different may be just about to happen. If you do decide to wear your full ritual costume while working with one person or a small number of people, be sure to let them know beforehand and explain the reasons why you will be wearing it.

The full ritual costume can come into its own if you are leading work for a group of people, and especially if some of these people have never attended a ceremony before and do not know what to expect. Wearing your full ritual costume will heighten the sense of drama and emphasize the fact that everyone is within a sacred space; therefore, they should be respectful and pay attention to any instructions that you are going to give them. Conversely, if it is a group of experienced people with whom you have worked before, and you are confident they understand what they are doing and will follow your directions, you may decide it is unnecessary to wear your full costume. The key is to know your audience.

For those who are just beginning to learn seiðr, a complete ritual costume is certainly not required. A full set of shamanic armor can be quite expensive to assemble, and it makes sense to wait and see if you are seriously going to pursue the practice of seiðr before rushing out and buying anything.

The most effective shaman's armor for use in seiðr is based on ninth-century Norse, Saxon, or Germanic costumes. Therefore, it is important to do some historical research into these styles of clothing and the materials that were used in their construction. Although it will cost more, it is important to have your own costume made from natural materials—preferably authentic ones, such as linen,* wool, leather, and fur (do not forget, this is also supposed to impress your audience with your knowledge). You should not hesitate to spend as much as you can afford on your ritual costume, even if this means buying it one piece at a time and slowly putting it together over a longer period. A good quality costume will last a lifetime if looked after properly.

Synthetic materials, such as polyester or acrylic, should be avoided if possible. Poor-quality imported "Viking reproduction" clothing made from such fabrics can be purchased very cheaply online these days from some well-known discount retailers. In addition to being detrimental for the environment, this sort of mass-produced clothing is often manufactured in sweatshops that exploit their workers, which is not the best type of energy to be introducing into your ceremonies. On a spiritual level, clothes made of synthetic materials do not hold the power of the wights well either, which thereby defeats some of its purpose as shaman's armor.

We will now look at three special components of the seiðr-worker's costume: the hood, the belt, and the sax.

---

*Cotton will do in a pinch, although it is a New World plant that would not have been known by our heathen ancestors in Europe. That being said, and bearing in mind my earlier comments about the necessity of pragmatism, cotton is significantly less expensive than linen if you are on a budget, while still being a natural material that works well with spirit.

The Seiðr Hood

The one piece of ritual costume that it is vital to have from the start is the seiðr-worker's hood. Why does one don a hood? By cutting out or reducing external visual information from Midgard and the middle realms, it becomes much easier for the shaman to focus on what is happening in the spirit realms. The name *shaman* (*šamān*), which derives from the Siberian Tungus language, has been interpreted by some to mean "one who sees or knows in the dark." Therefore, it is not surprising that many Indigenous shamans either work in the dark or wear some sort of eye covering, such as the beaded eye-curtains used by numerous Siberian tribes or the scarves and bandanas that one finds in more modern practice. The account of the seeress Thorbjorg in *Eirik the Red's Saga* makes it clear that the eye covering of choice for Norse seiðr was a hood. This hood was large enough to cover the face while directly engaged in a seiðr working but could be pulled back when not in use.

Theoretically, any medieval-type hood could suffice for this purpose, provided it is large enough to pull down to cover the eyes. Various designs can be found for purchase online, but it would be even better if you are able to construct and sew the seiðr hood for yourself. A good set of instructions on how to go about this can be found in appendix B of Evelyn Rysdyk's book *The Norse Shaman* (2016, 210–18), though you may want to modify the dimensions to fit your size and needs. Here again, natural materials are best. Wool is an excellent choice for a fabric as it tends to be thicker than linen or cotton and thus will exclude external light more effectively. The idea is that the hood should keep out as much light as possible while you are journeying, which makes it much easier to see the wights.

The Seiðr Belt

The graves of several ancient seiðr-workers have yielded remnants of small pouches and amulets that were presumably attached to a belt made of leather or some other natural material. The pouches could be used to hold things needed in the practice, such as the seeds of entheogenic plants. Two archeologically attested examples are the seeds of *Hyoscyamus spp.*, or henbane, and *Cannabis sativa.* These seeds may have been utilized in several ways in seiðr—and not necessarily for ingestion.* The belts also had metal charms attached to them, for example small *Mjöllnir* (Thor's hammer) pendants that probably served as a form of protection.

Although this item of costume is not vital to have in the long term, if you take seiðr seriously, you should consider making yourself a belt to further enhance and empower your work.

The Sax

I find it essential to keep a small traditional knife as part of my armor. The Norse called this single-edged knife a *sax*, and the corresponding Anglo-Saxon term is Old English *seax.* The sax can be used as a tool for directing energies in shamanic work, for cutting herbs, carving runes, and even for obtaining small amounts of blood if needed in a ritual. For heathens in the early medieval period, the sax would have also been used for eating, butchering small game, carving wood, and a host of other everyday tasks—metal being too expensive generally for a person to have a range of knives dedicated to specific purposes, such as magic. Above all, therefore, a sax always had to be kept sharp. A blunt knife is of no use to anyone, and a blunt ritual knife is worse than useless—it is an affront to the gods!

A small, sharp sax, the type of blade used by our Germanic ancestors, is an ideal ritual knife for seiðr. A suitable sax can be found for purchase on the internet or even commissioned directly from a heathen metalsmith. Like some other elements of your ritual costume, this will not be cheap and it is probably not necessary for beginners. But a good, well-maintained sax will last for a lifetime's work.

---

*Given the toxicity of henbane, experimenting with ingestion is not something I would recommend today.

4
Varðlokur and Protection

And when the (next) day was far spent, the preparations were made for her which she required for the exercise of her enchantments. She begged them to bring to her those women who were acquainted with the lore needed for the exercise of the enchantments, and which is known by the name of Weird-songs, but no such women came forward. Then was search made throughout the homestead if any woman were so learned.

Then answered Gudrid, "I am not skilled in deep learning, nor am I a wise-woman, although Halldis, my foster-mother, taught me, in Iceland, the lore which she called Weird-songs."

"Then art thou wise in good season," answered Thorbjorg; but Gudrid replied, "That lore and the ceremony are of such a kind, that I purpose to be of no assistance therein, because I am a Christian woman."

Then answered Thorbjorg, "Thou mightiest perchance afford thy help to the men in this company, and yet be none the worse woman than thou wast before; but to Thorkell give I charge to provide here the things that are needful."

Thorkell thereupon urged Gudrid to consent, and she yielded to his wishes. The women formed a ring round

70

about, and Thorbjorg ascended the scaffold and the seat prepared for her enchantments. Then sang Gudrid the Weird-song in so beautiful and excellent a manner, that to no one there did it seem that he had ever before heard the song in voice so beautiful as now.

The spae-queen thanked her for the song. "Many spirits," said she, "have been present under its charm, and were pleased to listen to the song, who before would turn away from us, and grant us no such homage."

—*Eirik the Red's Saga,*
Chap. 3 (Sephton 1880, 13–14)

VARÐLOKUR

Now that you have your staff, we are going to start gathering the allies necessary for seiðr work. To do so, you will need to obtain your own varðlokur. The word *varðlokur* (pl.) comes from Old Norse and can be interpreted as "ward songs" or "guardian songs."* The presumed singular form is *varðloka*, which is a compound of *varð* ("ward, guardian") and *loka* ("lock," but with an extended meaning of "song or chant").

Before getting underway with the practical work, it would be worthwhile to read the entire seiðr account in *Eirik the Red's Saga* (*Eiríks saga rauða*), a portion of which is quoted at the beginning of this chapter.† What concerns us here is description of the actions of the seeress Thorbjorg in chapter 4 of the saga.‡ Thorbjorg is a völva and a prophetess (spákona) who travels from farmstead to farmstead, revealing

---

*In the translation of *Eirik the Red's Saga* by John Sephton, which is quoted from at the beginning of this chapter and several other times throughout this book, he chose to render *varðlokur* as "Weird-songs" but this a fanciful interpretation.

†Several older translations can be found for free on the internet, and there is an excellent modern translation by Keneva Kurz in *The Sagas of Icelanders* (Smiley 2005, 653–74).

‡The original Old Icelandic spelling of her name is Þorbjörg. In the saga she is also referred to by the epithet *lítilvölva*, "little völva."

the future for the people who live there (and in cases where she is not shown sufficient respect, changing that future to a negative one for the people on the farm). We will be returning to the story of Thorbjorg several times, so it is best to become familiar with it now.

In the tale, Thorbjorg talks about the varðloka as a type of song or chant used to bring in the spirits (*náttúrur*). In the practice of seiðr, the rhythm of these varðlokur, along with the beat of the staff, is the main way of achieving a shamanic state of consciousness.

Other sources make it clear that there are a range of varðlokur (in the original saga text the word is always used in the plural). In this regard we may note that similar practices from other cultures, including the icaros or healing songs of the Amazon, show that not only are there different icaros for achieving different shamanic techniques, but these icaros are also often unique to each shaman.

ICAROS, OR MEDICINE SONGS, AND OTHER PARALLELS

The shamans of several Indigenous groups in the Amazon use icaros, or medicine songs, in their healing ceremonies, but perhaps the most studied are the Shipibo. These songs are often accompanied by the sound of a palm-frond rattle called a *shacapa*, which is used to create a specific rhythm. With respect to the icaros themselves, some are given to the shamans by their teachers, but the most powerful songs are said to be gifted directly by the spirits during a period called *la dieta*, in which the shaman undergoes physical isolation, celibacy, and abstinence while also adhering to a strict dietary regimen. During this time, the shamans build their relationships with the unseen; for example, a shaman may undertake journeys to the spirits to receive the icaros, or the spirits may visit the shaman in dreams and give the icaros to the shaman directly.

Icaros may be hummed, whistled, whispered, or sung. They are a kind of language of their own, which enables the shaman to communicate with the spirit realms and thereby to empower people or objects. The songs may be in Spanish, in local tribal languages, or even composed of sounds from no known human language, like speaking in tongues. They can be used for healing; love magic and battle magic; apprenticeship and initiation; purification, blessing, and protection; as well as for closing shamanic treatments, ceremonies, and dieta (Sammarco 2010, 22). Each type of work requires a unique and individual icaro, and experienced shamans may have several hundred of these songs at their disposal.

Shamans also use icaros to receive an *arkana*, an invisible energetic protection, which can then be used for both the shaman's own protection as well as that of the other participants in a ceremony. Here is an example of an English translation of an icaro, originally in Spanish, from the Shipibo shaman Don Adriano:

> Now that I have extracted this black spirit from you,
> I can call for the good spirits to come.
> I want them to arrive like a whirlpool,
> I want the good spirits to arrive here as a whirlpool and
>   enter with power inside your body.
> I want this whirlpool to rise above you, to be strong.
> I am going to finish with this, but first I want to charge
>   this arkana with more power, so that other people
>   or evil spirits may not take it away from you.
> I ask the plant spirits to help me,
> I call the spirits,
> I call my spirit protector.
> May nothing enter,
> May no evil spirit enter this body and may all be
>   cleansed and pure. (Sammarco 2010, 22)

Similar techniques to those used by Indigenous Amazonian groups like the Shipibo can be found in other shamanic cultures worldwide.

For example, in the documentary film footage of the southwest Native American Pomo shaman Essie Parrish described in chapter 2, she re-enacts a healing ceremony in which she sings medicine songs (though not, of course, in this case called icaros) and wields a pair of staffs (not the shacapa). Shamans from Indigenous groups in the Amur River basin in Siberia also intone their own type of medicine songs, although in this case they are usually sung to the beat of a drum. Thus, it appears that the use of spirit or medicine songs, often together with some sort of rhythmic instrument, is relatively common among shamanic cultures around the world. And as the saga account of the seeress Thorbjorg shows, similar techniques involving spirit songs (varðlokur) and likely rhythmic accompaniment (which could be generated by the beating of a staff) were essential to the work of a heathen Norse völva, seiðkona, or seiðmann.

There are no examples of authentic varðlokur that have survived from any ancient northern Germanic culture. However, as we have noted above, it is evident that shamans who use medicine songs, such as the Shipibo with their icaros, receive them from a variety of different sources—and the most powerful songs are, in fact, gifted by the spirits. Therefore, it should be relatively straightforward for someone working in the heathen Norse tradition to use shamanic methods to receive their own spirit songs for use in the context of seiðr.

We may ask, then: Which shamanic methods are best suited to receive varðlokur—for example, would something akin to dieta be appropriate? The dieta, which constitutes a sort of spiritual fast, is a specific element of the cultural shamanism of the Amazon River basin and it does not occur elsewhere, including in other shamanic cultures that use medicine songs. In the ancient Norse texts, there is no men-tion of fasting in connection with varðlokur, nor is fasting generally seen as a common practice in older Germanic cultures. Thus, it would seem that fasting is not a relevant historical practice in the context of seiðr (though you could certainly incorporate it into your practice if you found it effective). In my experience, varðlokur can be recovered through direct journey work as in other shamanic cultures.

✤ Gathering Your First Varðlokur

In what follows I am going to explain how you can use shamanic techniques to claim your own varðlokur. Once you have accomplished this, you will be able to start training yourself in further techniques of seiðr work.

We all have to start somewhere, and this means using the resources that are available to us. In ancient times it was probably the case that the potential seiðr-worker received his or her first varðloka from their teacher. Once this had been done, the apprentice seiðr-worker would have been able to begin journeying in the spirit realms on their own. In our modern world, by contrast, seiðr is a shamanic tradition that is still in the process of being rediscovered and revived, and it is unlikely that you will have direct access to an experienced teacher.

Some readers may already have a background in core shamanism and, therefore, some experience working with a drum. If this is the case, then at this early stage in seiðr training you can make use of the drum (or a prerecorded shamanic drumming track) to help you receive your first couple of varðlokur. *Once this is accomplished, however, you should set aside the drum, as it is not a traditional tool of seiðr work.* Once you have successfully received your initial varðloka (or varðlokur), you can then use the one(s) you have been given as the means to get any further varðlokur that you may need in future.

There are two methods by which you can get your first varðloka. With either method you will need to cover your eyes. You can use a scarf, bandanna, or blindfold if you want, but the traditional method— evident from both the archaeological evidence and the literary description of Thorbjorg in *Eirik the Red's Saga*—would be a hood, as discussed in the previous chapter. This large hood is pulled down to cover the face and seal out light during ceremonial work.

1. With your eyes or head covered and in darkness, undertake a fifteen-minute trance journey using whichever method you are comfortable with (either by using a drum or a prerecorded drumming track). Set your intention "To journey to a guide to get a varðloka to call the spirits." The guide may appear in human or animal form; once you have identified the guide, ask if it has a varðloka for you. If it does, ask if there are any specific instructions on how you should use the varðloka, and then ask the guide to teach it to you.

2. If you have already done some successful journeying work using your staff to tap a beat for inducing trance, you can repeat the method in tandem with the chant given below. It is difficult to use the staff lying down, so you will find it preferable to sit comfortably or stand. You can even walk around, as some people find this helps facilitate the experience—but remember that your vision will be restricted, so make sure you are in a safe space where you are unlikely to bump into anything, and move about slowly. Beat the staff on the ground while chanting the following:*

> *Æsir nornir,*
> *visa vanir,*
> *thursamøyir,*
> *thrá valkyrjur*
> *alvar dvergar*
> *disir völvur*
> *vordar vergar,*
> *Yggdrasil.*

---

*To learn the pronunciation of these phrases, you can listen to the song they are taken from. Search for "Rotlaust tre fel" by Wardruna on YouTube. The chant begins at approximately 2:40 in the song.

These words come from a modern song, "Rotlaust Tre Fel" (A Rootless Tree Falls), by the Norwegian group Wardruna, but they serve well—unintentionally, I suspect—as an effective invocation to most of the classes of Norse wights and spirits. Translated into English, the words mean:

> Æsir, Norns,
> Wise Vanir,
> Thurse-maidens,
> Resolute valkyries,
> Elves, dwarves,
> Dísir, völur,
> Warders guarding
> Yggdrasil.

As a means for calling in the wights, this is certainly enough to get you started. (Since it is a very general chant, however, it may not be especially suited for other aspects of seiðr work.) This verse also has the advantage that it is relatively short and easy to remember. It also shows how an effective varðloka can be obtained from a wide range of different places.

Eirik the Red's Saga also makes it clear that völva often had a "chorus" of other people who sang the songs for them. Such assistance was not always needed, however, and there are other references in the literature that show seiðr-workers operating very much alone. So, just as it is possible to drum for yourself for a shamanic journey, it is also possible to use the staff and varðlokur to journey alone.

The best method for developing the ability to journey using varðlokur is to practice it. Try it on your own, unaccompanied, and if you find it difficult at first, do not give up. Keep persisting, and it will suddenly click. Alternatively, you can also record yourself singing the chant—or, if you really don't like the sound of your own voice, get someone else to record it for you. This has the advantage that, like a shamanic drumming track, you can repeat it for a specific length of time, say fifteen or thirty minutes, so you know the length of a journey. (Setting a time limit is not necessary, however, as a journey will often take as long it needs to.)

At first at least, it is also good to have a "callback"—for example, a specific sound or spoken formula—which can help to bring you back fully into ordinary reality. The callback should be something that sounds different from the normal rhythm of the staff and varðloka. I have attached metal rings to my staff (see chapter 3), which can be quickly shaken back and forth to produce the callback. Another callback that I like to use is a recitation of stanzas 77–78 of the Eddic poem "Hávamál":

> *Deyr fé, deyja frændr*
> *deyr sjálfr it sama;*
> *en orðstírr deyr aldregi*
> *hveim er sér góðan getr.*
> *Deyr fé, deyja frændr*
> *deyr sjálfr it sama*
> *ek veit einn at aldri deyr*
> *dómr um dauðan hvern.**

[Translation:
Cattle die, kinsmen die,
the self must also die;
but the glory of reputation never dies,
for the man who can get himself a good one.
Cattle die, kinsmen die,
the self must also die;
I know one thing which never dies:
the reputation of each dead man.]
(Larrington 2014, 22–23)

---

*If you choose to try using this for your practice as well, you will need to spend some time memorizing it with proper pronunciation. There are YouTube videos by scholars of Old Norse that can be of further help in this regard.

A varðloka need not be a full song; it can be a single line repeated over and over, or even just a series of seemingly random tones—so do not journey to the other realms expecting to come back with a full choral work for fifty voices (if you do, great, but don't be disappointed if you don't)! Many of the most powerful icaros are one or two lines of very simple verse sung repeatedly. Whatever you come back with will be right for you. Also, it may sometimes take several journeys to get the whole of a varðloka, as you may only be given small pieces of it at a time to make it easier to remember. Therefore, when returning to visit your guide on later journeys, it is always worthwhile checking if there is anything else. When you journey it is also a good idea to have a pen and paper nearby so that you can write down and record anything you are given. Better yet, you might want to keep a dedicated journal for the purpose of recording all your varðlokur.

⬡ Gathering a Varðloka to Awaken Your Seiðstafr

After you have successfully accomplished the preceding exercise and have obtained your own first varðloka, you can repeat the basic procedure, this time using your initial general varðloka to gather a second varðloka for a specific purpose. In this case, your intention will be "To journey to a guide to receive a varðloka to awaken and empower my staff." You can then follow the detailed instructions in chapter 3 on how to activate your staff.

PROTECTION IN SEIÐR

In seiðr workings, as in most shamanic modalities, the standard methods of protection that one might use in other esoteric traditions are ineffective. As we have mentioned earlier, there is a very simple reason for this: in most forms of magical practice, protection tends to be either fixed in space and time (as is the case when casting a circle) or focused on the physical body (as with most of the visualization practices involving protective "eggs" or "cloaks"), whereas in trance work, by very definition, the spirit leaves the physical body and the current place in the middle realms, and it can be highly mobile. The spirit realms are also not subject to the same rules of time as the physical realms, and it is even possible for the spirit to transcend time.

Therefore, we must adopt certain special practices to make sure we are protected when carrying out trance work. Journeying in the upper and lower realms is relatively safe most of the time. However, you may occasionally have to visit specific areas of these realms that can be quite hostile to humankind. In a Norse context, the classic examples of such inhospitable regions are Muspelheim and Niflheim, both of which we will discuss in more detail later (see chapter 5).

Arguably, the most dangerous place to journey is the spiritual dimension of the middle realms, and Midgard in particular. There is a very specific reason for this as well. It is because many different types of entities tend to get trapped here, and some of them are potentially unfriendly to people. Giants (*jötnar*; also called "etins"), trolls, elves (*álfar*), dwarves (*dvergar*), and the wights of the restless dead all pass through Midgard and occasionally find themselves unable to leave for various reasons. They are stuck in the wrong place and at the wrong time and—like a spider trapped in the bath—just want to get "home." While these entities are not specifically out to target people, they have no qualms about trying to take advantage of anyone who could potentially be able to help them—say, apprentice seiðr-workers, for example. That's why journey work in Midgard is generally considered to be an advanced-level practice. It is best to avoid it until you have more experience, especially with regard to using protection.

Protection in trance work is done in a very specific way, by actively "merging" with a wight that is one of your guides or allies. This essentially constitutes a low-level, voluntary form of spirit-possession, but one in which you remain in complete control.

The *hamr* is the Norse term for the energetic body and forms one part of the greater soul complex.* When our hamr is whole and balanced, it forms a perfect shell around our soul, and if the soul is inhabiting a physical body at the time, the hamr encloses that as well. When the hamr is whole, it is strong and smooth like an eggshell—in fact, some have described it as being "egg-shaped." In this state it is very difficult for any wight, or even the gods, to get a decent grip on the shell or break it and gain access to what is inside.

However, the hamr is rarely in a perfectly balanced state. During modern daily life, we are often exposed to negative energies that are thoughtlessly put out into the world at large by other people. With prolonged exposure, these negative energies can attach to the hamr and pull it out of shape. This then unbalances us and can affect our emotions, making us angry or depressed, and so on. The altered shape of the hamr also gives other wights something to be able to latch onto. In a worst-case scenario, when we become extremely unbalanced, a part of the soul complex can break away, leaving a huge hole in the hamr. This provides the perfect opportunity for other unscrupulous wights to enter through the hole and take shelter within our soul complex (a lot of Norse sorcery, including battle magic, is centered around trying to break another person's hamr in order to infect their soul complex with foreign wights).

But we can also choose, quite consciously and deliberately, to *allow* another wight to enter our soul complex. The soul complex then becomes a bit of a combination of the owner's and the new wight's spirit, which can be advantageous for both parties. For example, the owner gains some additional energy from the wight, which helps to support and reinforce the hamr and can temporarily fill any holes; in return, the wight gets to experience for a short period what it is like to have a physical body. This allows the wight to eat, drink, and feel other sensations that are only associated with physicality and therefore

---

*The various parts that make up the Norse soul complex are presented in detail in the section of chapter 8 titled "The Germanic Soul or Spirit."

normally inaccessible to the wight in its abode in the spirit realms. The seiðr-worker becomes full of power from the wight—and thus more "power-full"—but must always remain in full control of this relationship so that the wight will leave when asked and not try to take over. There is very little chance of the latter happening if the wight is a guide or ally, as these usually have our best interests at heart, but other wights may try to attempt it. The merge usually takes place in the spirit worlds, but experienced seiðr-workers can bring this merge into the physical world for short periods, thereby extending to the physical body the protection that it provides.

This is a very direct example of why—contrary to some popular misconceptions—shamans in general and seiðr-workers in particular are not necessarily working while in some kind of heavily drug-induced altered state. Seiðr-workers need to maintain control, which would be virtually impossible if they were intoxicated in the manner of recreational drug or alcohol use. The wights will simply take over in such a situation. This is not to deny that the use of entheogens is an important part of shamanic practice in many cultures. However, in these cases, the shaman will have undergone many years of training in how to maintain this type of control and to work with a particular plant spirit, so that it is known intimately, before the shaman gets to the stage of ingesting the plant itself. (This is yet another reason why "ayahuasca tourism" is so dangerous, as it puts people who have not had this training in direct contact with a very powerful plant spirit.)

Here we should reiterate a point that we noted in the introduction regarding a common misconception about seiðr. The shamanic technique of merging with a wight was probably a primary reason why male seiðr-workers in ancient Norse culture were often believed to be involved with "lewdness" or "perversity" (ergi). The wight can be seen as effectively "penetrating" the seiðr-worker's energy body, in a similar way to one partner penetrating the other during intercourse, and the energy used in shamanism is closely akin to the sort of energies generated during sex. In the ancient Norse world, a male who would allow himself to be penetrated was therefore seen as weak and submissive, probably in all aspects of his life—and in a violent world dominated by the warrior caste, submissive behavior was not considered a worthy trait for men.

But the act of shamanic merging with a wight is not the dominant-submissive relationship that it might appear to be from the outside. At its best—and not unlike any good sex—it is a balanced relationship between both partners, a meeting of souls rather than just a coming together of physical body parts. And if anything, it is the practitioner rather than the wight who maintains the upper hand and can determine exactly how far the relationship goes and when it ends.

✤ Finding a Wight and a Varðloka for Protection

A varðloka can be used to both call our spirit allies and to ease the merging process. Although it is not vital for accomplishing the merge, it will likely make the work significantly easier.

Find a location where you will not be disturbed for at least thirty minutes. With your staff and hood, prepare to journey as you have done before. For this journey you also need to use the original varðloka that you obtained in the previous exercise. Set your intention "To journey to the lower realms to find a wight and ask for a varðloka that will help protect me."

Journey downward to the lower realms and spend some time exploring there. Be open to different types of wights—your ally, when it comes to you, may be in animal form, plant form, humanlike form, or some other form. You may also come across several or more wights, but there is a general rule of thumb: if you see the same wight—or part of that wight—three times, then it is probably the one you are looking for.

Once you are confident that you have found the right wight, greet it and confirm that it is there for you. This is done by asking the wight if it is the one that will help protect you. If the wight confirms this, you can ask it to teach you a varðloka that will help call it to you and aid with the protection. (Be sure to write down the varðloka in your journal after you have finished journeying.) Ask the wight how to use the varðloka and if there is anything specific the wight needs you to do. (Again, make careful notes later and be sure to do anything it requests of you.) Ask the wight any other questions that might come to mind. While you are doing this, pay particular attention to any usual sensations, feelings, smells, or other perceptions that your body may experience while you are with the wight. These sensations are unique to that particular wight and can therefore serve as a form of alert to danger. Even when we are not journeying and are just getting on with everyday life, if we are threatened, our wights will come to our aid. Sometimes, if we are busy, we may not notice them—but if we suddenly feel a particular physical sensation associated with a wight, we know that wight is around and thus there may well be some sort of danger present.

At this point you should ask the wight to merge with you. If it agrees, remember that it can only do this with your explicit consent. Consciously lower any defenses you might have subconsciously put up, any mental barriers, and tell the wight it is welcome to enter you. Watch as the wight approaches you and moves into your spiritual body. Again, become aware of any sensations, smells, or other perceptions as it merges with your energy body. Spend a few minutes merged with the wight before thanking it and gently but firmly asking it to leave your body.

Repeat the exercise several times, each time extending the period you spend merged with the wight until you can remain merged quite easily for at least a full thirty-minute journey.

Once you have gotten to this stage, you can ask the wight if it will come back with you into the physical realm. If the wight agrees, while still maintaining the merge, you will come back into the physical world as you would on any other journey, slowly and deliberately retracing the route you took to go down to the lower realms in the first place.

Once you are back in the physical realm, try to maintain the feeling of the merge and the presence of the wight inside of you. This is where you can also begin to repay the wight for its support. As we have noted earlier, wights generally do not have a physical body (although some may have had one the past). Therefore, they do not often get the chance to experience physical sensations and they really enjoy the opportunity when it comes up. So, while merged, there may be certain activities that the wight likes to experience, such as eating or drinking (unless you are already a regular smoker, I would respectfully but firmly resist any requests to smoke). Always remember that *you* are in charge of the relationship!

One activity that a wight will enjoy especially is if you dance with it. You may want to have a music player of some kind (CD or MP3) prepared and a bit of space cleared in the room before you do your usual journey and merging. When you come back to the middle realms and into Midgard, put on some suitable music and allow the wight to have a degree of physical control over your body—just enough so that it can begin to move your body in time to the music, while you retain sufficient control to prevent yourself from bumping into things. Allow as much time for this as you both feel comfortable with, or you can continue it for as long as you are able to maintain the merge. At the end of the process, thank your wight again and gently but firmly ask it to leave.

The use of varðlokur gives the seiðr-worker a slight advantage over other shamans: whenever you are in situation where you are threatened or in danger, you can begin to sing your varðloka. If it is able to do so, your wight will then be with you instantly—wherever you are, in ordinary or non-ordinary reality.

5
Traveling the Nine Realms

Then said Gangleri: "Where is the chief abode or holy
place of the gods?" Hárr answered: "That is at the Ash of
Yggdrasill; there the gods must give judgment every day."
Then Gangleri asked: "What is to be said concerning that
place?" Then said Jafnhárr: "The Ash is greatest of all
trees and best; its limbs spread out over all the world and
stand above heaven. Three roots of the tree uphold it and
stand exceeding broad: one is among the Æsir; another
among the Rime-Giants, in that place where aforetime
was the Yawning Void [Ginnungagap]; the third stands
over Niflheim, and under that root is Hvergelmir, and
Nídhöggr gnaws the root from below. But under that root
which turns toward the Rime-Giants is Mímir's Well,
wherein wisdom and understanding are stored; and he is
called Mímir, who keeps the well. He is full of wisdom,
since he drinks of the well from the Gjallar–Horn. Thither
came Allfather and craved one drink of the well; but he got
it not until he had laid his eye in pledge."

—Prose Edda, "Gylfaginning,"
chap. 15 (Sturluson 1916, 27)

Shamans around the world generally agree that the spirit realms are split
into three levels. The lower worlds (not "underworld") are generally said
to be below us, under the ground. These are the chthonic realms of the

Earth spirits, the ancestors, the dead, and the Earth mother. They are likewise the realms of the plant allies and animal allies—thus, where we also find "power animals." Many people report that these are places from which we can receive very practical and pragmatic advice about our everyday lives. From a Norse perspective, the lower realms include Niflheim, Helheim, and Jötunheim.

The upper worlds are the realms above, "in the sky"; the realms of the spiritually enlightened, of angelic-type energies; the realms of the gods and the sky father. They are the realms from which we humans seek guidance on spiritual development, although the advice received tends to be more enigmatic and "*koan*-like," to draw a parallel to Zen, and often requires much more interpretation before its meaning is fully understood. These are also the realms of "teachers in human form." In Norse cosmology, these realms are Muspelheim, Vanaheim, and Asgard.

The middle realms are the ones that exist at the same level and alongside us in the physical world. These are places where the energies of both the lower and upper worlds are integrated, places of the physical body and of healing. But for various reasons, some of which we discussed in the previous chapter, the middle worlds are also the most dangerous regions for the shaman to operate in. Therefore, one of the best methods of protection for beginners is to avoid the middle realms altogether until they have gained a considerable amount of experience in shamanic work.* For the Norse, the middle realms are the two Álfheims (Ljósálfheim and Svartálfheim) and Midgard.

There is not just a single upper world, lower world, or middle world; each level is divided into an infinite number of realms or spiritual "rooms," rather like the layers of an onion. From a shamanic perspective, the nine realms are simply the ones that seiðr-workers journey to the most, but they are not the only ones available.

---

*The upper and lower realms are generally much safer for a beginner to journey in. There are exceptions to this, but the dangerous places are relatively difficult to find and impossible to stumble into by mistake.

There is a permeable barrier between each realm, which shamans can pass through at will. These barriers are sometimes experienced as a cloud, thick fog, or mist; or as water, rivers, or ocean. They mark the boundaries between realms. Occasionally, a very powerful spirit guardian of a realm can decide to close this barrier for their own reasons, to prevent other spirits from entering; even more occasionally our own spirit guides can prevent us from passing through a barrier if we are not ready to face what lies beyond or if they decide it is not in our own best interest.

From a general shamanic perspective, all realms are connected by the axis mundi, the world axis. This is often a World Tree, the primary Germanic equivalent of which is Yggdrasil.* In most shamanic arboreal cosmologies, the upper realms are considered to be in the branches of the tree, the middle realms along the trunk, and the lower realms among the roots. Traveling along the axis mundi thus enables the shaman to gain access to any of the realms of the spirit world. Tribal shamans report that if you continue to travel upward for long enough, you will eventually find yourself coming into the lower realms from below. Similarly, go down for long enough and you will come into the upper realms from above.

Many maps have been drawn that envision the arrangement of the nine realms. These range from early medieval maps, which show the worlds as branches of the tree Yggdrasil, to more modern maps that more closely resemble a diagram of the Sephirot of Kabbalah. Much like a modern subway map, no diagram of the realms is going to be geographically accurate. Such representations are metaphorical, but in the same way that a subway map will enable a rider to easily reach a certain station, a map of the nine realms can be useful for helping the seiðr-worker to journey to one realm in relative relationship to the others, in the shortest possible time.

---

*From a continental Germanic perspective, the World Tree was also symbolized by the Irminsûl, the "Great Column" of the Saxons.

One of the maps I find most useful was developed by Edred Thorsson for the Rune-Gild; it takes the form of an octahedron that leans slightly to one side (Thorsson 2016, 49). One of the corners of the horizontal plane (Vanaheim) sticks upward into the upper level, and one (Jötunheim) slopes downward into the lower realms. I have personally found this map to be useful because it provides a three-dimensional framework that not only shows the realms themselves but also the connections—the pathways of travel, so to speak—between the worlds. I like to combine or overlay this map with a more traditional representation of Yggdrasil. However, the map in itself is not so important—what matters is the *effect* that the map produces on your own consciousness. Therefore, you will want to find a map that calls to you and effectively helps you to navigate the realms. If you cannot find an existing map that suits you and serves you in your work, it can be a very useful exercise to draw or create your own. Over time you may continue to refine it based on your experience.

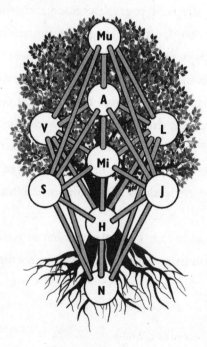

A = Asgard
H = Helheim
J = Jötunheim
L = Ljósálfheim
Mi = Midgard
Mu = Muspelheim
N = Niflheim
S = Svartálfheim
V = Vanaheim

Map of the nine realms used by the author

WORKING WITH THE GODS

Although working with the gods is one of the seven functions of shamanism, and therefore can be seen as an important part of seiðr, it is not a major focus of this book. There are some very specific reasons for this. It is perfectly possible to work with the gods through seiðr, but when one is just starting out with this work, most encounters with gods will take place through sheer chance and synchronous events. It is unwise and even potentially dangerous for the novice spirit worker to try to force these encounters or their outcomes. The gods usually choose when and where to work with us, and it is not our lot to try to force the gods to follow our agenda.

I would be surprised if, during your early work, you did not have encounters with at least a few deities—and potentially not only the Germanic ones. I am firmly of the belief that we exist in an infinite universe, or multiverse, which is likewise home to a vast number of god-like beings. Hindus, for example, would put the number of divinities in the millions. This allows the potential for all the gods from all the pantheons from around the world to exist in the spirit realms. And there is nothing in heathen lore that contradicts such a belief. I simply choose to follow the Germanic gods because for some reason I feel closer to them than to the gods of other pantheons, and they provide me with everything I need. Although I may have no personal reason to turn to other pantheons, I would never assert that such pantheons do not exist. In fact, it seems that it is only the jealous Abrahamic god who denies the existence of other gods!

In my own UPG I am aware that I have come across gods from other pantheons during my journey work. Gods tend to be very busy beings, with fingers in many pies and interests in many worlds. They travel quite freely through the spirit worlds, and if you journey long enough you are bound to come across them at some point or another, if only briefly. We may not always recognize them at first, or even at all—especially if they are from a pantheon that is very unfamiliar to us.

THE UPPER REALMS

Muspelheim (Múspellsheimr or Múspell)

The fiery realm of Muspelheim is home to the fire giants and their leader, Surtr the black. Muspelheim is one of the two primal worlds that existed in Ginnungagap before any of the others. In the creation myth, the fires of Muspelheim melt the ice of Niflheim, thus starting the cosmogonic process that leads to the creation of the other worlds. Therefore, Muspelheim, which existed long before humans ever existed, is, alongside Niflheim, one of the most hostile and least hospitable realms for people to visit. In the UPG of many people it is often described as a realm of volcanoes, lava fields, burnt land, ash, and random fires; the air is thick with smoke and sulphurous vapors. The land has its guardian in Surtr, whose flaming sword brings disaster to the gods and destroys the rest of the realms at Ragnarok.

No friend to either gods or men, Surtr keeps vigilance on the borders of Muspelheim. Never assume that you can cross the border without Surtr knowing that you are there. Nevertheless, it is sometimes necessary to cross the border for various reasons. On most such occasions, Surtr will *not* try to stop someone from crossing. This is arguably because he does not consider that anyone could possibly be a threat to him and his kind, and he would not lower himself to acknowledge such a person, so instead he ignores them. In all likelihood, you will not even be aware of Surtr—but he will know that you are there, and if you do anything wrong, he will make his presence felt. So, while working in Muspelheim, it is best to get in, do what you need to do, and get out quickly, trying to disturb the inhabitants as little as possible. Besides, as it is one of the least hospitable realms, traveling through Muspelheim tends to be an uncomfortable experience and people are generally not inclined to linger anyway. It is not exactly painful—the spirits realms are places devoid of physical pain—but it is not particularly welcoming either.

Asgard (Ásgarðr)

The realm of the Æsir, which contains the twelve major halls of the gods, is described in the lore as a rich landscape of mountains, hills, plains, woods, rivers, and marshes. Asgard is enclosed by huge walls broken by a single gateway that forms the fortress Himinbjörg, Heimdal's hall, and is surrounded by ocean. Heimdal acts as guardian and gatekeeper and, unlike Surtr, he will generally challenge everyone who tries to enter personally. Also, unlike the fire giants, the gods tend to not tolerate random people wandering around their halls, so you generally need to have a very good reason or even an invitation to be allowed to pass through the gate. Never try to sneak past Heimdal—you cannot, and you will only end up antagonizing him! If you are refused entry, there is no other choice. Just accept it and perhaps try again another day when the situation may have changed.

Vanaheim (Vanaheimr)

Vanaheim is the home of the Vanir gods. In contrast to Asgard it is not walled, but like all the realms it has its own guardian. The lore is not clear about who this guardian is. Personally, I see the guardian as being the ancient Germanic goddess Nerthus, although based on the lore of the Eddas, it could equally be the Vanir god Frey—at least when he is not in Álfheim. In Vanaheim people seem to be able to pass the borders freely and are generally made much more welcome than in Asgard, but the guardian will still be aware of all who cross and will no doubt intervene if there are any problems.

Vanaheim is not described in detail in the surviving mythological lore, but the people who visit it often experience a pastoral landscape of fields and hedges, meadows and livestock pastures, cereal crops mixed with orchards, and light woodland teeming with life and birdsong. It also seems to be very well populated as the Vanir are a fecund and fertile folk, and often quite welcoming to visitors. Good basic, tasty food and clean, crisp, cool water are always freely shared there.

THE MIDDLE WORLDS

Midgard (Miðgarðr)

Midgard is the spiritual counterpart of the physical realm we work in every day, so it appears exactly as the physical world and is subject to the same sort of conditions. However, I will reiterate the warning that journeying in Midgard is one of the most dangerous things that you can do. Midgard sits at the intersection of all the nine realms; wights often pass through and sometimes they become stuck. People also die, and often not realizing they have died, they become earthbound. Earthbound wights or ghosts (called *haugbúar* in Old Norse; sg. *haugbúi*, literally a "cairn dweller") will often try to take advantage of living folk who have become weakened in some way. They do this to be able to have the physical experiences they enjoyed in life—eating, smoking, drinking, sex, and so forth— or potentially just to find shelter from a world they can no longer interact with or understand. Other wights may try to get the attention of those people whom they think can help them move on, such as the more psychically inclined. But today it is often the case that even people who have some psychic sensitivity tend to ignore their perceptions for fear of being ridiculed; as a result, their abilities atrophy and they find it increasingly difficult to pick up on the unseen. So, many of the wights become increasingly frustrated and resort to more desperate measures to make their presence felt. Working shamanically in Midgard is like lighting a torch in a dark place—it can be seen for a great distance and all the "moths" (spirits) in the surrounding area suddenly make a direct beeline for the light. On the whole, the earthbound wights should not be seen as actively evil; they are simply trapped in the wrong time and place. Nevertheless, they can appear quite frightening to those who are not expecting them to be there.

In fact, they just need help to move on, and shamanic practitioners of all traditions spend a large proportion of their time working in the middle realms doing just that.

Shamanic work in Midgard requires a great degree of control. Instead of being like a torch in the darkness, you must become a laser with a highly focused beam, so that the light only shines in one direction. In this way you can work directly on the thing you need to, and your "light" cannot be seen from elsewhere. This sort of work also requires a high degree of protection. Until you have mastered such skills, it is therefore best to avoid working in Midgard. Nevertheless, there will be times when it is necessary, as all the land wights (*landvættir*) tend to be denizens of Midgard.*

Like the other realms, Midgard has its own guardian placed there by Óðinn the Allfather (*Alföðr*). This is the world serpent Jörmungandr, whose purpose is to create a barrier to keep the worst of the wights out of Midgard. This barrier is not perfect, however, and consequently some entities get through. Moreover, since the barrier was intended to stop things from the outside getting in, it provides no defense against things that are already trapped inside, such as earthbound wights or haugbúar, for example.

Ljósálfheim (Ljósálfheimr, Álfheimr)

Ljósálfheim (also called Álfheim), the realm of the light elves (*ljósálfar*), is often described as a place of mystery and wonder. It is a heavily forested land of mists, lights, and wonderful sounds, wind, birdsong, and music floating among the trees. It is a bit like Midgard but "more so"— colors seem more vibrant, sounds are clearer, and tastes and smells are more potent. The residents, the *álfar* (elves, sg. *álfr*) themselves, are more like Tolkienesque elves or the descriptions of the supernatural Tuatha Dé Danann in Irish myth and legend, rather than the diminutive folk with flower caps and pointy shoes that were so beloved in the Victorian

---

*The land wights are discussed in detail in chapter 7.

imagination. This not all that surprising, as Tolkien based his depiction of the elves on the old Germanic lore. The elves typically choose to appear as tall, elegant, refined, and good-looking beings, strongly connected to nature and highly skilled in the esoteric arts. They can be haughty, with a tendency to arrogance, and are easily offended and quick to anger. They generally have no great love of humans, but they are not actively antagonistic, so it is often possible to talk to them to try to win them over. But be careful—the álfar are masters of glamor, misdirection, and deception!* Nothing is ever quite as it seems, both with the álfar themselves and the land they call their own.

Ljósálfheim has a guardian in the Vanir god Frey, who according to the Eddic lore was given Álfheim as a teething gift and now rules as king of the álfar. However, as Frey divides his time between Asgard, Vanaheim, and Álfheim, he may defer this rulership to one of the other powerful álfar if he is not around.

Svartálfheim (Svartálfheimr)

Unlike the situation in most of the other realms, there may be two different types of wights that call Svartálfheim home. It is certainly the home of the *dvergar* (dwarves; sg. *dvergr*) but may also be home to the *svartálfar* (dark or black elves), who are mentioned a few times in the mythological lore. The information about them is contradictory, however, and it is not entirely clear whether the svartálfar are a separate race of beings unto themselves, perhaps a subset of the álfar, or if "svartálfar" is just another name for the dvergar. So, there is a big debate over this among both historians and heathens. If these are indeed two distinct types of beings, then it is possible that the svartálfar live on the surface of Svartálfheim, while the dvergar are mostly subterranean. And if the svartálfar do exist separately, this means they are very hard to engage with and shun contact, so I will concentrate mainly on the dvergar.

---

*For more on the magical concept of glamor (glamour), see the section "Variants of Gandr" in chapter 10.

Svartálfheim tends to be experienced as a desolate and dreary place: craggy, rocky, hilly, and mountainous; cold, often dark and murky, and full of geography and geology rather than biology. Certainly, most activity seems to take place below ground. The lore states that the dvergar themselves were created by Óðinn, Vili, and Vé from maggots they found burrowing in the flesh of Ymir, and as such they prefer to live in subterranean caves and tunnels where they can also find the raw materials they need. It is also interesting to note that the lore never describes their height, so the modern English "dwarf" may not be a fitting translation.

Surely, the stubborn and strong dvergar tend not to bother with social niceties and can be blunt to the point of rudeness. They are shrewd businessmen and always know the value of their goods, but they can also be quite self-centered and are often seen carrying out very "negative" acts to further their aims. The story recounted in the *Prose Edda* of their involvement in the death of Kvasir and the creation of the mead of inspiration is a good example of this. They are, however, craftsmen and creators beyond compare. They excel at incorporating magical attributes into physical objects; indeed, most of the objects we most strongly associate with the gods were made by dwarves. For magical "crafting" projects, then, one could find no better allies than the dvergar—if you can get them on board and are willing to pay their price!

Like the other realms Svartálfheim has its guardian, and this tends to be the current king of the dwarves. Due to internal politics, however, the one who holds this post can change from time to time.

THE LOWER REALMS

Niflheim (Niflheimr)

Alongside Muspelheim, Niflheim is one of the two primal realms responsible for creation: it is the realm of ice opposed to Muspelheim's fire.

Also, like Muspelheim, Niflheim is one of the most inhospitable places for people. It is very cold, craggy, misty, icy, and snowy, yet with lots of flowing water as well. This is the site of the well called Hvergelmir, from which nine rivers flow—the ultimate source of all water in the nine realms. This is the home of the rime thurses (*hrímþursar*; sg. *hrímþurs*) or frost giants, implacable enemies of the gods and especially Thor. In contrast to how these giants are often portrayed in modern popular culture, the original lore makes it clear that they are far from being just big, dumb giants with crude weapons. Highly intelligent and cultured in their own way, some of the cleverest rime thurses—especially their kings—were known to nearly rival Óðinn in terms of wisdom. Great strategists as well as warriors, they also tended to have some of the best weapons and armor available. Thjazi, father of the goddess Skaði, was a king of the rime thurses before being killed by the gods, and Skaði herself is technically a rime thurse and not one of the Æsir.

The frost giants are not generally inimical toward people, mainly because they find us to be insignificant beings, not worth bothering with and best ignored. Like the fire giants, the rime thurses will tolerate people entering and passing through their land for short periods, probably because they figure that we represent no real threat, and it is beneath their dignity to acknowledge us. But Niflheim is no place to linger, both due to the environment and the inhabitants. And although they may start out rather indifferent with respect to their disposition, the rime thurses are very easy to antagonize. In going about their daily activities, they are also oblivious concerning any collateral damage that they might inflict on people who happen to be nearby.

The guardian of Niflheim is the king of the rime thurses. Similarly to the situation with the dvergar in Svartálfheim, however, the giant who holds this position can sometimes change.*

---

*Due to their ongoing battles, the king will occasionally lose his life at the hands of Thor.

Jötunheim (Jötunheimr)

Jötunheim or "Etin Home" is the third of the realms that belong to the giants. Often experienced as a wild and untamed place, its landscape consists of huge mountains, high waterfalls, rivers, and lakes, and dense, dark forests of towering conifers in which the gloom of night never really lifts. There is every imaginable shade of weather, often in random succession, so it is possible to have blizzards followed by baking heat, followed by tropical downpours—all in a single day. In Jötunheim it is really the size of things that catches the attention: everything is on a vastly grander scale than in Midgard. The land itself tends to be chaotic and unstable, with a tendency to shift and change each time you visit, very much like the inhabitants.

The land is home to "jötuns" (*jötnar*, sg. *jötunn*), trolls, and all the other etin kin and their relations. This is a very mixed bunch, and the usual English translation of "giant" may be a bit misleading. Even the true jötuns are described as varying in height from slightly above average human size to truly giant and towering over the largest trees; moreover, many are masters of the hamr and thus able to adjust their sizes and shapes. Jötuns are all descended from Ymir and are therefore very close relatives of the fire and frost giants, but unlike the latter two groups, true jötuns tend to have mixed and highly variable forms. For example, the children of Loki are all jötuns, yet one is a giant serpent or wyrm (Jörmungandr), one is a massive wolf (Fenris), and one is more or less human-size but appears partly as a beautiful maiden and partly as a rotting corpse (Hela). The jötuns tend to be named after and therefore representative of the forces of nature and the wilderness—especially those forces that are uncontrolled and chaotic.

The mother of the children of Loki is Angrboða, who is referred to as the "bearer of wolves" and "old lady of the iron wood." Together with Útgarða-Loki (a giant who is unrelated to the true Loki), these two may act as guardians of the realm. Although the jötuns seem to be more free-spirited and lack the formal hierarchies and social structures that mark the other races, Angrboða and Útgarða-Loki hold a position of great respect among the inhabitants of Jötunheim.

The jötuns are chaotic, powerful, sometimes aggressive, and undoubtedly dangerous. While they harbor great resentment toward the gods for the killing of their primordial ancestor, Ymir, they are not necessarily antagonistic to humans and should not be thought of as "evil." Unless someone really enrages them, most of the injuries the jötuns inflict on people seem to be the result of "collateral damage," because they often do not register that we are even there. But the jötuns are very much individuals and on a personal level some of them really do not like humans. If you come across one of these, I strongly advise that you get out of the way, quick! Others are much more open and even curious about us, and therefore a lot easier to talk to and engage, or potentially negotiate with.

Helheim (Helheimr)

The last of the lower realms is Helheim. Despite the similarity of the name with "hell," this realm has nothing in common with the fiery place of punishment in the Abrahamic religions.* The general impression in the Germanic lore is that Helheim is described in ways not dissimilar to the physical world. Life there seems to carry on much as it does now in Midgard, apart from the fact that there may be less hard work required of anyone in Helheim. The spirits of the dead get more peace and rest, and arguably are better fed. Helheim is under the rulership of Hela,† who is the daughter of Loki and Angrboða.

Today many people seem to have gotten the impression—perhaps from reading internet articles depicting it as the abode for the

---

*In fact, the missionizing Christians in Germanic-speaking areas of Europe stole the name Hel and applied it to their own vision of an afterlife for sinners in an attempt to demonize heathen beliefs.

†In the original Old Norse texts, the name of both the realm and its ruler are identical: Hel. In this book, however, we will refer to the realm as Hel and its ruler as Hela in order disambiguate the two for the reader.

"dishonorable dead"—that Helheim, if not actually a place of punishment, is akin to the classical conception of Hades: a cold, gloomy realm where the depressed dead sit around tiny fires in meager shelters with little food, cursing their fate. This is certainly not the case. Helheim is not the destination of the dishonorable dead, but rather of all who are not chosen to join the *einherjar* (the slain warriors that comprise Óðinn's army in Valhalla)—which probably means over 99 percent of people.

As mentioned, Helheim is described much like Midgard, with a couple of notable exceptions. The biggest of these is the climate, which is said to vary greatly across space rather than over time. In one part of Helheim it is summer, while in other parts it is winter, spring, or autumn—and it is even possible to walk between the seasons. This means that somewhere in Helheim, at any given time, a portion of Hela's apple trees—and, presumably, of other crops as well—are always in flower, some always in fruit, some losing their leaves, and others just bare branches. So, the dead always have food available and there is no glut or shortage as the seasons change. Hela takes good care of her guests.

Helheim is surrounded by high walls. At its border is a river, the Gjöll, that is crossed by a single bridge, the Gjallarbrú, which passes into Hel's gateway. The bridge is guarded by the giantess Moðguðr and the hound Garmr, who together act as gatekeepers. The walls themselves are not intended to keep the dead in, but rather to keep the living out, so that the peace of the dead is not disturbed by a constant stream of relatives demanding to know where granny buried the family fortune. The dead can pass freely over the bridge, but Moðguðr and Garmr stop the living from entering.

This has led some people to suggest you cannot get into Helheim unless you are dead. This is not supported by the lore, however, as chapter 49 of the "Gylfaginning" section of the *Prose Edda* describes how Hermoð was able to travel across the bridge to talk to Baldr in Helheim. It is usually the case that you will not be allowed to go in unless you have either an invitation or a very good reason. However, something to keep in mind for the shamanic practitioner is that in my experience people who have undergone *La petite mort* are changed energetically so that they more closely resemble the dead. In certain circumstances this enables them to pass as the dead, and in this way they are able to travel through the gates of Helheim.

❖ Exploring the Realms

Using the following exercises, you can spend some time visiting and exploring as many of the nine realms as possible. At this point it is advisable to avoid Midgard for the reasons explained earlier. It may also be the case that you are unable to gain access to either Asgard or Helheim at this time, but you should at least be able to visit the other six realms. If you already have a relationship with any of the Æsir, you can journey to them beforehand and ask if it is possible for them to take you to Asgard.

Many people believe that you should not ask the gods for petty favors like this, but this is a shortsighted view. As multifaceted beings, the deities are dealing with countless people and other things at the same time. Even if they choose to answer you—and they certainly will only grant the request if they themselves deem it important—you will only be getting the merest fraction of their attention, anyway.

As for gaining entry to Helheim, it is not impossible, but it is difficult and better left to seiðr-workers who have mastered certain more advanced techniques than the ones presented in this book.

There are two different ways you can journey to one of the six remaining realms: (1) you can either obtain a single varðloka that can take you to all the realms, or (2) you can obtain a different varðloka for each of the realms. The second method is more complex and takes longer, but has the benefit that it will provide you with a personal key to each of those realms. It can also be of help when you come across wights from those realms in other parts of the nine worlds—perhaps in places where they should not be!

The technique for obtaining a varðloka is explained in the previous chapter. Once you have your varðloka (either for journeying to the realms in general, or a specific varðloka for a particular realm) your intention will be "To journey to the realm of _____ to explore." Merge with your spirit helpers for protection and then carry on as you would normally.

THE WIGHTS OF YGGDRASIL

Alongside the wights that inhabit the nine realms, there are several other wights that are specifically associated with the World Tree, Yggdrasil. None of these wights is particularly hostile, but they may not be all that friendly either—they usually keep to themselves. However, in certain situations they can provide support and insight, and occasionally you may want to approach some of them for information.

Ratatöskr

> Ratatosk [Ratatöskr] is the squirrel who there shall run
> On the ash-tree Yggdrasil;
> From above the words of the eagle he bears,
> And tells them to Nithhogg [Níðhöggr] beneath.
> —GRÍMNISMÁL 32
> (BELLOWS 1923, 97)

Ratatöskr is the squirrel that runs the length of Yggdrasil, taking messages, gossip, and taunts between the eagle that sits at the top of the tree to Níðhöggr, the wyrm (serpent) at the roots. The Old Norse word *rata* means "to travel, fare, journey," and *tösk* means "tusk," so the name Ratatöskr can be interpreted as "Tusk the traveler" or "Tusk the climber."* As the messenger of Yggdrasil, he knows the tree and its secrets intimately and has access to all of the nine realms.

Ratatöskr is a generally cheeky, chatty, and mischievous wight who likes stirring up petty arguments for his own entertainment. But there

---

*See Cleasby and Vigfusson 1874, under "*rata*" and "*rati*."

is no better guide than him to the pathways of Yggdrasil, and if you are struggling to find something or to journey along the great tree's branches by yourself, it is sometimes possible to hitch a lift by riding Ratatöskr. Be aware, however, that he will always demand something in return, so it is best to "fix the fare" before you start the journey. To begin any relationship with Ratatöskr you will need to obtain a varðloka for calling him.

The Deer of Yggdrasil:
Dáinn, Dvalinn, Duneyrr, and Duraþrór

In chapter 16 of the "Gylfaginning," we are informed: "Four harts run in the limbs of the Ash [Yggdrasil] and bite the leaves. They are called thus: Dáinn, Dvalinn, Duneyrr, Durathrór" (Sturluson 1916, 29). These four harts (deer) that graze in the World Tree are an enigmatic group of wights. At first thought one might assume a connection to the four seasons or the four directions, but as the Norse only had two seasons (summer and winter) and the four directions were not a central part of their beliefs, this is unlikely to be the case. Finnur Magnússon (1824, 144) suggests that they may be connected to the four winds: Dáinn (The Dead One) and Dvalinn (The Unconscious One) suggesting gentle breezes, while Duneyrr (Thundering in the Ear) and Duraþrór (Thriving Slumber, perhaps a reference to snoring) may be kennings, or poetic circumlocutions, for strong winds. In my own experience journeying, I have found they are wights that can be approached for weather workings.

However, there is another theory based on stanzas 141–42 of the "Rúnatál" (Óðinn's "Rune Listing," a section of the Eddic poem "Hávamál"):

> Hidden Runes shalt thou seek and interpreted signs,
>   many symbols of might and power,
>   by the great Singer painted, by the high Powers fashioned,
>   graved by the Utterer of gods.

For gods graved Odin, for elves graved Daïn [Dáinn],

Dvalin [Dvalinn] the Dallier for dwarfs,

All-wise for Jötuns, and I, of myself,

graved some for the sons of men. (Bray 1908, 103)

As there are four deer and the names of two of them, Dáinn and Dvalinn, look identical to the names of two rune masters of the four nondivine races (elves, dwarves, jötuns, and men), it has been suggested that the deer may be the rune masters transformed into animal form, hiding from something unknown. Personally, I find this unlikely— why would they choose to hide in Yggdrasil? But I have never directly approached the deer about working with the runes, so perhaps it would be a worthwhile experiment!

The Eagle and Veðrfölnir

Another line in chapter 16 of the "Gylfaginning" tells of two raptors in the branches of the World Tree: "An eagle sits in the limbs of the Ash, and he has understanding of many a thing; and between his eyes sits the hawk that is called Vedrfölnir [Veðrfölnir]" (Sturluson 1916, 29). This pair of birds is even more enigmatic than the four deer. We know very little about them; for example, we never learn the eagle's name. However, it is clear they are somehow associated with knowledge and wisdom. It is thought that similarly to Óðinn's ravens Huginn and Muninn, the hawk Veðrfölnir may act as the eyes and ears of the eagle, traveling the nine realms and bringing back any information it finds, which is then reported to and remembered by the eagle. But unlike the god Óðinn, who has his own distinct agenda and may only share knowledge if it suits his purpose, the eagle may be an easier source from which the journeying seiðr-worker may glean information. Presumably, though, the eagle may not have quite as great a level of understanding as the god of wisdom.

Níðhöggr

Níðhöggr (often anglicized to Nidhögg) is the serpent or wyrm that lives among the roots of Yggdrasil. As chapter 15 of the "Gylfaginning" informs us: "The third [root] stands over Niflheim, and under that root is Hvergelmir, and Níðhöggr gnaws the root from below" (Sturluson 1916, 27).

Níðhöggr and its children are the source of venom in the nine realms. Venom is a very specific spiritual substance—it is the essence of entropy, the element of rot and decay, and the energy behind all toxins and poisons in the middle realms.* It is strongly linked to the presence of disease in the human body, and several of the early Germanic healing charms were used to repel or destroy venom.

Venom is a much misunderstood and maligned substance. It is not "evil"—it is pure, blind energy with no consciousness, and its basic function of destruction is necessary to the correct functioning of the multiverse. The old, that which blocks progress, must always be cleared away to make space for the new. Venom is the substance that does this, breaking things down into their constituent elements so that they are ready to be recycled and reused.

Like all energy, venom itself is neutral but can be directed for positive or negative purposes. It can cause disease or the destruction of things that people are not yet ready to part with. But it can also dissolve blockages and barriers, links to people and things that hold us back, and it can even be applied in healing to target the causes of illness. The use of chemotherapy in cancer treatment is a good example of a modern application of venom in healing.

Níðhöggr is the undisputed master of venom and the keeper of knowledge about its use. Níðhöggr also has lessons to teach us about the importance of breaking down the old to produce the material for new growth, and of recycling as part of overall sustainability.

---

*See chapter 10 for a discussion of venom in the context of *gandr* magic.

6
Wyrd and Divination

Wyrd is a specialized term I will be using to refer to the ancient Germanic concept of fate. To work effectively with seiðr, you need a basic understanding of how Wyrd works. The word itself comes from Old English, and therefore our modern understanding of Wyrd largely derives from Anglo-Saxon sources, such as the poem "The Wanderer," rather than Norse texts. Wyrd is a noun that originated from the Old English verb *weorþan*, "to come to pass." Its Norse cognate and equivalent is *urðr*, which loosely translates as "fate" and is related to the past tense of the verb *verða*, "to become." There are indications that the Anglo-Saxon and Norse cultures shared a roughly similar understanding of fate, so Wyrd is generally considered to be a pan-Germanic concept today.

Wyrd has been compared to other pagan conceptions of fate such as the classical Roman *fatum* or Hellenic "destiny" (μοῖρα). While there are some similarities and overlap between these notions, Wyrd also works in subtly different ways. It is arguably closer to the Eastern concepts of karma and dharma, but it is not identical with them.

Let us start at the beginning. The Eddas speak of three women, or more specifically three giant maidens. Maidens in this sense may mean "untouched" or "unsullied," rather than implying a certain age, because they are spoken of in the literature as appearing as different ages, from young to elderly. They are, in fact, ageless. Their names are Urðr (That Which Has Become), Verðandi (That Which Is Becoming), and Skuld (That Which Should Become), and together they are known as the greater Norns or simply the Norns. And it is the Norns who determine how Wyrd works. They themselves are not, however, the masters or rulers over Wyrd—when they "lay out" Wyrd, it seems they must follow certain rules, and they cannot change the course of Wyrd on a whim.

In our modern world of cause and effect, we tend to see events in the past as dictating what happens in the future. There is strong evidence that our ancestors did not quite view it this way, however. Many heathens today consider Urðr to be the oldest and most important of the Norns, while the other two may just be later aspects of Urðr. I prefer to see them as separate and individual beings, but it is entirely for you to decide how you can best connect and work with them.

The Eddas also speak of three wells. Here, as with the three Norns, we have an example of a sacred Germanic triplicate. The well Hvergelmir in Niflheim is the ultimate source of all the waters of the nine realms. The Mímisbrunnr (Mímir's Well), guarded by the severed head of the jötun Mímir, is where Óðinn sacrificed his eye to gain all the wisdom of the world. The Urðarbrunnr (Well of Urðr) is also often referred to as the "Well of Wyrd." All three wells are said to lie beneath the World Tree, Yggdrasil.

The three wells are thought to be the ultimate source of Wyrd and to represent an initiatory sequence. Wyrd enters the nine realms through Hvergelmir, indicating that it potentially originates from somewhere outside the nine realms, which raises some intriguing possibilities. It flows through the Mímisbrunnr, which may represent the collective subconscious of all beings of the realms—the place where wisdom originates—and finally begins to manifest in the physical realm through the Urðarbrunnr. The three wells, connected by Yggdrasil's roots, can therefore also be seen as collectively forming a Well of Wyrd.

The Eddas describe the Norns as tending the Urðarbrunnr. Every day they take pure white clay from the bottom of the well and spread it over the roots of Yggdrasil to heal and repair the damage caused by the serpent-wyrm Níðhöggr (an agent of atrophy and decay) and prevent Yggdrasil from falling. Yggdrasil—and thus all of the nine realms and every being that exists within them—is, in effect, being held up and supported solely by Wyrd. The Eddas do not ever refer to the Norns as weavers, only as tenders of the well.

Alongside the Anglo-Saxon Wyrd, we have a related concept in the Norse tradition called ørlög. Wyrd and ørlög are often conflated in modern popular consciousness even though they originated from different cultures and their connotations are not identical.

Ørlög operates at two different levels. At the higher level, ørlög is effectively the set of rules according to which the greater Norns lay out the overall pattern of Wyrd, which can be likened to a tapestry, for all the nine realms. Because ørlög effectively dictates the overall pattern, which include the routes that the various threads take through the tapestry, at a lesser or lower level it becomes a proxy for the fated course of each of our individual lives: our unique ørlög.

For each individual, ørlög is set at birth. Again, perhaps surprisingly, this is not done by the greater Norns, who are presumably too busy setting out the Wyrd of entire realms to be interested in the ørlög of individuals. It is made clear in chapter 15 of the "Gylfaginning" section of the *Prose Edda* that, in addition to Urðr, Verðandi, and Skuld, "there are many more norns: those who come to each child that is born, to appoint his life; these are of the race of the gods, but the second are of the Elf-people, and the third are of the kindred of the dwarves" (Sturluson 1916, 29).

For humans, the lesser Norns appear to be a subcategory of the *dísir* (sg. *dís*), the wise female ancestors who take an interest in and help to guide the lives of their descendants. But there are also norns of álfr-kin and of dvergr-kin, and presumably of jötun-kin as well.

The much later fairy-tale figure of the Fairy Godmother may have developed from a folk memory of these lesser Norns—the classic example being Sleeping Beauty where three (or in the original Perrault version, six) good fairies bestow a set of "gifts" including beauty, wit, grace, and so forth on the young princess. But Sleeping Beauty also contains a stark warning about Wyrd and the power of the Norns. The bad fairy, unhappy that she was not invited to the party, "curses" the baby princess to die—the equivalent of giving her a very short ørlög. The combined power of the other fairies cannot entirely undo this curse, but they are able to modify it so that instead of dying the princess falls into a very deep sleep from which she can only be awakened by a true love's kiss. This children's story seems to reflect a half-remembered truth about fate: in some situations, Wyrd is highly malleable and can be changed easily, but in others it is completely unchangeable and not even the gods can affect it.

The closer we follow our ørlög through life, the easier that life becomes. We are in "flow" with the universe—our hamingja (integral luck) ensures that events go in our favor and things just seem to work out. But if we try to move away from our ørlög, life becomes harder. Things get sticky and take a lot to work through, and our luck begins to run out.

So, our ørlög flows through the tapestry of Wyrd, and where it touches the ørlög of another, it forms a node or knot in the tapestry, and an event in the physical realm—a meeting of two people, perhaps. That event may completely change the direction of any or all threads of ørlög involved.

In cases where it involves just two or a very few threads, this forms a simple event, one that can be changed through a process of physical action. For example, two people arrange to go for a coffee to discuss some new project ideas; with respect to Wyrd, the most likely outcome of this meeting is the formation of a new business partnership. But at the last minute one of them suddenly calls off the meeting, the partnership never forms, and both people go their different ways. Two threads that should have come together touch briefly, but the knot, the event, does not hold, so they separate again. There has been a slight change in the pattern of Wyrd, but because it is so small in the overall tapestry (two lives set against billions) it would probably be imperceptible to anyone but the Norns. For the people involved, however, the partnership would have bought some financial security, so for the rest of their lives they struggle with money—because they moved away from their original ørlög, their lives become a little bit harder.

If a few more threads come together at the same place, then that event becomes tied much tighter into the pattern of Wyrd and cannot be changed by physical action alone. In this case, it needs either magic or the intervention of the gods and wights to change things—this is where seiðr comes in.

Finally, if enough threads come together in a single place or event, no power—not even that of the gods—will suffice to change them. The most obvious example of this would be Ragnarok, the cataclysmic end of the world. Athough the Allfather knows exactly what will happen—for he has consulted a völva, who has prophesied what is to come—he is completely unable to change the events no matter how hard he tries.

Stories related in the Icelandic sagas make it clear, however, that magic can be used to change events in the lesser ørlög of people's lives. Once this is done, however, it is very hard to change them back again. A prime example is found in *The Saga of Arrow-Odd* (*Örvar-Odds saga*). The family of Arrow-Odd (Örvar-Oddr) invites a völva onto their lands to prophesy how things will go for them over the next year. Everyone is quite excited about this and cues up to receive a prophecy—except for Arrow-Odd, who insults and even attacks the völva. Once he has been subdued by his friends and family, the völva reveals the prophecy to him anyway, but in revenge changes it subtly: instead of what should have been a positive ending, she condemns Arrow-Odd to die on the land, killed by his own horse.

The young Arrow-Odd tries as hard as he can to avert the prophecy by killing the horse, burying it, and then leaving the land far behind to become a Viking. But whatever he does, he cannot escape the Wyrd that the völva has set. Eventually, he is forced to return to the farm and is indeed finished off by the horse that he himself had earlier killed and buried. In the end, it becomes clear that his attempt to avoid the prophecy by killing the horse is what led to his final demise—if the horse had remained alive, it certainly could not have hurt him in the same way. So, what we do to avoid Wyrd will sometimes only bind us more tightly to it.

From a Germanic perspective, divination—whether done through seiðr or by consulting the runes—may be thought of as an attempt to see more of the pattern of Wyrd than is otherwise visible, whereas magic is the means by which the vitki or vitka can attempt to change some aspects of Wyrd in accordance with his or her will (potentially as a consequence of what was revealed in the divination). But the limitation here is that we are not Norns: although we may be able to get a glimpse of the "bigger picture," particularly with respect to our own ørlög, we will never have a full perception of the greater Wyrd.

Wyrd is extremely complex. If you live in a city, or even a town, you might conceivably interact with hundreds of people on a given day. In some cases, this may be a mere moment of eye contact in the street, but often it is much more—some words over coffee with a colleague at work, a meal with a friend, a long discussion with your partner in the evening. Each time you encounter someone else, both of your ørlögs "touch" and thus have the possibility of affecting each other. But the network of ørlög extends much further than this, as the person with whom you are interacting has also encountered dozens of other people that day who may have in some small way affected *their* ørlög right up until the point of your interaction. Thus, the ørlögs of these people can have an impact on yours as well, albeit indirectly.

Consider the following hypothetical situation. Your partner has had a bad day at work—perhaps due to a run-in with a colleague—which has impacted his or her ørlög. Your partner comes home tired and irritable and takes it out on you: their ørlög touches yours and changes it, perhaps dampening your otherwise good mood, making you irritable as well. Multiply this sort of interaction by the more than eight billion people in the world and you will begin to see just how complex the overall pattern of Wyrd may be. Billions of threads of ørlög, each of which is continually intertwining with others to a varying degree. If we then consider the additional impact of other, less-visible factors—for example, influences from the past actions of the dead, or the power of subconscious feelings to affect behavior, or the use of magic to change the course of events—and add these to the mix, we begin to get a sense of how truly terrifying this all may be.

Even if we employ the most powerful divination methods, as humans we cannot possibly see where all of these threads lead. And if we use magic to pull on and change one thread—either ours or somebody else's—we in turn pull on thousands, if not millions, of others that are loosely or strongly connected to it, changing things in small or large ways. Successful magic has consequences—often ones that we did not and could not foresee. The more powerful the magic, the more unintended consequences there will be, some of which will undoubtedly be negative. This should not stop us from doing magic, but it should always make a responsible vitki or vitka stop and think before carrying out any magical working: Will the cost of inaction likely be greater than the cost of using magic to change the current situation? Each situation will present a unique set of circumstances, and only you can balance that equation.

It is also important to remember that whether a consequence is positive or negative is a highly subjective question. For example, if your magical working makes the tool that someone is using to try to do you damage break at a crucial moment, then that may be of great benefit and so overall seem very positive to you—whereas the person holding the now broken tool in their hand would see this in an entirely different way!

Carrying out a healing is always positive, right? Not necessarily. What if the person who would have died instead heals well, but then goes on to hurt many others? And if the latter occurs, is *that* always negative? If the action prevents these people from hurting you or those you love at some time in the future, then perhaps not. But what if the healed person goes on to hurt someone who was otherwise destined to develop the next antibiotic that the world sorely needs, and consequently the antibiotic is never produced? Which is the greater negative cost: the loss of a single life or the potential damage to many more? And how can you foresee any of this at the time when you must decide whether to perform the healing?

The examples presented here are admittedly extreme and unlikely. But they are not impossible, and I mention them to highlight a point: when it comes to a magical working, there are an array of unforeseen consequences that can and will occur. In Germanic magic there is no higher moral "judgment," no absolute black and white, only shades of gray. There are only actions and the consequences they bring about.

✤ Exercises with the Norns

Here we will present some seiðr techniques for engaging with both the lesser and the greater Norns to learn more about your own ørlög and the greater workings of Wyrd.

ᚷ Contacting Your Lesser Norn

Using your staff and your original varðloka, you can undertake a journey to contact the lesser Norn that set your own ørlög at your birth. Remember, the lesser Norns vary from race to race. So, as a human, your individual Norn will likely be a *dís*, in which case she may be found either in Helheim or an ancestral burial mound. However, there is an outside chance that if your family has nonhuman blood, your lesser Norn may also not be human, and very occasionally I have come across people with álfr, dvergr, or even jötun Norns. Therefore, I would advise you to avoid prejudging the situation and keep an open mind. If the lesser Norn is of a different race than the *dísir*, then it is also likely that it will be found dwelling in another part of the nine realms. In such a case, looking for the Norn in Helheim would be a waste of time, for example.

Set your intention "To journey to the nine realms to speak to my lesser Norn." Using your staff and your early varðloka, journey as you normally would, and you will be taken to the right place.

There are several questions you could potentially ask your Norn, or things you can try:

1. Ask for a specific varðloka that will help you to contact your lesser Norn immediately when you need to do so.

2. As a type of divination, ask your Norn to show you more about your own ørlög: Why was it originally set out like it was? What are the "reasons" for your life as it stands?

3. Try to find out if you are currently in alignment with your own ørlög or if there have been any major changes to it over your lifetime that you should be aware of.

4. Merge with the Norn and ask it to make changes to your own ørlög if it seems that the latter is going in a direction you do not like. You cannot make these changes yourself, so do not try to do so. Accept that your Norn is wiser than you are and has more awareness of what the final outcomes could be, so if it refuses your request, do not try to force it. But if it agrees, then listen to what it says: it will tell you exactly what you need to do to make these changes happen.

ᚷ Visiting the Greater Norns

It is relatively easy to journey to Asgard to visit the Urðarbrunnr and the greater Norns. Based on my own experiences and UPG, I would say that they are even rather partial to receiving guests. It is possible to help them with their work with the clay to support Yggdrasil, and I have found this a good way of building megin, which will always be a significant help when trying to work with lesser Norns and Wyrd. They are also sometimes not averse to merging with a seiðr-worker to return to Midgard and experience a physical body for short time—again, not a bad way of potentially building megin for Wyrd work! Be respectful; listen closely to what they say and sometimes they will provide little gems that can really increase your understanding of how Wyrd operates.

However, what they will *never* do is provide specific details about any individual strands of Wyrd, any individual ørlög, or any events tied into the tapestry, the past, or the future. So, do not even try to get this information out of them—it is very easy way to anger them. Trust me, the last thing you need is an angry Norn that even the gods are afraid of!

DIVINATION IN SEIÐR

To understand how divination works in seiðr, you need to have at least a basic understanding of Wyrd (*urðr* in Old Norse) as explained at the beginning of this chapter. The problem is that the average person can only see a very small part of Wyrd at any one time. Those who are more psychically gifted might have a slightly wider picture, but it is still quite limited. How can we take action to improve Wyrd if we cannot really see it and thereby gain a sense of what changes might be needed?

Divination, in a Germanic context at least, is about trying to gain as wide a view of Wyrd as is possible at a given time. Unlike the Norns, people will never be able to see Wyrd in its entirety—this would simply be too much for the human mind to take and would damage us beyond repair. But we can use certain techniques to get a glimpse of parts of Wyrd beyond our usual and limited horizons.

Seiðr offers a variety of methods of divination. The most well known of these is probably the high-seat rite performed by the seeress Thorbjorg in *Eirik the Red's Saga*, which we quoted from in earlier chapters. In this rite the seiðr-worker opens herself or himself to the wights and allows one to step into their energetic body and take control; other people then ask questions of the wight through the seiðr-worker. This is essentially a type of voluntary possession and is not without dangers. It is therefore an advanced technique and certainly not something I would recommend that anyone try when they are just starting out with seiðr.

Here we will instead look at some more basic methods of divination that are often ignored. The first of these involves the use of the staff, while the second is a technique based on a shared personal gnosis (SPG) that many people have found to be effective.

Divination Using the Seiðstafr

On most ancient seiðstafir, about two-thirds of the way up the staff and just below the four arched metal pieces that archaeologists in the past often called the "handle"—but which we now know had a completely different purpose—there was a strange feature: a flat and usually triangular structure through which the central shaft of the staff passed. One point of the triangle was generally longer and stuck out slightly farther than the two others. This point was pierced through with a circular hole. There are two theories about function of this feature:

- The structure could be used somehow for navigation, enabling the seer to find their way from farm to farm at night, perhaps by focusing on the pole star.
- Alternatively, the structure could be used for divination, similarly to objects that are found in certain other shamanic cultures.

As a practicing seiðr-worker, I tend to favor the second explanation. The Chukchi are a tribe from the very northern and eastern edge of Siberia, which makes them part of the wider circumpolar culture that may have also influenced the development of seiðr. Many of the Siberian tribes had an unbroken tradition of shamanic practice until the early twentieth century. However, Siberian shamanism was very strongly suppressed by the Soviet authorities, and this was especially the case with the Chukchi. Despite their resistance to Soviet rule, unfortunately only certain fragments of Chukchi shamanism survive. Nevertheless, we can use some of these fragments to start to fill in certain gaps in our knowledge about seiðr.

For example, we know that the Chukchi, like the Norse, tended to use a staff in their shamanic practices. And accounts from surviving elders of the community, who were alive when the last Chukchi shamans were still working, reveal that they also had an interesting method of divination. The shamans would take a weighted string or cord and attach it to the end of the staff, and they would then employ this as a type of pendulum for answering straightforward yes-or-no questions.

The elders also remember a significant technique whereby the shaman would tie the cord of the staff around the head of a fresh corpse before rigor mortis set in. The shaman would then use this to lift the head off the ground while asking it questions, and the way the head lolled and moved from side to side would give some indication of the answer to those questions. The theory behind this was that an ancestor who had just died would have one foot in the spirit worlds, and thus have access to more information, while also still having a vestigial connection to their physical corpse, through which they could relay the information to others.

Needless to say, I am definitely *not* going to recommend that you tie the head of your recently departed grandmother to your staff, even if your family is very understanding of your beliefs! But there are some very effective ways in which the basic technique of a divinatory pendulum attached to your staff can be used, as we will explore below.

❈ Divination with the Seiðr Staff

1. Carry out a journey as you have done before to retrieve a new varðloka. The intention this time is "To retrieve a varðloka for

use in divination." Travel to the upper worlds or lower worlds, as directed by your wights, and follow the same process as you have used on earlier journeys. When you get a varðloka, remember to note it in your journal so that you will be able to recall it in future.

2. On your return, tie a weighted cord to the appropriate fitting on your staff. Begin to sing the varðloka you were given and try to enter a very light trance state, with most of your consciousness still in the middle realms, in Midgard.

3. As with any form of pendulum divination, you will first need to establish how it is going to respond to your questions. Silently, in your head, ask for it to show you the response for "yes," watching very carefully how the pendulum moves (and make a note if it helps). Repeat the process, asking the pendulum to show you the responses for "no" and "maybe"/"unlearn."*

4. While continuing to sing the varðloka and maintaining the light trance state, silently ask the questions for which you seek answers, carefully watching how the pendulum moves in response.

5. At the end of the process, stop singing and gently bring yourself back to full consciousness. Thank the spirit of your staff for helping you in your work, ground yourself, and make any notes in your journal before you forget the answers.

Weaving the Threads

What follows is not my own method, but rather one developed from the shared personal gnosis (SPG) of several practitioners. There is no evidence from the lore that this was used as an authentic practice by our ancestors. Nevertheless, it is in keeping with the link between seiðr and the Norns, and to weaving and textile work. It has also been used quite

---

*It is best to repeat this exercise at the outset of every divination session. For some people, the responses of the pendulum never change no matter how many times it is used. For other people, the responses may be different every time. Therefore, it is always best to check.

successfully by several different practitioners. Therefore, I recommend that you experiment and give the method a try.

❁ Method for Mapping the Ørlög

The varðloka that you obtained for divination may work here as well, or if you feel like you need a specific varðloka for the practice, you can use the same method as before to get this.

1. Take a spool of woolen yarn.* This must be pure wool and not polyester or some other synthetic fiber. Preferably, the yarn should be dyed red (using natural dyes), which represents blood and ancestral ties, but other colors of yarn can be used if red is unavailable.

2. Using a sterile needle or diabetic lancet, prick the thumb and press a small drop of blood onto one end of the thread. The blood provides the spiritual link to the ørlög of the person who is looking for the answers. (So, if you are doing the divination for someone else, then you will need to use their blood.)†

3. Once the blood has dried, use the woolen yarn to crochet or knit a thin strip of material. Enter a light trance while singing or chanting an appropriate varðloka. Set your intention "To map the ørlög of _____ [person's name]," merge with your guides, and begin to make a strip of material nine stitches wide by as long as your feel is necessary (ideally, this should also be a multiple of nine, so, for example, ninety rows long). When finished, you should end up with something that resembles a very thin scarf. You need not be an experienced knitter to accomplish this;

---

*If have experience in the fiber arts and enjoy working with wool, you may spin this yarn yourself. Ideally, you should try to do so in a ritual way while singing a varðloka and holding a visualization in your mind of the person for whom you are spinning the thread.
†Regardless of whether you are drawing a drop of your own blood or are obtaining it from another person, be sure to follow sterile procedures and safe practices, as blood can act as a transmitter of certain diseases.

it is also fine to use the most basic crochet stitches to make it. The simple shape also makes it relatively easy to do, and it does not matter if the result looks a bit rustic. What is important is not how it looks, but how it feels—and what information it conveys.

If you are doing a reading for someone else, it is preferable that the client crochet or knit this strip themselves, provided they have the necessary skills. As they do this, they will add their own energy to the strip, which will in turn heighten the accuracy of any readings that are done with it. You can, however, do the crocheting or knitting on their behalf as long as the client provides the blood.* If you are making the strip for someone else, you will constantly have to focus your intent on that person, visualizing them and keeping them in your mind as you crochet or knit it.

Once the strip of material has been finished, you can use it in divination. In this case, you will be setting your intention "To determine the ørlög of _____ [person's name] from the strip of wool." For this form of divination you will be working in the middle realms, in Midgard, so bring in any guides and wights for protection that you feel necessary. Begin to sing your varðloka and enter a light trance while holding the strip; if it helps, you can get someone else to beat your seiðstafr at the same time. While still in the trance state and holding the strip of material in both your hands, move your fingers up and down the length of the material. You should begin to feel all the lumps, bumps, and unevenness in the wool—these distinctive features represent "events" tied into the ørlög of the person you are doing the reading for. Ask your wights to give you a sense of what these "events" actually mean in the life of that person, and be able to advise them accordingly. Once the reading

---

*Obviously, I would not recommend handling other people's blood, but this can be minimized. Once the yarn has been "blooded" in one spot, the energy from the blood will permeate the entire length; after it has dried, you can cut off the bit at the end of the yarn that contains the blood and dispose of it safely, making sure you do not touch it.

has finished, thank your wights. Make any necessary notes about the reading in your journal while it is fresh in your mind.

This strip of wool is a direct link to the ørlög of the client or person for whom you have done the reading. Therefore, if someone with negative intent gets ahold of the strip, they can do a significant amount of damage. So, once the reading has been completed, *always return the strip directly to the person who provided the blood*. The choice is then theirs: they can either keep the strip so that it can be used again for future divination, storing it safely in a place where no one else will ever get ahold of it, or they can burn the strip and destroy it to make sure no one can use it against them. If they choose to do the latter and then want the same type of divination in future, they will have to create a new strip.

❋ Changing Ørlög

This is a one of the methods that can be used to change the ørlög of the person for whom you have done the reading, if they do not like what they find out. It involves the use of the woolen strip that you created in the previous exercise. Set your intention "To journey to change the ørlög of _____ [person's name] in accordance with their instructions." Carry out a journey to the client's lesser Norn, merge with it, and return in that state to the middle realms and Midgard. While still merged with the Norn and singing an appropriate varðloka to help maintain the merge and keep you in semi-trance state, take up the client's woolen strip and begin to unpick the crochet/knit. Once it is completely unpicked, maintain the merge and the varðloka and re-crochet or re-knit the strip using the original thread while following any instructions from the Norn, while all the time maintaining a visualization of the perfect situation for your client in your head. The thread represents a direct physical connection to the client's ørlög, and "as above, so below," when you change the physical strip, you witness the changes happening to the ørlög. You will find that maintaining the merge is hard work, and unpicking the strip and remaking it a long process. You need not try to complete all of this in one session; it may take several separate sessions, restating your intention and re-merging with the Norn each time. During the interim between sessions, however, the unfinished strip and yarn must be kept somewhere safe where no one else can find or interfere with it, and once the re-crocheting or re-knitting is complete it must be returned to the client.

If someone else were to find the strip, it would give them a very direct link to the ørlög of the person to whom it belongs. Thus, the finder could use the same method as you did to change a person's ørlög without the latter's consent. This would be a highly unethical practice and would inevitably come with consequences for the perpetrator. But because the perpetrator has the strip, which is directly linked to the person's ørlög by blood, there is very little the victim could do to resist it. This is why, once created, a strip should be very closely guarded or destroyed after the work is completed, lest it fall into the wrong hands.

ᛊ A Second Method for Changing Ørlög

A more traditional method of changing a person's ørlög without their consent is the one that occurs with Arrow-Odd (Örvar-Oddr) in the aforementioned *Saga of Arrow-Odd*. However, because it does not make use of a fetish or object with a direct link to the victim's ørlög that can be manipulated, this procedure is more difficult and it is also more easily resisted by the victim.

In something akin to the high-seat rite, the seiðr-worker once again merges with their own lesser Norn and, remaining in the merged state, brings the Norn back into the middle realm of Midgard. The seiðr-worker then allows the Norn to speak prophecy through them exactly as they would in a high-seat rite, but while it is doing so the Norn can subtly change that prophecy to affect the ørlög of the person concerned.

If the "victim" becomes aware of this at the time it is being done and knows what is going on, they can themselves merge with either their own Norn or potentially with other wights to become full of power (power-full) and try to resist this. Whoever finally emerges as the victor in this type of confrontation becomes a direct case of the balance of power between the two sets of wights. But because of the law of sovereignty,* things are heavily weighted in the favor of the "target," so it becomes relatively easy to resist and turn this kind of working—if the target understands the situation and can act quickly enough.

If the victim is unable to resist the negative working at the time it is being carried out and it does take hold, there is still another way to counter it: the revised ørlög can also be "unpicked" by another seiðr-worker using a method similar to the one outlined earlier that makes use of a crocheted or knitted "Wyrd strip." The victim creates a strip of cloth tied to their own ørlög, and the seiðr-worker, merged with the victim's Norn, can then ritually unpick and remake the strip to rebuild the ørlög in the original pattern.

Although it is never easy, it is sometimes possible to merge with a greater Norn when attempting this type of work, either as attacker or victim. This will obviously lend much more power to whichever side the Norn is on: if it is on the side of the attacker, change will be almost impossible to resist; if it is on the side of the target, it will be almost impossible for the change to take hold. But all power must be paid for. If you can persuade a greater Norn to get involved—which would be extremely tricky, and the Norn would have to have their own very particular reason to do so—the cost would also be great.

ÚTISETA

Perhaps the most powerful divination rite that can be practiced by beginners is *útiseta* or "sitting out." Historically, this was resorted to

---

*The law of sovereignty is common to all shamanic modalities. It basically says that you are the sole ruler of your body, mind, and spirit (soul complex). Because of this no other spirit can affect any of these without your express consent.

when someone had a very important decision to make. For example, in the year 1000 when Iceland was under pressure from the neighboring Christian kingdom of Norway, the law-giver (and lore-keeper, in many respects) of Iceland, Thorgeir, used útiseta to determine whether the island should remain pagan or convert to Christianity. Thorgeir spent a night sitting out under a cloak, beneath a local waterfall, communing with the spirits. By the morning he had decided that, politically, Iceland should officially convert to avert the threat of invasion, but people could continue to follow the old gods in the privacy of their own homes if they wished and there would be no retaliation against those who remained pagan.

Practices similar to útiseta are also evident in some neighboring cultures, particularly among the Celts. An example is a ceremony used by the high kings of Ireland on the night before their coronation at Tara. First, they would partake of a ritual feast of horsemeat.* The king was then covered with a flayed horsehide and sat out all night on a local burial mound in order to receive the ancestral spirits.

Like the Native American practice of vision quest, útiseta needs to be performed outside. It cannot be done indoors. The reason for this is that the person undergoing útiseta must be cold, uncomfortable, and physically suffering to some degree. The wights then take pity on the person and are more likely to help them with their trickiest problems. But this also makes útiseta a potentially dangerous practice— especially for those not used to spending long periods outdoors—and one which requires a certain level of preparation. And while a certain level of discomfort and suffering is necessary, there is no need to push this too far. It will not help anyone—least of all yourself—if you are unable to return with the information you went to such efforts to obtain!

Even during summer in the United Kingdom, where I live, tempera-

---

*A similarity might be seen here with the ritual feast prepared for Thorbjorg the seeress in *Eirik the Red's Saga* before she undertakes the high-seat rite.

tures can drop rapidly at night, and wind and rain can soon soak clothing, leaving a person vulnerable to exposure and hypothermia. Fires are
not part of the útiseta procedure, so there will be no external source of
heat or light. The sites for útiseta are often isolated, and getting to them
is not easy, with uneven ground, rocks, and tree roots that must be traversed. Trips, falls, and other accidents can easily occur if one is wandering around in the dark. There are also potential dangers from other
people, who probably will not understand what you are doing and—
especially if they happen to be lurking around in the early hours—may
not have your best interests in mind.

You should always wear appropriate outdoor clothing and dress in
several layers. You *will* get cold when you are sitting still outside in the
middle of the night, even at the height of summer. Ritual clothing can
be worn but it is certainly not necessary—any decent outdoor clothes
will do. If you do wear ritual gear, make sure it is heavyweight and
appropriate, so it will help to protect you from thorns and scratches
without ripping. Ritual clothing made of wool is preferable over cotton or linen, as it will better retain your body heat, even when wet.
Cloaks made from raw wool felt (which have not had the lanolin
removed) may be expensive, but they are also relatively waterproof and
perhaps worth the investment if útiseta is something you start to do
on a regular basis. Bear in mind that if wool clothing does get wet, it
can also become extremely heavy. A sturdy pair of hiking boots is also
essential.

You should always let someone else know where you are going to
be—although not necessarily *what* you are going to be doing—and
when you should be expected back. That way they can alert the emergency services if you do not return within a reasonable time frame.

When first performing útiseta, for the intitial few times at least,
I strongly advise that you do it as a group with a few other people. A
suitable site that you find for the group should allow each participant
to have their own individual space while remaining in sight of one

another. You do not want to be so close that you can hear each other's varðlokur. If there is someone who would like to be involved but does not necessarily feel that they need to be performing útiseta, they can serve as a dedicated fire-keeper. This person will keep a fire going all night just outside the sacred area, and—assuming it is allowed and safe to do so—help to create an overall sacred space. They can meditate, sing, or even play instruments quietly while they tend the fire, as long as it does not intrude on the people taking part in útiseta. This individual will help to keep watch over everyone, and they can also be entrusted with a first-aid kit. While it should only be done as a last resort, if anyone engaged in útiseta does get too cold and is at risk from hypothermia, they can leave their spot and warm up by the fire for a while. And a fire and some warm food is always welcome the next morning before traveling home!

For the actual performance of útiseta, you will need a varðloka. For this you can use any varðloka that you think is appropriate, or you can obtain a specific varðloka in the usual way. If you are hoping to use a dedicated varðloka, then I recommend obtaining this ahead of time and learning it well before you go out. It can be difficult trying to remember a varðloka when you are alone on a lonely hill in the dark, with the wind and rain battering your face!

Útiseta is traditionally done from dusk until dawn, sundown to sunup. In more northern lattitudes this obviously will be a much shorter period in summer than in winter, so if it is an extremely complex issue about which you are seeking guidance, you might not have sufficient time to get to the root of the problem on a single summer night. In winter, by contrast, the period of darkness is much longer—but the weather is also likely to be much colder. On the physical level, this will mean that you need much better protective clothing and longer preparation, but on a spiritual level getting colder for longer will induce more suffering and consequently arouse more pity among the wights. Always remember to balance this potential benefit against your personal safety. It is your responsibility to assess the risks and decide if it is worthwhile.

Nowadays útiseta is typically done on the Celtic model. If you are in England or Europe, this could even take place on an ancient burial mound or other sacred site. In places where you have no access to anything of this sort in your area (which will be the case for most people), a burial site or graveyard can be used. The goal is to engage with ancestral spirits, which again are more likely to help. The age of the burial site does not actually matter, nor even what religious denomination it is. People have quite successfully performed útiseta in relatively recent Christian and multi-denominational graveyards in urban areas (provided of course that you have access to one where you will not be accosted by anyone demanding to know what you are doing in a graveyard in the middle of the night!). Closed-circuit TV or other security measures are another consideration. Engaging in útiseta in a graveyard obviously rules out any use of a campfire.

⁂ Procedure for Útiseta

You might choose to start útiseta with a ritual feast before you leave, perhaps with certain food that has a symbolic connection to the purpose of the rite. In the Celtic version, the Irish king ate horsemeat before sitting out—horses being very closely associated with sovereignty and the power of the land and its wights. It is not necessary that your feast include horsemeat (which would be hard to come by in many countries) or any meat at all—the symbolism of various beverages, fruits, grains, or vegetables, or prepared dishes, can also be connected to the reason why you are performing the rite. During the rite itself, however, you will try to strictly observe a fast without food and with only limited water. You are supposed to be hungry and thirsty during the rite, which again helps to induce pity in the wights.

Just before the sun begins to set, you should take your hood, staff, protective clothing, a journal and pen, a flashlight, and some water (and perhaps some food to eat afterward) to your site. Make a small offering to the local wights and get as settled as you can. You can adjust your physical position slightly during the rite if you need to, but you should not be moving around excessively nor walking from place to place. As the sun begins to set, set your intention "To perform this útiseta to find out _____." Then begin to sing your varðloka and merge with your protective wights. You should try to sing or chant your varðloka for most of the night, but you need not do it constantly; you can take short breaks of 5–10 minutes to rest, particularly if your throat is hurting. There is also no need to be loud. Intoning the varðloka quietly under your breath is fine as long as you can hear it. People often find that the pitch of their varðloka naturally changes throughout the night. In any case, just go with the flow.

In addition to the varðloka, you can tap your staff in rhythm. Another action that often helps is to pick up a stone and grind it against another stone in rhythm with your chanting. (Obviously, if you are sitting on an ancient mound, burial place, or in a graveyard, you do not want to be grinding a stone in any way that might damage the monument itself.)

After chanting for a while, you will probably find yourself falling naturally into trance for short stretches, then coming back into ordinary reality. During these trances, the local spirits may begin to approach and will try to assess you; just be open to anything that comes along. It can take several stretches of trance before the spirits will feel sufficient pity and approach you fully, at which point they will answer your questions. It is often just before dawn that this happens, when you are in your most exhausted state, hungry and cold. (If, however, the spirits do answer your questions at some point before this, you are free to leave as soon as you have the information you sought.) Always remember to thank the wights before you end the rite and depart. You should also make notes in your journal as soon as it is possible to do, so you do not forget any important information the spirits impart.

In most cases, it is ancestral wights that will approach and provide you with help. Occasionally, other classes of wights may come forward, and it is not unheard of for even the gods to do this. Therefore, you should be open to whatever decides to speak to you. Obviously, if it is a god then that usually means what they tell you carries extra weight; any requests they make should be followed to the letter, if possible.

7

The Hearth Cult, Cofgodas, and the Landvættir

The work discussed in this chapter is very basic and can only loosely be considered seiðr. Indeed, the historical and literary sources about seiðr make no mention of it. The material presented here falls into of the category of "folk conjuring" or *trolldómr* ("witchcraft"), and likely would have been the province of the local village herbalist or cunning woman or man who received very little formal training at all. Ideally, it should be an aspect of general practice for most heathens today. It is included here for several reasons. First because it *is* an often-overlooked part of seiðr practice, and second because, if done well, it can teach you a lot about working with the wights in general.

What we are dealing with is a group of basic services that bring several benefits to individual households in the local community. Historically, these works could be conducted by the local goði or ritual specialist, or even by the head of a family, without the trance-work elements and they would still be effective. The addition of some trance work, however, can make them easier to carry out and more likely to be successful the first time around. Today even experienced pagans may be unfamiliar with these practices and will therefore need to seek help from someone who is qualified to teach them. The latter role can be a very positive one for the experienced seiðr-worker to have.

COFGODAS

The term cofgod (pl. cofgodas)* comes from Old English (*cōfgod*, *cōfgodas*) and literally translates as "chamber god" or "household god." Cofgod can be used to refer to several different types of wights, but generally it concerns lesser spirits that have a protective function for a house and those living within it. House spirits of this kind have been recognized even into the modern era—for example, the Scandinavian *tomte* (pl. *tomtar*), the Scottish brownie, the *kobold* (which derives from *kofewalt*, a "spirit with power over a room") of German folklore, or the Irish leprechaun, often described as a shoemaker for the family. This general category of beings includes certain ancestral wights who are interested in the home and the private life of its inhabitants and their descendants.† Even the Yule Lads of later Icelandic folklore may be thought of as a type of cofgod that comes at certain times of year, giving small rewards for following the rules of the household or punishing those that transgress.

Cofgodas generally do not include the major powers of divine pantheons such as the Æsir or Vanir. These higher gods may be patrons to individual household members and be honored through certain practices of the people in the house, but they are generally thought to be too important to be concerned with the day-to-day running of a single house. When it comes to the latter sort of activities, however, "power" is a relative term. Although the power of the cofgodas is surely insignificant compared to that of the gods, they are still quite capable of causing serious problems for anyone who slights them. In extreme cases they have even been known to cause the deaths of those they believe have wronged them.

Cofgodas are the spirits with influence over the household processes

---

*The pronunciation of the word is "COAF-goad" and the plural "COAF-goadas."
†For a useful cross-cultural overview of these spirits, see Claude Lecouteux's *The Tradition of Household Spirits* (2013).

such as the cooking of food, the brewing of ale, housekeeping and clean-liness, making clothes and shoes, watching over children, protecting the animals of the house, and generally keeping things in good repair and order.

If treated well, the resident cofgodas may help to ensure there is enough food and warmth when times get tight. They may even assist with household tasks, making the housework and upkeep much easier and family life more agreeable. They will also help protect individual family members from other wights that may want to exploit them or cause harm. Having a happy household spirit in your house can bring a whole host of such benefits. Conversely, if household spirits are not happy, they will find lots of ingenious little ways to show their displea-sure before they finally move on and abandon the place entirely. For example, what if the milk in your fridge is constantly turning sour or your food is spoiling? Today if all your food had gone rotten it is gener-ally not a matter of life and death, as it potentially could have been in earlier times. Nevertheless, you still must spend time and money replac-ing it, which means using resources that could have been put toward something more productive. And if it happens repeatedly, it will soon impact your bank account. Having disgruntled wights in your house-hold can quickly make day-to-day life much more complicated and difficult.

Not every house necessarily has its attendant spirits. New houses may not have had sufficient time for household wights to find them. Tomtar and brownies are well known for following families that they like when they move house, leaving the old house behind. They are even more well known for abandoning houses where the resident family has failed to treat them with respect, usually after causing a fair amount of mischief. But this also means that there are often free household spirits available in the area that can be attracted into an empty house if you know how to do so. Once you are sure that you have cofgodas in the house, the focus should be on maintaining a relationship of mutual respect, and making sure they are happy.

You can begin to see why building a relationship with the cofgodas, while unlikely to change the world at large, will directly improve day-to-day life in your immediate sphere. Building a mutually beneficial relationship with the cofgodas is also an excellent way to gather megin. Just as caring for domestic animals and pets can teach you to have greater compassion for all living beings, keeping the cofgodas happy is a useful first step in learning how to interact with different wights in a relatively safe environment—and this, in turn, will teach you a lot about building relationships with other more powerful wights in the future. Keep your promises to the cofgodas, and the other wights will begin to trust you more.

✤ Working with Cofgodas

As a rule, the first step in working with cofgodas is to determine whether they are currently present or not in your home. If you start making offerings to the cofgodas and there are none in your house, all you are doing is wasting time and food! So, do not just assume that they are already there. This is often not the case, particularly in newer houses.

If you determine they are absent, you can then decide whether you want to try to attract them or not. There is no rule that says you must do so. Even avowed pagans might worry about the idea of constantly having to keep the cofgodas happy, not to mention what could happen if things go wrong. Generally, however, the benefits that the presence of cofgodas will bring outweigh the hassle it takes to look after them, so it is worth it. And for the aspiring völva or vitki, it brings other advantages.

If you determine that you already have household wights, I would caution against trying to attract more. While it is possible to have several household spirits in a single house and some of them will get on with each other, they are often also quite irascible. So, what you do not want to do is upset the resident cofgod by introducing another that it dislikes. The last thing you need is two household spirits fighting it out over your home!

It is possible for additional household spirits to arrive of their own accord. For example, if you already have one wight living comfortably with you, this can serve to demonstrate that the house is potentially a good place to live and it may become more attractive to other spirits. If this happens, then at least there is an opportunity for the wights to work out between themselves whether they can get along—before they are actually living together, and without anyone else trying to force the issue! The benefits of having two cofgodas in your house are only slightly greater than having one, and do not outweigh the issues if the two start to fight each other.

⚅ Steps for Working with Cofgodas

There are three basic steps with respect to establishing and maintaining a mutually beneficial relationship with cofgodas:

1. Determine if there are wights already living in your house. (If there are not, then you must decide if you would really like them sharing your home and invite new ones in if necessary.)
2. Find out what they need from you.
3. Maintain the relationship by making sure that you satisfy their needs and keep up with your side of any agreements.

✳ Checking in on the Cofgodas

The following method is one that uses a seiðr technique to determine whether cofgodas are present in your home. Similar results may be achieved with other techniques that do not involve seiðr, for example by meditating to see if you can pick up on the presence of any spirits in the house. One can also use various methods of divination, such as that of the runes, or simply ask for a sign that the cofgodas are present.

However, a request for a sign may not receive an immediate response. It can take some time before a sign manifests. Moreover, a further limitation of these non-seiðr methods is that the information you receive will be sparse. Using seiðr, on the other hand, will allow you to have face-to-face communication with the house wight, which in turn lets you directly find out what it wants to keep it happy. Therefore, I recommend the use of ecstatic trance as the best way to check in on the cofgodas.

Make sure you will remain undisturbed for the duration of the exercise. Donning your hood and using your seiðstafr, prepare to journey as you normally would. Set your intention "To travel to find a varðloka to work with the cofgodas." Follow any wight that shows up to guide you, obtain the varðloka, and spend some time repeating it upon your return. It is always a good idea to record any varðlokur that you were given in your journal.

If you feel ready, you can undertake a second journey right away; otherwise, you can wait to do so at a more convenient time. Your second journey should be done using the varðloka that you obtained in the first one. Your intention is "To journey into Midgard to find out if there are any cofgodas in this house—and, if so, to find out what they want." As you are journeying into Midgard, it is important that you call and merge with your guides for protection (you should be doing this as a matter of course!). Carry out the journey and spend some time talking to any house wight you come across. Most importantly, ask them whether there is anything specific that they need you to do to ensure they will remain in the house. Be sure to follow any instructions once you have come back.

✤ Calling a Cofgod by Means of a Spirit House

If your house does not already have a cofgod then it is possible to set up a call to see if you can attract one from the local area. It should be noted that this working is borrowed from general shamanism and there is no historic evidence that it was ever done in seiðr. However, it is effective. We know that our Germanic ancestors dealt with house wights, so this feels in keeping with the tradition even if it may not reflect the exact methodology that they would have used.

This procedure requires that some additional materials be obtained in advance, for it concerns the construction of what in other traditions would be called a "spirit house" (one example is the Mongolian ongon). There are several materials that can be used for this: it can be made from a specific stone, or small pile of stones in the form of a small cairn. Today many practitioners use an individual crystal, typically one of clear quartz (the only crystal used in shamanic practice). Personally, however, I favor a small model of an actual house, made of metal or wood, perhaps akin in size to the little "weather houses" (*Wetterhäuschen*) that were popular in Germany in the eighteenth and nineteenth centuries.* There is a possible spirit-house parallel in the Norse tradition: the archaeological record has at least one example of a völva's staff with a metal finial in the shape of a traditional longhouse; one explanation for this would be that it served as a temporary home for the völva's guides and wights.†

When constructing and maintaining your spirit house, there are three things to keep in mind. First, it should be built so that it is portable—which means small enough that it can be easily lifted and carried. Second, as with your other seiðr tools, it should be made from natural materials and not plastic. Third, whatever materials you use should

---

*These miniature wooden houses were mainly from the Black Forest region. They usually have two doors: if the weather was going to be fine, the figurine of a woman in a summer dress would come out of one door; if it was going to rain, a man with an overcoat and umbrella would come out of the other door. It all worked by means of a very simple mechanism that measured atmospheric pressure like a barometer. Many illiterate peasants believed that these were some kind of spirit house—the spirit could sense the weather and would send out the appropriate figure. Perhaps this hearkens back to an earlier Germanic belief that spirits could live in small model houses?

†A spirit house can also serve a function in healing, particularly with extractions (see "Intrusions and Extractions" in chapter 8).

be clean, and the spirit house should be kept that way. Cleanliness in the household is particularly important from a Germanic perspective, overseen by the goddesses Frigg, Holda, or Perchta, who in the spring often assessed the effectiveness of people's cleaning techniques and punished those they found to be slovenly. There are also several stories of household spirits leaving houses that were not kept clean enough. Dirty houses are not welcoming, and the same goes for spirit houses. So, if you are using a natural rock, for example, you will want to expend some time and effort to make sure it is clean and not coated with mud or soil. In fact, before doing any working to attract a house wight, you may want to think about doing a spring clean throughout your own house! It is also important that whatever you decide upon as material for a spirit house has not been used for any other purpose previously—and particularly not anything magical, as lingering energies can also put spirits off.

Once you have constructed your spirit house, you will again need to find a place where you are not going to be disturbed. Take your spirit house there, along with your hood and seiðstafr. Your intention should be "To create a spirit house that will attract a house wight." If you are doing this for yourself, it is likely to be a one-off working. So, unless you plan to do this lots of times for friends, any general varðlokur could be used. You do not need to have a specific varðloka for creating a spirit house (although you can of course obtain one if you want). Begin singing the varðloka to journey and merge with your wights. While trying to maintain at least a semi-trance state, return to the physical realm and pick up your spirit house, lifting it up above your head. As you do this, visualize a hole or portal that opens above you into the upper worlds. As the spirit house in your hands goes through this portal, you witness a very bright light and see the spirit house begin to fill with light. When you perceive that the house is full of light and warmth, thank the wights and begin to pull your hands and the spirit house back down through the hole.

The light and warmth that fill the house act as a form of spiritual cleansing, simultaneously making it an inviting place to stay, which calls in the spirits. Keep the spirit house in your home in a spot that is preferably calm and quiet, where it will not be disturbed by children, pets, or visitors. Ideally, this should be somewhere with a bit of additional space so that, if necessary, you can make any offerings to the cofgodas. You can also put it on your home altar if you have one.

A spirit house can also be useful if you are moving to a new home and you want to take your existing cofgodas with you. It is not absolutely necessary—as a determined house wight will follow you regardless of whether you have a spirit house—but creating one can help them to make the journey safely and ensure that they are ready to start their work in your new home as soon as you move in. There is a caveat here: you will need to make sure that they *want* to move with you and your family, lest you force them into the spirit house and abduct them against their will! I would also recommend that you prepare the spirit house at least a few weeks before the intended move, so the wights will have a chance to get used to *their* new home and feel safe in it before you relocate it to *your* new home. Once in the new place, you may find that the house wights still prefer to live in their own spirit house inside your home, so continue to treat it with respect.

❖ Creating an Altar to the Cofgodas

There is some evidence that heathen households in Anglo-Saxon England had a small space devoted to the cofgodas. There are also indications in the Norse sources that the two main "high-seat pillars" of a house—which supported the roof and typically stood at either side of the high seat, where the head of the household sat to receive visitors and guests—served as a locus of spiritual activity and worship in the home.

You could combine an altar to the cofgodas with your main altar to the gods, or keep them separate. Indeed, many people today do like to keep a space near to their hearth or fireplace for the house wights, hence the term "hearth cult." Although there is limited evidence for this from a historic Germanic perspective, it was common in other traditions. An altar or *vé* ("holy enclosure") for the cofgodas can be as simple or elaborate as you wish, and it may contain whatever objects you feel are sacred and significant. There are no specific rules. The only essential components are the spirit house, if you have one, and a small offering bowl that is reserved specifically for the cofgodas (and thus kept separate from vessels used for other deities or spirits); everything else is up to you.

An altar provides a place for you to make regular offerings to show your appreciation for the cofgodas. When doing so, be sure to ask them what they want and when, and then follow their wishes to the best of your ability. If you are uncertain about what they might enjoy, I can offer a bit of advice: regardless of the place or the tradition, the folklore about house spirits consistently suggests they are quite partial to regular offerings of freshly made porridge with lots of milk and honey!

LANDVÆTTIR

The Norse landvættir or land wights are the *animae loci*, the spirits of the land, in Norse mythology and cosmology. Considered neither gods, jötuns, álfar, dvergar, nor people, they are an entirely different sort of wight. They can vary in power from the spirit of an individual plant to the spirit of a major region. They can also be the spirit of a specific geographical feature like a lake, mountain, or vast forest, and function as the mother spirit or master spirit of all the other wights that live within or upon that feature. They are exceedingly common and there is not an inch of the planet on which we move that lacks a corresponding wight.[*]

Although they are not seen as deities per se, the oldest, largest, and mightiest land wights are—much like the jötuns—easily equal in power

---

[*]For a cross-cultural survey of these entities, see Claude Lecouteux's *Demons and Spirits of the Land* (2015).

to some of the gods. But unlike the gods, whose power can be universal, the power of a land wight is geographically restricted. It is limited to the feature with which the wight is associated and the surrounding area under the influence of that feature—a mountain, for example, can affect wind and rainfall patterns over a wide area around it. Whether such limitations exist because the wight is uninterested in anything outside of its immediate area and chooses of its own will not to extend its power beyond certain boundaries, or whether there are actual spiritual barriers or restrictions in place that prevent the wight from doing so, we will probably never know. Within its own geographically limited sphere of influence, the land wight is the sovereign power and can even overrule the gods.

Although this fact is often overlooked, the land wights can have a correspondingly forceful effect on the people who move into or through their sphere of influence. They can bring blessings to support those they like and can curse and make life unbearable for those they dislike. This was the reason for the intricate carved dragon heads set on the prows of the Norse longships, which were designed to frighten away the landvættir from any shore they approached, thus preventing the local land wights from supporting the raiders' enemies. These same heads would often be covered, removed, or turned inward when the ships returned to their home ports, so as to avoid frightening the local wights. This is also the basis behind the use of the *níðstöng*, a "nithing" or cursing pole, which was used to inflict damage upon an enemy remotely.* Effectively, the pole served to frighten away the land wights and stop them from supporting the person who has been cursed.

Given their prevalence, the land wights can have a considerable effect on human affairs. Depending on their relative size, every piece of farmland, every house, every garden, and every building and structure created by man may be under the influence of one or more land wights.

---

*Several sagas report the use of a níðstöng, most famously *Egil's Saga* (chap. 60). In recent years such cursing poles have also been raised against politicians and others in Iceland and Norway.

Since buildings and fields generally stay fixed in one place and tend not to move around the landscape too much, they will usually fall under the permanent influence of the same local wight. That wight can therefore wield considerable power over day-to-day life for the human owner(s) of that building or field. The more time you spend in your home, for example, the more time you are under the influence of the wight that controls the land on which your house is built. If you go to work in an office, there will be another wight that has dominion over the land on which your workplace is built. You can begin to see why it is very important to forge good working relationships with the local wights! This is something of which our heathen ancestors were quite aware, but many modern pagans seem to have largely forgotten about it in their race to engage with the gods and other spirits.

The land wights are tied to a specific place but their sway is dynamic and not static. Anyone who has passed even briefly over or through a certain area of land has been exposed to the energy of the local land wights and has absorbed some of that energy every time they eat anything, drink anything, or use anything that originated on that land. Thus, they begin to come into alignment with the energy of those land wights, as well as with the energies of local gods and other spirits. Regardless of where you live, every drop of water you drink has passed through the land; all of your food is grown or raised on the land; and all of the materials you use ultimately have their source in the land, even if they have been highly processed before being turned into any final product—for example, the rare-earth elements and metals that go into mobile phones, computers, and countless other high-tech devices were once part of the land somewhere in the world. All of these things have been influenced by and carry the energy of the land wights.

In these days of globalization, multinational trade, and the internet, each of us is exposed to the energy of countless local wights from all around the world. Ideally, we are habituated to it, able to use and under-stand it, feel at home in it, and so can adapt to it and any spiritual path that developed alongside it. Generally, there are no longer any spurious barriers—based, for example, on categories like race, gender, or sexual orientation—that should prevent anyone from following any spiritual path, anywhere in the world.

The land spirits are an essential part of Norse cosmology and exemplify the animistic nature of heathenism. In animism nothing can exist in the physical world without a spirit behind it, "dreaming it into being," as it were. This means that everything in the physical realm is ultimately spiritual in origin, and every event has a spiritual cause.

So, if we turn our attention to the current climate crisis, like everything else, this reflects an underlying spiritual situation. And ultimately, if the local land wights have sway over our environment and climate, then the land wights must also be responsible for climate change. In spiritual terms it is our failing relationship with the land wights, our loss of respect for them, that has finally spurred them to act. They have been patient with us; they have watched as millennia of technological advancement have drawn us slowly away from our relationship with the Earth and with the wights that inhabit it. But now the situation has reached a stage where they can no longer continue to abide it and must take action to stop us destroying both ourselves and every other spiritual being that shares this planet with us.

We will explore this in more detail when we begin to look at disease theory, but for now we can say that the situation with our planet is like that of the human body with the common cold. The coughs and sneezes we experience are simply physical symptoms that alert us to the presence of the underlying rhinovirus itself—the actual root cause of the sickness. Climate changes, rising temperatures, disturbances in global weather patterns, and so forth represent a range of physical symptoms in the body of the Earth; they are a response to the underlying spiritual imbalance—an imbalance this time not caused by a virus but by human activity. On a planetary level, then, we all need to do more than simply reduce our carbon footprint and our impact on the planet.

We also need to take spiritual action to repair the relationship between people and the land wights.

When it comes to dealing with the land wights, the first and most important step is to build a spiritual relationship with them. Often this means first "waking" the land wight. This should not be taken literally. Although the activity of the wights can change with natural cycles—just try talking to a meadow spirit on a drowsy summer afternoon, or a tree spirit in winter—they are never fully asleep and are always concerned with their business.

In historical pagan times, the people were very aware of the presence of the land wights, for they interacted with them every day. These wights were not considered members of the family per se, but they were treated as close neighbors. However, with the coming of the Abrahamic religions, the authorities began to deny the existence of the land wights altogether, or label them as devils. Interacting with them was viewed as contrary to God's will, and various laws and precepts were established to curtail such practices. People began to fear the land wights and ceased to directly engage with them. Eventually, they forgot how to do so entirely.

For their part, the wights grew tired of being ignored and began to ignore people in return. Often, we became irrelevant to them; sometimes they lost all awareness of our presence. So, when we talk about "waking" the wights, it's not about rousing them from complete torpor but rather waking them again to the presence of people.

Reciprocity is the key here. In many cultures around the world, it is considered essential to try to live in sacred reciprocity or balance with the local nature spirits; the Q'ero people of Peru, for example, call this state *ayni* and certain similarities can be seen in the modern Norwegian concept of *dugnad*, which refers to a tradition of voluntary communal help.* The historic Germanic people were no

---

*The word derives from the Old Norse *dugnaðr*, "aid, assistance, virtue."

exception, and this is seen in the meaning of the X-rune. This rune was known as *gebo* in ancient times, and in Old English as *gyfu*. The "Old English Rune Poem," composed over a millennium ago, has the following verse about it:

> *Gyfu gumena byþ gleng and herenys, wraþu and wyrþscype*
> *and wræcna gewham ar and ætwist, ðe byþ oþra leas.*

> Generosity brings credit and honour, which support one's
> dignity; it furnishes help and subsistence to all broken
> men who are devoid of aught else.
> (Dickins 1915, 14–15)

The basis of building relationships with the landvættir is about making offerings in gratitude. In Germanic terms, this essentially means offering blót.

✤ Waking the Landvættir

One of my teachers noted that when we visit a sacred site, it often feels like a "dead battery," and it is very hard to contact the local wights. This is especially the case if that site is not used regularly by pagans, or not used respectfully. Many people find this to be true, for example, at a place like Stonehenge, which had been ignored for centuries but when it finally came back into usage was abused by every New Age mystic who could get to it. People are often disappointed when they first visit because they are expecting to feel the spectacular "energies"—but then cannot experience anything. They may feel more, and have a better energetic experience, walking along their local river. Why? Because at that local site the land wights have not completely given up due to the people having turned their backs on them—indeed, they may even be slightly curious about the person who recognizes their presence.

Whenever my teacher visited a sacred site, and especially if it was a "dead" site, he would always chant the twenty-four-rune sequence of the Elder Futhark. He would do this in a multiple of three—either three, six, or nine times, depending on how far "removed" he felt the local wights were—thus bringing sacred Germanic numerology into the equation. He felt that chanting the futhark was an effective way to attract the attention of the local wights. They would begin to see that this is a person who not only acknowledges their existence but is also willing to take the time to communicate with them. As a result, they suspend some of their indifference and give in to their curiosity just for a moment—but long enough to start to communicate with us. This serves to "wake" the site and its spirits so that the engagement process can proceed more deeply.

This is hardly an example of high magic. It is something that can be done by anyone—or at least anyone who can remember the futhark order (which most can accomplish with a bit of practice).* What follows next will depend on how the chanter wishes to communicate with the spirits. Obviously, the means to do this will reflect one's skill and knowledge level, but there are simple methods whereby even someone with no magical experience at all can enter into communication with the local wights.

The Blót

The basic way of showing gratitude to any wight is to make an offering. This is done formally through the heathen ritual of blót or "sacrifice," often performed by a ritual leader called a goði (male) or gyðja (female). It is important for all heathens to understand how to perform blót, as it is the main way of interacting with the gods (and for many ordinary

---

*Here, for reference, are the Elder Futhark rune names: *fehu, uruz, thurisaz, ansuz, raiðo, kenaz, gebo, wunjo, hagalaz, nauðiz, isa, jera, eihwaz, perthro, algiz, sowilo, tiwaz, berkano, ehwaz, mannaz, laguz, ingwaz, dagaz, othila.* For more on the pronunciation of the rune names and the various historical rune rows, see Thorsson, *Rune-Song* (2021, 15–20).

heathens, this is as close to magic as they like to get). From the perspective of seiðr, blót is a fairly basic ritual, but it provides the first stage of interaction with the wights—especially the landvættir.

While those who serve in the capacity of a goði or gyðja are indeed spirit workers in their own right, this does not mean they are practitioners of seiðr. In most cases, they will not be. Some heathen ritual leaders may find the skills and practices of the seiðr-worker—such as allowing foreign spirits to work inside one's own body or manipulating spirits in the bodies of patients for healing or other purposes—discomfiting or dangerous. A goði or gyðja has to understand how to perform the basic rituals of blót and sumbl, and must be able to provide spiritual counsel and direction to their local group. They should know how to call spirits into a certain geographical area and how to interact with those spirits once present. And for many heathen ritual leaders, that is as far as it needs to go.*

So, while it is not essential for the goði or gyðja to know and use the advanced skills of the seiðr-worker, I would argue it *is* necessary for the seiðr-worker to know and understand the skills of the goði or gyðja, as these constitute the basic steps for working with spirits.

✤ A Blót to the Landvættir

Before you begin a blót, you will need to gather a few items. The main thing required is the offering itself. For informal sacrifices, anything may be used as an offering. However, the offering will carry more power if it is something you have created or made yourself: a piece of artwork,

---

*I do not say this to underplay the role of the goði. For the average member of the heathen community, the goði forms the first and most essential link between the "normal" people and the spirits. In fact, it is often the only link that is ever needed, since after they have seen the goði or gyðja do things a few times, they can even build those links to the spirits themselves (until things go wrong, of course). On the other hand, most "normal" people still harbor mistrust for magicians, witches, shamans, and seiðr-workers even today. At best we are seen as charlatans out to scam the unwary, and at worst as sorcerers in league with destructive forces.

a poem, a bowl of porridge or some home-baked bread, or a libation of mead. There are many possibilities.

A formal blót has six main stages:

1. *Create a sacred space or vé.* Historically, this was done in a very different way to anything found in modern witchcraft or ritual magic. We know from the literature that a vé was generally rectangular not circular, but practically speaking it can be established in whatever shape suits the area. Our ancestors did not call on the four quarters, the sacred directions, or the elements—none of this was particularly important in the Germanic mindset. Sometimes the ritual area was roped off, and even this modest barrier was sufficient to highlight the boundaries of sacred space in people's minds. Everyone subconsciously agreed that the "normal" realm lay outside the barrier, but the sacred prevailed inside. Sometimes sacred space was created by carrying a live flame around the boundary; sometimes people processed the boundary by chanting. (In contemporary heathenry today, chanting the rune row is one way to emphasize the sacred boundary.) It was also possible to use a combination of these methods. It seems likely that when our ancestors created sacred spaces, they choose spots in the landscape where the veil with the spirit realm was already thinnest, places that naturally felt more liminal. They probably worked with what was present in the landscape, adapting themselves to it rather than trying to force their will upon it.

   With this process, therefore, we can afford to be somewhat inventive. Once you get accustomed to "reading" the landscape and picking a spot that feels right, you can use whichever method you prefer to draw the boundaries. Whatever you do, the most important thing is to create an awareness for all who are present that the area within the sacred space is very different to what lies outside of it. So, if you are working with others, it is sometimes necessary to include a bit of theater, to put on a show. (Don't be afraid to ham it up a bit, especially if you're naturally a bit introverted.) This helps to establish and reinforce the boundary in people's minds.

2. *Set the intention of the ritual.* If working alone, it is important at this stage that you take a few moments to reinforce the intention to yourself, either quietly in your own mind or by speaking it out loud. The whole purpose of ritual is to raise energy and direct it to a specific target or thing—in this case, to send energy to the landvættir. The intention forms the framework of the entire ritual and directs the energy to the appropriate place when it is all complete. If you don't set an intention for a ritual, any energy is simply dissipated and lost. The ritual will not achieve its purpose and the whole thing will have been a waste of effort. Wights abhor waste, so this may also make it harder to engage with them in future. Don't worry about talking to yourself—only the wights will hear you (which is also true even if you are just reciting the intention in your mind!). If you are conducting the blót with others present, this is the point at which you should explain its purpose to them in the simplest terms possible. This is especially important if you have new people who may feel a bit overwhelmed by what is happening. Take the time to explain to them exactly where they should be, what they are supposed to do, and when they should do it. This will provide them with reassurance and confidence, which will also contribute positively to the atmosphere and efficacy of the rite.

3. *Invite the wights.* Once the intention has been set, it is time to ask the wights to attend and invite them to witness the proceedings. The operative words here are *ask* and *invite*—not force, demand, or even evoke and invoke. Nobody likes being forced to do something against their will. Besides, it is impossible for humans to *force* the wights to do anything in the first place. Attempting to do so will only earn you their deep enmity—and wights have exceed-

ingly long memories! Fortunately, the wights generally like a good party as much as anyone, and especially a party at which they are the guests of honor and the center of attention. If you extend an invitation, they are generally inclined to accept (assuming they do not have pressing business elsewhere). The invitation is particularly important from a shamanic perspective, as the spirit worker can do nothing and the wights do everything. The goði or gyðja does not bless the offering—the wights bless the offering, working through the goði or gyðja. The goði or gyðja does not direct the energy—the wights direct the energy, working though the goði or gyðja.

The ritual leader generally decides on their own wording to invite the wights in. This might be done using a passage from the lore that relates to the purpose of the ritual, perhaps with additional words composed in alliterative verse.

4. *Bless the offering.* Modern heathens generally use mead as an offering in blót. This can be store-bought, but it is always best if you brew it yourself. At this stage in the ritual, the goði asks the gods to bless the offering. Again, the goði chooses some suitable words to *invite* the gods to do this.

5. *Make the offering.* The offering is usually put into a blót *bowli*, a wooden or metallic bowl reserved specifically for the purpose, and after the ritual the contents are poured onto the ground or the roots of a nearby tree.

6. *Closing.* Thank the wights and any other participants and allow them to depart. In heathenry there is no need to "close" the sacred space, especially if it is somewhere that is not going to be disturbed or used again for ritual. The energies around the sacred space will dissipate slowly over time; in the process, they will continue to provide some additional energies for the local landvættir.

Immediately after conducting a blót to the local landvættir, it is best to spend a few minutes in the sacred space quietly trying to "tune in to" them, to feel their presence and get a sense if they are satisfied with your efforts.

Note: If you conduct the blót with a group, there may be first-time participants who have no idea what to expect. They may be disappointed by the lack of excitement and "fireworks," and think that the blót has somehow "failed." This is because they are looking *externally* for their experience. With blót the answer is generally *internal*, and you must go to the quiet place within to find out whether it was successful.

8

Basic Healing in Seiðr

In any culture in which shamanism occurs, one of the basic functions of the shaman is healing. We may further recognize that shamanism as a cross-cultural phenomenon is remarkably conservative, and similar healing techniques—although they may have different names and terminology—were used in very different parts of the world. Since seiðr is a shamanic modality, it will come as no surprise that it can also be used for healing.

The sagas are full of reports of seiðr being used to heal, but unfortunately none of these written sources provide much methodological detail about how it was done. This is another area where archaeology can play an important role in reconstruction. For example, there are certain features that archaeologists have found on the tools of seiðr-workers—particularly the seiðstafr, the most important piece of equipment—which might suggest how seiðr healing was carried out.

I cannot guarantee that the techniques presented here are identical to those used by the original seiðr-workers, since the latter kept no records. They have been developed from a study of both the original sources and the archeological findings, together with some educated guesswork and practical experimentation. The most crucial thing, of course, is that the methods *work*. The ones described here have been tested by myself and a few others and we have found them to be quite effective in shamanic healing. (But here, too, there are no guarantees—

and, unfortunately, nothing can overcome someone's Wyrd if it is fully against you.)

When practicing shamanic healing, it is important to always remember that you are not a trained medical professional, and it is not your place to provide medical advice. Shamanic healing works on a spiritual rather than on a physical level, and it is certainly not a replacement for conventional medicine. Although they work in different ways, shamanic and medical healing methodologies are in fact quite complementary. They often function well together in a mutually supportive manner. If someone is genuinely ill, then my advice to them would be to get as much support from as many different sources as possible. As a seiðr-worker you should not be providing any advice whatsoever about the use, disuse, or dosages of prescription medicines or drugs. It is important to recognize when someone needs to be referred to a medical professional. You should not hesitate to do so, nor should you view this as any sort of failing on your part as a healer. It is usually possible to continue working with and helping that person while they are consulting a doctor as well.

Many shamanic cultures share quite similar views regarding the causes of illness and disease, and it could be said that there is a common shamanic theory of disease. Comprehension of this theory will shed light on how the corresponding healing techniques work, and indeed it will help you to determine which techniques should be applied in a given healing.

First, however, you need to gain a basic understanding of the soul or spirit, particularly from a Germanic perspective, as this does differ slightly from other models. This is essential because, as seiðr-workers, we are operating within a fundamentally animistic worldview. Everything has its basis in the spirit realms, which means that to get to the root cause of something, you must deal with it on a spiritual level. If you participate in a healing, you are basically trying to heal the soul.

THE GERMANIC SOUL OR SPIRIT

Shamanic cultures worldwide do not see the soul or spirit as a single, indivisible unit. Instead, the soul is usually conceived as a complex made up of several parts. Under certain circumstances these parts can split off and go in their own separate directions. They may also have separate fates after the final dissolution at death. The number and function of these parts varies from culture to culture. The Germanic soul model is just one such example. Modern heathens have identified between a minimum of four and a maximum of nine different parts of the soul: there are at least four major parts that are generally recognized, while the rest are mentioned in the lore and may or may not play a significant role. It may also be the case that some of these are subdivisions of one of the major soul parts, and it is debatable whether they are technically separate. Here I will attempt to list them all and leave it up to you to decide, through your own experiments, which are truly separate soul parts and which may be considered a subdivision of another part.

We will start with the four major soul parts and then look at the minor ones.

The Lík (Lich)

The first major part of the soul to consider is the *lík*. The Old Norse term has an archaic English counterpart in the word *lich* (from Old English *līc*). The lík refers in some respect to the physical body but it has several unique attributes. It is the only soul part with a physical component. Due to this aspect, the lík is also the only part of the larger soul complex that has a limited life span. It is loosely connected to the other soul parts. The connecting element that ties the lík to the rest of the soul complex is the *önd* or "sacred breath," the gift of Óðinn.*

---

*See the description of Óðinn's gifts to humanity in the Eddic poem "Völuspá."

Önd permeates the lík and provides it with animating force.* Upon death, önd is returned to the Allfather (Óðinn). This releases the rest of the soul and separates it from the lík. At this point, with nothing holding it together any longer, the lík usually begins to collapse and decompose, its physical components returning to the Earth from whence they originally came. In certain circumstances, however, if önd has left the lík but the will remains strong enough, this can prevent the rest of the soul complex from departing—leading to the creation of a *draugr* (pl. *draugar*) or revenant. A draugr is basically a spirit that maintains contact with—and a certain amount of control over—the lík, the body. It is more akin to a zombie than a disembodied spirit or ghost, which was distinguished by a separate name in Old Norse (*haugbúi*). The main difference between a draugr and a classical zombie is that zombies are said to be mindless, with no recollection of their former lives, whereas the Icelandic sagas describe draugar as not only having memories of their prior existence but also retaining their intelligence, which makes them much more dangerous.

The Hamr

The Old Norse word *hamr* literally translates as "shape" or "skin." In spiritual terms, the hamr is the energetic or ethereal body that surrounds and penetrates the lík. The hamr is seen as the "shape" because it is the spiritual "blueprint" or "plan" that determines the shape and form of the lík. The terms *hamr-craft* or *shape-craft* describe the shamanic art of shapeshifting: practitioners must first learn to change the shape of the hamr, which controls and determines the shape of the lík.

An example from the lore of a "hamr-crafty" person is a shapeshifter like Bödvar Bjarki, who physically walked the battlefields as a bear in *The Saga of King Hrolf Kraki* (*Hrólfs saga kraka*). This is, however, subtly different from the behavior of the wild Odinic warriors known as ber-

---

*Önd has been compared to other concepts of sacred breath or vital energy such as prana or chi. While there are some similarities, they do not function in the same way.

serkers. Shapeshifters do not enter a "berserker frenzy," and they retain their human reasoning and logic while in animal form. It is all about control. The berserkers do not actually change their physical form; they always appear as human regardless of their mental state (they do strive to lose their human intelligence and replace it with that of the spirit animal). The difference could therefore be described thus: shapeshifters use the hamr to influence the lík, whereas berserkers use the hamr to influence the *hugr* ("mind"). Berserkers are sometimes incorrectly referred to as "shamanic warriors," but at best they might be seen as failed shamans. In contrast to the unbridled fury of a berserker, the shamanic trance worker strives to maintain control at all times, for to lose control is to fail. Shapeshifters are better described as shamanic warriors.

It is the hamr that the seiðr-worker sends forth when journeying.

The Fylgja

The *fylgja* ("follower") is sometimes called the "animal soul" of a person. An alternative term used for the fylgja in modern heathenry is the archaic English word *fetch*. Though generally of limited intelligence and higher thinking, the fylgja contains all of our instinctual responses and basic survival impulses that enable us to function in the physical realm. The fylgja, along with the ørlög, is presented to the newborn soul of a person by their lesser Norns nine days after the birth of the body. The fylgja is inherited from a direct blood ancestor. It is also the seat of power of the berserker or *ulfheðinn* ("wolf-coat") and takes over the body during the berserker rage. When seen and engaged with, to its owner the fylgja either takes the form of a specific animal or a person of the opposite sex. The fylgja is an intrinsic and fully integrated part of the soul complex, though it is capable of a semi-independent existence. It is an intimate part of the person and—similarly to a vital physical organ like the liver or stomach—if it fails or leaves, this means the failure and eventual death of the person.

Although it may take on the form of an animal, the fylgja should not be confused with a spirit animal. A spirit animal is a distinct, independent wight in its own right, more like a friend or ally than an internal organ. The spirit animal may voluntarily choose to work with a person for a time, but it is not controlled by the soul complex. It makes its own decisions; it can be persuaded to carry out certain actions, but it cannot be ordered to do so. Spirit animals also come and go as they please. When a spirit animal leaves a person, it may weaken them temporarily—until it is replaced by another spirit animal—but it does not mean the death of that person.

Treating the fylgja like a spirit animal can be exceptionally dangerous. Because it is capable of independent existence, the fylgja can be sent out from the soul complex by the magician who knows how to accomplish certain tasks, as can the animal spirit. But if either of them come across certain other wights or encounter another person with some magical knowledge while they are away from the soul complex, they can be severely damaged. If the spirit animal is damaged, it may only weaken the sender, whereas if the fylgja is damaged, it can kill the sender. A large part of battle magic involves specifically targeting the opponent's fylgja.

Working with the fylgja is also dangerous for anyone who is not a spiritual specialist. The sagas make it clear that "normal" folk will only meet and experience their fylgja once in their life: at the moment of death, the fylgja turns up to claim the rest of the soul complex and direct it to the appropriate place in the afterlife. For the average person, then, the fylgja is the ultimate psychopomp and will play a more prominent role than the valkyries or Óðinn with respect to the afterlife. Immediately after death, the fylgja itself breaks away from the rest of the soul complex and returns to the Norns, where it may be given to one of your own descendants in a new life.*

---

*While reincarnation did exist for the Germanic peoples, cases of this are a relatively rare occurrence in the lore. From a heathen perspective, the phenomenon of "past lives" is better explained by the inheritance of the fylgja from an ancestor, rather than outright reincarnation.

Engaging with spirit animals is a basic technique in most shamanic modalities, but working with the fylgja is a very advanced technique that should not be attempted by anyone but experienced seiðr-workers. Only those with spiritual knowledge can work safely with the fylgja and avoid it taking their souls away.

The Hugr

The Old Norse word *hugr* translates as "thought" or "mind," but what it refers to is probably closest to what most people would consider the classic immortal soul. The hugr contains all those "invisible" mind-related elements that make each of us unique: our personal free will, psychic abilities, and emotions, along with our thoughts, memories, and experiences. It is the id, ego, and superego—in other words, our basic or "true" self. On death, it is the hugr that generally retains its wholeness and integrity and which passes to the afterlife—either in Helheim, or the ancestral mound, or on very rare occasions into Valhalla (*valhöll*).*
It is the hugr that first inhabits the newly born lík.

The following is a list of the minor soul parts that it has been suggested may make up the hugr.

The Munr

Munr is generally translated as "memory." There are some indications that hugr and munr may be separate. Óðinn's ravens, Huginn ("Thought") and Muninn ("Memory"), have names that share the same root as hugr and munr. They fly out each day to gather information for the Allfather. Thus, the ravens are distinct from one another and seem to have an independent existence—so is Óðinn sending out parts of his own soul complex?

---

*There are debates as to whether the hugr itself is a single, unified entity or is made up of separate parts that retain their general tendency to cluster and stay together even after death but which can under certain circumstances be forced apart.

Certain imbalances and diseases would also point to a separation of the munr and hugr. Amnesia, for example, may result from physical damage or illness and specifically affects the memory while having no impact on the ability to think. Similarly, dementia is a condition that attacks the munr but may leave the hugr largely unaffected.

The Vili

The *vili* ("will"), which can also be described as the free will, is the gift of Hœnir to Askr and Embla (see stanza 18 of the poem "Völuspá" in the *Poetic Edda*). The vili enables us to process information from the hugr and the munr, and to make decisions based on that information. Without the vili, we cannot engage and interact with the outside world, nor indeed influence it. Depression could be seen as a condition that specifically targets the vili over other soul parts.

The Vé

The vé ("holy enclosure") encompasses psychicism and the sixth sense. It is the ability to become aware of, assess, and interact with the unseen spiritual realms. It is the gift of Lóðurr to Askr and Embla (see stanza 18 of the poem "Völuspá"). Everyone has a vé to a greater or lesser extent, but it can atrophy through lack of use or be strengthened from constant practice. In Tantric traditions a concept similar to the vé is the *ajna* or "third eye" chakra situated behind the forehead.

The Móðr

The *móðr* ("mood") is the emotional body, the seat of all emotions. It is usually thought to center on the heart and be associated with the endocrine system. Some people assert that the móðr is inherently associated with the lík—after all, would we truly feel emotions without all those hormones sloshing around? However, experience shows that you can still feel very strong emotions while journeying in the spirit worlds and thus separated from the physical body. Therefore, I am more inclined to include the móðr within the hugr rather than the lík. That being said, journeying concerns only a temporary separation from the lík, so whether we will still experience the móðr after we have permanently lost our connection with the lík at death is something we are all going to find out for ourselves one day.

Hamingja

As we explored earlier in chapter 1, the hamingja (sometimes referred to as "luck") is a kind of internal power bestowed on the spirit by the lesser Norns at the time of birth. Although hamingja is certainly connected with an individual soul, the question as to whether it technically constitutes an actual "soul part" is open to debate. Is it "borrowed" from some external source, to which it returns at death, or does it remain with the soul throughout the latter's existence? Since some people do view the hamingja as part of the soul complex, I am including it here as a possible subcomponent of the hugr.

Megin

Megin, which I defined in chapter 1 as "honor," is very similar to hamingja in function, albeit not in generation. It is not presented by the lesser Norns at birth, but we can build megin over our lifetime. As is the case with other soul parts, we may also wonder: Does megin dissipate at death or does it remain an intrinsic part of the spirit?

THEORY OF DIS-EASE

In an animistic worldview, for anything to exist in the physical world, it must have a spirit or wight "behind" it, which holds it together,*

---

*In terms of the human being, spirit provides both the blueprint for the body, holding the physical material that comprises the body in the required form (hamr), and the animating principle (önd), which drives physiology and enables living beings to move.

and the same is true of disease and illness. All diseases have a spiritual cause. While physical methods of healing can tackle the physical symptoms or side effects that result from an illness, if the root causes of the condition are not addressed, it will likely return or reoccur. Therefore, to get at the root cause of any disease requires healing on a spiritual level.

Many minor illnesses, especially those of a chronic nature, are caused by some sort of imbalance, or "dis-ease," in our own spirit or soul complex. More serious diseases start with an imbalance in the soul complex that is then taken advantage of by other external spirits for their own ends, which makes the conditions much worse.

Basically, if the spirit or soul complex of a person is whole and empowered (that is, "power-full"), these imbalances do not occur in the first place. Power acts like an armor. Similar to an egg, it forms a perfect shell around the body, both hard and slippery. Other spirits find it had to find a place to grip onto that shell without slipping harmlessly off, but even if they do manage to get a hold, it is impossible for them to break through the tough shell to the vulnerable bits underneath. Power creates a spiritual pressure from inside to out that is difficult to grip and damage, like a fully inflated beach ball. If some of that power dissipates, however, it is like the air going out of the beach ball—suddenly it becomes floppy, loose, and much easier to grasp. This gives an external entity or energy much more time and opportunity to then create holes in the skin and penetrate inside if it wishes.

The easiest way to combat disease is to prevent it from developing in the first place—in other words, to avoid the conditions that lead to an imbalance or power loss, which in turn allows the disease to get hold. Generally, this is achieved by living a healthy lifestyle: engaging in regular strong exercise, getting enough sleep, avoiding tobacco, drinking alcohol in moderation if at all, and eating well. We maintain our power by not abusing our bodies or spirits in any way, through moderation.

In the poem "Hávamál" (The Words of the High One) Óðinn himself counsels moderation in all things, but particularly in food and drink. Stanza 21 reads:

> The herds know well when home they shall fare,
> And then from the grass they go;
> But the foolish man his belly's measure
> Shall never know aright. (Bellows 1923, 33)

But none of us are saints (at least while we are alive!) and we often struggle to maintain this sort of healthy lifestyle in a consistent way. So, while we should be able to forgive ourselves for our own failings in this regard, it is also important to be aware that every time we slip up, we potentially expose our spirit to external attack.

The health situation is made worse by external environmental factors. There are numerous spiritual elements in the external environment that can take advantage of us in a weakened state and it is nearly impossible to avoid them all.

"Heavy energy" is an especially prevalent potential source of debilitation.* Every time someone has had a bad day on the way home, as they go over events in their own mind, they are generating heavy energy that is released into the environment. Although most human beings are not especially well suited to deal with heavy energies—and may be damaged if too much heavy energy builds up in the body—there are specific beings in the other worlds that feed on these heavy energies, positively thriving on them, and in the process give off light energies as the waste product, which we in turn need to thrive. It is a similar process to that of plants, which take in carbon dioxide (a metabolic poison

---

*Here I am employing the terminology of "heavy" and "light" energy that is used in Andean shamanism. This is preferable over more popular English phrases that describe energy as "negative" or "positive," which suggests a subjective viewpoint with shades of good and evil. Our ancestors did not think in this way.

to most animals) and excrete oxygen (which is essential for animal respiration) as a waste product. To these beings, heavy energies are not "negative" in any way. This is why the term "negative energy" is subjective and highly anthropocentric.

Let us return to the scenario I described of people having a bad day. When this has occurred, these people are quite literally generating heavy energies as they walk down the street. They may not be directing these energies at other people—except, perhaps, at their boss!—but they are nonetheless releasing them into the atmosphere, albeit subconsciously, as a type of spiritual pollution. Anyone who happens to be following along behind one of these people will then find themself passing through a cloud of their heavy energy, much like a cloud of exhaust from a diesel engine. And these clouds of spiritual pollution can take a very long time to dissipate.

How many thousands of people pass along a busy shopping street every day? What percentage of those are having a bad day, or wrestling with some mental dilemma, and creating this heavy energy? You can begin to see the scale of the problem. In daily life, in our increasingly hectic modern age, we are subjected to so much heavy energy that it is impossible to avoid. All it takes is a very small chink in our "spiritual armor" for this heavy energy to stick to our energetic bodies and being to accumulate. Moreover, what we are describing here is only *unconscious* energy. There are also conscious spiritual beings that exist in our midst, and which are actively looking to target and exploit any weakness for their own benefit.

It is important to recognize that healers, regardless of their skill level, are subjected to such heavy energies—and not just from the general environment. They are also exposed to the heavy energies that are directly afflicting their clients. As they are trying to remove them from their clients, healers are very vulnerable to picking up such energies themselves. Being client-focused, they often miss or overlook when energies become lodged in themselves. Therefore, it is recommended that every healer should take a regular opportunity to get checked out by another healer—just in case they have missed something.

SEIÐR HEALING TECHNIQUES

In shamanic cultures all around the world, basic healing usually takes two forms: extractions (to remove an intrusion) and soul retrievals. We will now discuss them in detail.

Intrusions and Extractions

When heavy energy finds a hole, a gap, in someone's power, it can penetrate that gap and enter the energetic body. The energy either takes advantage of an existing gap in the person's energetic body caused by a prior condition of soul loss or, if powerful enough, it can create its own space, which can directly bring about soul loss.* The energy becomes parasitic, forming a type of cyst or gall surrounded by the healthy energetic body, and it then begins to drain that person's energy, feeding on it and growing. This situation, which is called an *intrusion*, usually leads to low-level, chronic illness rather than anything acute.

Intrusions can occur on two separate levels: unconscious and conscious. In the former category, which is the majority of cases, they are merely the result of blind, unconscious heavy energy picked up from the environment. This is akin to a foreign body, a "spiritual splinter" if you like, which has broken through the protective shell of the energetic body. Since it lacks any form of intelligence, it should not be thought of as malevolent; it is simply in the wrong place at the wrong time.

In a small number of cases, an intrusion may be caused by energy that is conscious and has intelligent purpose. The combination of energy plus conscious intelligence equals a wight. However, even in the rare cases where a wight is involved rather than just heavy energy, it is

---

*Soul loss is specifically addressed in the next section.

very important to understand that this not the same thing as full-blown spirit possession. In an instance of true possession, the invading entity will invariably try to take over and completely control the person it is possessing. The behavior of the possessed person changes completely—sometimes beyond recognition. The possessing entity enmeshes itself in every aspect of the victim's life, and this needs significant unpicking. Intrusions, on the other hand, are only loosely connected to the person they afflict and therefore behavioral changes may only be slight, if they happen at all. Any behavioral changes that do occur are usually a by-product of the illness generated by the intrusion, rather than a result of direct action from the intrusion itself. For example, behavioral changes may be the result of depression that is indirectly triggered by the condition of intrusion, rather than any deliberate attempt by the intruding spirit to take over the person's hugr. The intrusion only seeks to feed from or hide in the "host" person, not to control the latter entirely. This means that while de-possessions are very advanced work indeed, intrusions are significantly easier to deal with. The extraction of an intrusion therefore falls into the category of basic healing.

Soul Loss and Retrieval

A second and slightly more serious cause of imbalance and illness is soul loss, which is often self-induced through trauma. "Soul loss" is perhaps a slight misnomer since it does not refer to the *entire* soul complex. As we explored earlier, the soul or spirit is not a single, uni-fied entity but is comprised of several different parts. Given the right conditions, one of these parts can break away from the soul complex, leave the energetic body, and move independently into different places in the spirit realms. Once a soul part has been "lost," this condition can severely weaken the person to whom it had belonged, as well as leaving behind a space or gap in their energetic body. The resulting space can then be exploited by an external heavy energy or spirit in the form of an intrusion, which can lead to secondary complications.

Soul loss often occurs suddenly and can precipitate serious and acute illnesses.

The cause of soul loss is deep emotional and mental trauma. Any significant traumatic and emotional event can lead to soul loss. Abuse (sexual or physical), PTSD, discrimination, bullying, bereavement, and guilt are just a few of the many factors that can lead to such a condition. In psychological terms, soul loss is described as "disassociation": part of the self "runs away and hides" rather than facing the constant emotional pain it is in. Many centuries before Freud ever appeared on the scene, however, shamans were calling this soul loss and treating the condition.

Soul loss is dealt with and remedied through soul retrieval: the shaman must set off into the spirit worlds to locate the missing soul part and bring it back to the owner. This is not as easy as it sounds, since the soul part is often reluctant to return and again face the emotions that caused it to leave in the first place. The soul part must be persuaded that the situation has changed and that it will no longer face the same pain if it returns. As part of this process, the soul part often demands very strict conditions from the owner, which it expects the latter to follow to the letter. Failure to ensure any of these conditions will generally result in the soul part immediately leaving again.

Soul loss is an important affliction to understand and a crucial one to heal. In addition to causing serious illness in a living person, it has ever greater postmortem repercussions. If a soul part is missing at the time of a person's death, the rest of the soul complex cannot penetrate the barriers and make the transition to whichever afterlife it is destined. It remains stuck in the middle realms—in Germanic terms, in Midgard. It becomes a disembodied earthbound spirit, a ghost or a haugbúi.

Soul Theft

Soul theft is a very specific subset of the larger phenomenon of soul loss. Soul theft refers to a situation in which, instead of wandering away of its own accord, the soul part is "taken" by another person or wight. "Theft" is perhaps a misnomer as it implies that this action can occur without the victim's consent. In fact, the law of sovereignty ensures that no one, no wight, nor even a god can have an influence over someone else's body or soul complex without their direct consent. However, that consent does not have to be given consciously; it can be given unconsciously as well. This is often seen in victims of domestic abuse who refuse to report their abuser or leave, and instead continue to suffer in silence. The victim has subconsciously surrendered part of their soul complex to their abuser, and this gives the latter more power over them.

It is also possible for a seiðr-worker to act as a "soul thief" by taking and holding part of the soul complex of their victim. This gives them much more leverage and influence over that person: the victim is significantly more likely to agree with the seiðr-worker and follow the wishes of the latter. In fact, this is often the basis of gandr or wand magic, which we will cover in chapter 10. But the seiðr-worker cannot accomplish this without the consent of the other person. The soul part needs to be given freely, so the seiðr-worker will often have to seduce the person involved, rather than intimidating them into it.

In the long run, however, this does as much damage to the thief as the victim. Similarly to the situation in which a person who dies with missing soul parts is unable to penetrate the barriers between the worlds, someone who dies holding additional soul parts also remains trapped in Midgard until those soul parts are released. To remedy the situation often involves a very complex process, swapping a series of soul parts between several different people before any of them can move on to the afterlife.

❖ The Diagnostic Journey

Before you can decide on any treatments, you need to know what's wrong—in other words, there must be a diagnosis. However, as we have said before, the seiðr-worker is not a trained medical practitioner and therefore should never make that diagnosis on their own. As in all things, the seiðr-worker is just the "hollow bone" and does not carry out any work themselves. It is the wights upon whom we must rely to make this diagnosis.

Before you do any diagnostic journeying, you need to obtain a varðloka specifically for this type of work. Gather your seiðstafr and hood, and any other equipment you require, find somewhere you will not be disturbed for at least thirty minutes, and make your preparations to undertake a journey. Your intention in this case is "To find allies who can help me with diagnostic journeying and to ask them to give me a varðloka to help with diagnosis." At this stage you can use any general varðloka that you think is appropriate until you obtain the varðloka specifically for the diagnostic journey. Carry out your journey and be sure to record your results, particularly the new varðloka, in your journal.

Once you have your new varðloka, it will be possible to do a specific diagnostic journey to find out what the underlying issues are for another person. Using the same method as above, with your seiðstafr and specific varðloka, in this case you will set your intention "To carry out a diagnostic journey for _____ [person's name], to find the root causes of their issues and determine the treatment plan to overcome those issues."

On this diagnostic journey the wights may reveal to you some very personal information about the person you are working for. This is particularly likely if you are dealing with a situation concerning soul loss. You may hear about some very deep emotional traumas, stories of abuse, and so forth—things that the client has never revealed to other people and certainly would not want spread around. It may even concern things that the client themself has suppressed and done their best to forget. Confidentiality and tact are therefore of paramount importance. What is given to you must remain solely between you and the client. Carefully determine whether you should make any written notes or records, and only do so if it is absolutely appropriate. If you do make any notes, store them in a locked, secure place, to which no one else has access but you, and make sure they are destroyed at the earliest opportunity after their purpose has been achieved. You can also write down the planned approach for treatment. In fact, I would encourage you to do this because if you forget a certain part of the plan and fail to follow through exactly as the wights have described, then it is unlikely that the plan will work. Again, it is good practice to both anonymize the treatment plan so nothing can link it back to that particular client, and to destroy it as soon as it no longer serves a purpose.

✵ Extraction

Before proceeding with an extraction, you need to engage with the wights that can help you to obtain a varðloka specifically for this type of work. Gather your seiðstafr and hood, and any other equipment you require, find somewhere you will not be disturbed for at least thirty minutes, and make your preparations to undertake a journey. Your intention in this case is "To find allies who can help me with extraction to ask them to give me a varðloka to help with extraction." At this stage you can use any general varðloka that you think is appropriate until you get the varðloka specifically for the extraction. Carry out your journey and be sure to record your results, particularly your varðloka, in your journal.

If the wights indicate that an extraction is required, then there is a further step before you can begin the extraction work itself: you will need to identify the exact locations of the physical intrusions in the body. There are several methods that derive from other shamanic cultures that can be used to do this, such as the Navajo "trembling hands" method, but here we are going to focus on how you can identify the locations of intrusions using seiðr practices.

When doing seiðr work for other people, it is always best to have an impartial witness present. This is for both your own protection as well as that of your patient. Many modern people have never experi-

enced any trance work being done on or around them, and they may
be understandably nervous about what is going to happen. Though it
is perfectly safe, you should always mention that anyone you are going
to be working on may bring another friend along with them, just to
provide a bit of support and comfort. This can really help with their
nerves. The friend/observer should be invited to sit quietly at the back
of the room and pay attention to everything that is going on, so it can
be discussed with the patient later. During an extraction session, the
patient will often become so relaxed that it is difficult for them to
recall afterward what happened during the treatment; they may even
fall asleep. And as mentioned above, the wights or the client will often
reveal personal information during the healing process, so you should
ensure before the procedure begins that any witnesses understand the
absolute importance of confidentiality. The observer should only ever
discuss the healing process with those in the room, and nobody outside
of it.

I understand it is often difficult or embarrassing for new trance
workers to perform in front of witnesses, but this is something you must
get used to. In traditional cultures, the entire village will often turn out
to see the shaman perform a healing. In places with limited access to
television, it is treated like a form of entertainment. There is no need
for confidentiality in such an intimate world, as the villagers are all very
familiar with one another. (Needless to say, in modern Western culture the social circumstances are quite different.) The situation seems
to have been similar with seiðr in ancient times. In several sagas there
is evidence that observers and others were present for a seiðr working.
In *Eirik the Red's Saga*, for example, the völva travels with a "choir," a
group of people whose function is to chant or galdr the varðloka, which
enables the völva not to worry about having to do this herself as she
enters trance. The ceremonies are usually witnessed by the entire household as well, so it is very rare that the völva and the client would ever
be in a room alone.

Today we typically have to work as solo practitioners, which means that very few of us will enjoy the advantage of having a choir—a group of people who have some understanding of what is going on and can show up for the ceremony to chant varðlokur. If you can enlist such supporters to assist you, it will be a brilliant way of teaching a group of apprentices and creating more impactful ceremonies. But you will definitely be in the minority. That being said, even if you are a solo practitioner, you will still need to get comfortable working with others present. If you discover that you are *unable* to perform seiðr with observers present, you may not be well suited to do this type of work.

❊ Procedure for an Extraction

Prepare your room by making sure it is clean. Light incense and candles if you use them; you may also want to close the curtains or dim the light to create a more relaxing atmosphere. Before beginning you need to prepare your seiðstafr by tying the weight you use for divination to the fixture on your staff (see chapter 6). Although this work can be done remotely, at a distance, it is often much easier if the person you will be working on is in the same room with you. If the patient is comfortable with this, they should lay on a blanket on the floor with a cushion or pillow under their head. If there are physical issues that make it difficult for the patient to lie on the floor, they can sit up in a chair, but you may have to modify your technique slightly. Explain to the patient that during this process you will not need to touch them physically at any point, but sometimes the wights can interact with the person and even touch the location point of intrusion and extraction. Therefore, if they experience a physical sensation, it is just the wights and nothing to worry about. Explain that you will be undertaking a journey, during which you will be chanting and using your staff near them. Explain that if they are experienced in trance work, they are welcome to journey alongside you. Otherwise, they should simply relax and be open to any sensations they may feel. The patient can keep their eyes open or shut, whichever they are most comfortable with. You can explain that if they do shut their eyes and happen to fall asleep, again this is nothing to worry about—you will wake them gently at the end of the process.

Using the varðloka that you obtained for extractions, begin to journey with the intention "To locate any intrusions in the body of _____ [person's name]." Enter the spirit realms and merge with your wights. Once you have merged, return to Midgard, maintaining a semi-trance as you do so. Take up your staff and slowly begin to pass it over the body of the patient; the bottom of the weight should always remain a few inches above the patient's body and not make any physical contact. Make sure the weight passes over every part of their body; if necessary, you may ask them to shift position (for example, rolling over onto their front, allowing you to check their back) to accomplish this. When the weight passes over an intrusion it will begin to react in whatever manner is normal for you (as seen from prior divination with your staff); for example, it may swing from side to side or spin in a specific direction. If you are sensitive enough, you may even experience a physical sensation in your hands in contact with your staff, or in another part of your body, as the weight passes over an intrusion. The type of sensation can vary from practitioner to practitioner. For example, some people experience a feeling of heat or cold. In my case, it comes as a tingling in my left palm below the little finger. The sensation itself can be extremely subtle; to notice it you may need to be deeply attuned to your own body, with a good sense of what is normal and what is not. Make a note about the location of all the intrusions in the patient's body. Unless there are a great number of intrusions requiring multiple sessions, it best to try to remove all the intrusions at once. Obviously, the more intrusions there are, the longer this will take. The removal of intrusions requires a fair amount of concentration, which in the long term can lead to fatigue, but you should be able to cope with eight or nine different intrusions in a single session.

Once you have located all the intrusions, you can then go on to start remove them in the same session, or you can arrange to do the removal at another time. If you are going to proceed with removing them in the same session, you will maintain the merge and begin with the extraction work as explained below.

If you decide to remove them later, however, you will want to thank your wights and enable them to leave, after which you can bring the session to a close. When the follow-up session takes place, you will have to completely restart the journey with a new intention and merge once again with your wights before continuing as explained below.*

In many cultures around the globe, the shaman removes intrusions by placing his or her lips on the patient's body, physically sucking out the intrusion and storing it in the mouth or stomach until it can be safely dealt with. However, this is a relatively dangerous practice, for it involves the shaman deliberately taking the heavy energies into their own energy field, which puts them at great risk of being affected by the intrusions themselves. Although these shamans train for years to do this and must spiritually modify their mouths or stomach to be able to hold the intrusion safely, they cannot eliminate the risk entirely, and sooner or later one of the intrusions will get through. Other shamanic cultures do this in slightly different way, whereby the shaman physically pulls the intrusions out with his or her hands. This means that the intrusion cannot enter the shaman's energetic body at any point, and it is therefore a much safer method.

The Norse, it seems, were uniquely one step ahead in how they handled these situations. There are features on the seiðstafr that suggest a seiðr-worker may have been able to use their staff to remove intrusions without having to touch them. At the top of the staff are the four handle-like objects that make a kind of basketwork arrangement. The objects are very similar to the handles on a distaff, used in spinning and

---

*It is vital to make sure you are merged at this stage. You will be exposing yourself to the intrusions inside the person you are working with and if you are not full of power, it is very easy for those intrusions to latch onto you instead.

the production of cloth. The raw wool is wrapped around the handles of the distaff, which keeps it untangled and safely out of the way. This makes spinning much easier as the yarn is drawn out and spun on the spindle.

In many shamanic cultures, intrusions are described as being long and thin. They may take the appearance of snakes, string, old rope, or arrows, but often appear as amorphous lengths of dark heavy, wispy material, very much like the fibers of cotton candy or un-spun wool. In fact, the appearance of the intrusions is solely designed to give the shaman information about them, and so varies from shaman to shaman. The appearance can also differ depending on the shaman's expectations. It may be that seiðr-workers were trained to see intrusions as skeins of un-spun wool that could be wrapped around the distaff end of the seiðstafr, keeping them well away from their own energetic body until they could be "processed."

All intrusions need "processing" after they have been removed. If intrusions are removed from a patient and then left lying around in the room, or thrown out into the street, they will try to affect the next person that comes along. In fact, this is exactly what certain unscrupulous Indigenous shamans used to do: they would leave the intrusions they had removed from a patient in a pile in the center of the village to infect the next person that happened along; in this way they ensured their services were in constant demand. We do not have to resort to these sorts of tactics today. In our modern society, intrusions are hardly rare. Many are made each day as light energy is converted into heavy energy. People will come across them quite naturally, without us having to deliberately leave any in their path.

The first law of thermodynamics tells us that energy can neither be created or destroyed, but it can change form. This happens quite naturally as the Earth takes heavy energy and converts it to light energy. The ocean and large bodies of water behave similarly. But what happens if you do not have the time to dig a big hole in the Earth in which to bury your intrusion, or to take it to the nearest ocean? Some shamans are specially trained to handle this energy internally—for example, Andean shamans who take the energy into their sacred stomach to digest and convert it—but again this is fairly dangerous, as it involves first bringing the heavy energy into your own energetic body. In the context of seiðr, we will take a different approach and instead rely upon wights who can also convert this heavy energy.*

First you will need to locate a wight with the ability to convert heavy energy into light energy. It may be the same wight that can help you with the extractions, or it may be a completely different one. It is important to clarify this *before* you begin to do any extractions, because if the extraction wight is unable do conversions, then you will need to have also enlisted a second wight that can.

Begin your journey using the varðloka specifically for extractions. Enter the other worlds and merge with your wights, then return to Midgard, keeping the merge and trying to maintain a semi-trancelike state. The wight that carries out the conversion of the energy may choose to leave your merge and prepare for what it is supposed to do.

Maintaining the merge with the wight that will help you with the extraction should allow you to visualize the intrusions at the points that you previously identified in the divinatory diagnosis. Pay close attention to the appearance of the intrusions, as it can give you information about them and their origins. As mentioned, the appearance can assume many different forms: people in the past have described worms, snakes, or old rotting string and ropes (typically, it is something unpleasant). It is very important that you avoid describing the appearance to the person you

---

*Many readers may recall the fairy tale "Rumpelstiltskin," which tells the story of an imp that can spin straw into gold. The tale was collected by the Brothers Grimm in the early nineteenth century, but it is undoubtedly much older. What if there is something deeper behind this children's fairy tale—perhaps a folk memory of a seiðr ceremony? Could the spinning of straw into gold be a metaphor for both the conversion of heavy energies into light ones and the spinning of fate or Wyrd?

are healing.* The appearance, which is not a true representation of the intrusion, is just there for your benefit, to provide the healer with information about how to deal with it. (If you really want, you can ask to be shown the true form of the intrusion. They usually appear as dark, wispy energy.)

Once you have established what you are going to be removing, bring the head of your staff over the intrusion and try to "hook" part of the intrusion on the basketwork handles of your staff. Because the handles are specifically intended for this purpose, you should find that parts of the intrusion begin to stick to them. Once a bit of the intrusion has been hooked, gently rotate your staff counterclockwise, so that the intrusion begins to wrap around the top of the staff like wool that is just about to be spun, and slowly start pulling it out of the person's body. Try to always keep the staff a few inches away from the body of the patient, so as to avoid physically touching them with it. Continue until you are sure that the entire intrusion has been pulled from the person's body and is now wrapped around the staff. Check the clean, empty space where the intrusion used to be to make sure it has been completely removed and that no bits of it broke off and remain in the energetic field. If there are any bits that were left behind, simply repeat the process until it is all gone.

Once you have the intrusion entirely on the end of your staff, call over your wight and ask it to convert the intrusion. Watch as the wight takes a bit of the energy, and slowly begin to wind your staff clockwise to unwrap the intrusion. As your wight receives the intrusion, the wight may begin to eat it, or spin it, or use one of several other methods to convert it.

---

*I have heard of several cases where the thought of having something unpleasant and potentially rotting inside the body has caused long-term psychological damage to a person. One case in America ended in a lengthy and expensive lawsuit after a healer described removing a dead and rotting rat from a client's energetic field. But this was information solely meant for the healer, and it did not refer to an actual rat. From a shamanic perspective, the dead and rotting "rat" is an indication of a nonsentient intrusion that can cause degeneration in the person it has affected.

The method does not really matter; what is important is that you witness it being converted into a thread of white, silver, or golden light. If there seems to be a hole or gap left in the energetic field of your client where the intrusion used to be, you can use some of this light to temporarily "plug" that gap; this will prevent anything else taking advantage of the gap until it is healed. Otherwise, you can just leave the string of light where it is to be picked up by anyone who needs it, or watch as it slowly dissipates into the atmosphere, helping to neutralize any heavy energy in the area and raising the vibration of the general area as it does so.

Repeat the above process until you have removed all the intrusions from the patient's body. Maintaining a merge over an extended length of time and focusing on the intrusions can be tiring, especially if you are not used to it. Therefore, if your original diagnosis reveals a large number of intrusions, you may want to divide the removals into two or three sessions. Once you have finished, remember to leave the merge and thank your wight(s). You do not need to escort them back to the lower worlds; they will be able to make their own way.

SOUL RETRIEVAL

The second major seiðr healing technique is soul retrieval, which is used in cases of soul loss. Soul loss or disassociation occurs because of trauma: the soul part that is unable to face the negative consequences of the traumatic event separates itself from the soul complex and flees into the other worlds, where it hopes to find a refuge. The soul part could go to any part of the spirit realms, so locating the lost part before it can be returned is not always straightforward.

Soul loss is much more likely to occur, and its effects will be more extensive, if the soul complex has already been weakened by intrusions. The two conditions often occur together, and certainly in our modern world it is rare to find a case of soul loss in isolation. Thus, extraction and soul retrieval often must be carried out at the same time to heal the afflicted person. Like intrusions, soul loss can occur multiple times over the course of a person's life. The first parts are often lost in childhood due to traumas that have been forgotten or even suppressed by the person over time. If no shaman is available to reverse previous soul loss, the number of lost soul parts can mount over the years, requiring multiple retrievals at once.

Soul retrieval in seiðr was undoubtedly done in a culturally specific way, and once again the methodology is suggested by specific features on the seiðstafr. In this case, it is not the basketwork structures but the finial at the very top of the staff. In the archaeological record the finial often has the form of a head, either animal or human, or in one case it took the form of a perfect scale model of a Norse longhouse. These forms all hint at the shamanic use of the finial structure. In several closely related Indo-European traditions, the head is viewed as the seat of the soul complex within the body. This is particularly evident in ancient Celtic beliefs surrounding the "cult of the head." One example of this was the practice in which Celtic warriors would decapitate their enemies and keep their heads in order to have some control over an opponent's soul. The skulls—which were believed to still contain the trapped spirits of the deceased—would be used to decorate the groves of the druids. The head was seen as the "home" of the spirit, and so the finials in the shape of a head at the top of the staff become a type of ongon or spirit house, which can be used to temporarily and safely store wights or soul parts while they are being dealt with. The finial in the shape of a longhouse suggests a similar usage.*

In an emergency it is possible to temporarily take hold of a single soul part in order to return it to its owner. The problem comes when

---

*In *Eirik the Red's Saga*, the finial of Thorbjorg's staff is described as a brass knob or sphere. In other shamanic cultures, a ceramic sphere, or one made of hollowed stone or small beads, is sometimes used as an ongon or spirit house. Clear quartz crystals can serve the same function, which is the only instance where crystals are really utilized in shamanism.

there are multiple soul parts that are being retrieved, as it is difficult to juggle several soul parts at once without losing at least one of them again. This is where the finial spirit house on the seiðstafr comes in. The spirit house can safely hold and protect multiple soul parts, enabling them to be easily transported until they can be dealt with.

✤ Empowering the Finial Spirit House

Use any general varðloka you feel is appropriate and begin to journey with the intention "To open and empower the spirit house on my seiðstafr." You do not need to find a wight that is specially dedicated to this task, so you may work with any that you think are appropriate. Call and merge with your wight(s). You will remain in the middle realms but "see" a portal to the upper worlds coming into being above your head. Thrust the top of your staff through the portal. Watch as it is surrounded by light, allowing the light to penetrate and suffuse whatever finial you are using as a spirit house, cleansing it and making it safe for visiting wights. When you feel the process is complete, withdraw your staff from the portal and watch as it closes. Once the portal has closed, thank your wight(s) and return to ordinary reality.

✤ Carrying Out a Soul Retrieval

You will need to engage with wights that can specifically help you with soul retrieval before you start this work. These could be any wights that have helped you with other aspects of healing, or it may be completely new and different wights—just be open to any possibility that presents itself. Do a journey in the normal way to find the wights that will support you with the process.

Make your preparations for journeying. Gather your equipment and find a location to work where you will not be disturbed. Light your candles and incense if you are using them. The patient should be lying on a blanket on the floor near you, with their friend/witness nearby.

Your intention for the journey is "To carry out a soul retrieval for

_____ [person's name]." Begin to journey and call your wights. Ask one of your wights to take you to the location of the first soul part. Follow the wight wherever it leads you and adhere to any instructions it gives you on the way. Once you have located the soul part, introduce yourself politely to it and explain what you are here for. Be gentle— remember that these missing soul parts are traumatized and probably afraid. Ask the soul part about its story and why it left. Ask the soul part if it is willing to return, and if so, does it have any conditions that must be met for it to stay once it has returned? Make careful notes about all these responses. (It is very important that you provide the owner with this information afterward because if any conditions are not met, the soul part will not stay and will leave again.) Not all soul parts will initially want to return to their owner, so you may have to negotiate and convince the soul part that the circumstances that caused it to leave in the first place are no longer present. But if all else fails, do not be tempted to try to coerce the soul part to do anything against its will, lest you risk becoming a soul thief with all the issues that involves.

If the soul part agrees to return, ask it to enter the spirit house on your staff and wait there until you can take it back to its owner. Repeat this process with all missing soul parts. If there are multiple soul parts that have become separated, you may have to do the retrievals over several sessions.

⅗ Reintegration of the Soul Parts

Return to the middle realms and to Midgard, and to the room where the person you are working for is waiting. Taking your staff, place the finial spirit house over the patient's heart and blow over the spirit house toward the heart. With each breath, witness the soul parts leave the spirit house and enter back into the person they left in the region of the heart. Witness as they rejoin and reintegrate with the rest of the soul complex. Once all the spirit parts have returned to their owner, move your staff to a position above their head and blow three times over the finial spirit house toward the crown of the head. This will ensure that any residual energies rejoin with the person. Once this has been done, shake your staff a few times over the patient lying on the ground and witness as it helps to seal and repair their energetic field.

After all of this has been completed, thank your wights and allow them to depart before ending your trance completely. Ask the patient to begin to get up and slowly bring themselves around. It is a good idea to suggest they drink some water and eat a small snack, as this will help with the grounding process. Explain everything that the missing soul part(s) revealed to you before they came back, especially anything that the owner must do to honor them and prevent them from leaving again. Check to make sure that the owner understands these conditions. You can also recommend that the person spend some time out in nature, preferably sitting nearby a favorite tree, while they try to reconnect and respond to the returned soul parts.

✣ Dealing with Soul Theft

Cases of soul theft should be treated like a (more complicated) version of soul loss: once you have access to the soul parts, they should be returned to the appropriate person using the methods above. But before you can get to this stage, you will have to locate the "thief" and persuade them to return the stolen parts. This does *not* require a physical confrontation with the thief. It should be done while journeying, so you are dealing directly with the soul complex of the thief rather than their physical body and their conscious mind—which will also prevent any danger to you of physical reprisals on their part.

It is not your place to form any sort of judgment about the thief. The reason why someone might consciously or even subconsciously try to steal parts of another person's soul is a highly complex matter and can be the result of many different factors. And as we noted earlier, it is impossible for a thief to take a soul part without the implicit agreement of the "victim," even if this does not occur at a conscious level. Soul theft is often done out of misplaced love and affection rather than any negative reason. It is common for people in love to exchange soul parts temporarily and freely; however, if that relationship then breaks down, one of the partners may subconsciously want to retain their partner's soul parts out of fear of loneliness and abandonment. People who have been together for a long time tend to be reluctant to completely release what has bought them comfort in the past, even if they have technically fallen out of love with the other person. Often the exchange of soul parts between lovers was mutual, so the "victim" may even be holding onto parts of the "thief's" soul complex as well, even though they are consciously unaware of it. This could be seen as a kind of "Stockholm syndrome"—the feeling of affection that sometimes develops between a victim and their captor in cases of kidnapping or hostage-taking.

It is also common for soul thieves to try to retain other people's soul parts because of soul loss that they themselves have suffered in the past. Subconsciously, they are trying to fill gaps in their own energetic body, although this is futile (because of the law of sovereignty, other people's soul parts cannot be integrated into the thief's energetic body). What this does typically mean, however, is that the soul thief themself is suffering and in need of soul-retrieval work; only after the latter is accomplished will they surrender the stolen soul parts. As we noted earlier, on death a soul thief cannot pass through the barriers between worlds if they are holding on to soul parts that do not belong to them. Therefore, the soul thief becomes a haugbúi, an earthbound spirit, a ghost trapped in Midgard. In many cases at the end of a relationship where one partner has died, both partners need to undergo soul exchange before they can find peace. In this scenario the earthbound spirit should be treated exactly as you would a living soul thief—even to the point that it may need soul retrieval itself before you then do further work to help it pass through the barriers and move on.

All of this makes dealing with soul theft extremely complex, which usually demands a great deal of unpicking before it can be resolved. Typically, this will also entail several sessions. But since all of this work centers around soul retrieval, it is still counted as basic healing work in seiðr.

⁜ Distance Healing

Although healing work preferably should take place with the patient in the same room, sometimes this is not possible. All the healing techniques we have looked at so far can also be done remotely, over a distance, but it requires the use of a stand-in—a "poppet," if you like. The poppet is an inanimate representation of the person being healed.* I generally use a small wooden artist's model figurine or "manikin" as my poppet.† It can be bent and posed, but it is also small enough to be kept on my altar after a working. For the purposes of remote healing with seiðr, you do not have to create a new poppet every time you work on a new person. The same poppet can be reused to represent a number of different people over time.

To use the poppet for remote healing, all you need to do is to state clearly at the outset, as part of your intention, that "the healing is for _____ [person's name]" and indicate that *the poppet is this person*. Throughout the working, treat the poppet exactly like you would the living person. At the end of the working, it is also good to thank the wight of the poppet for lending its strength to the working. Once the healing is over, the poppet should be cleansed with incense smoke. This returns it to a nonrepresentational state, no longer representing a specific person. Between workings you should keep the poppet clean and show it respect.

---

*Unlike in modern witchcraft, it is neither necessary nor advisable for the poppet to have a personal item—such as a lock of hair, bit of clothing, or some other small object—attached to it from the individual it is representing.
†These are available from any good artist's supply company.

9

Death, Dying, and Dealing with the Dead

For the northern Germanic peoples, the dead tended to fall into three distinct categories: the ancestors; the ghosts or earthbound spirits (Old Norse *haugbúar,* sg. *haugbúi*); and the draugar, undead revenants that are still connected to a physical body.

The ancestors are generally seen as kindly disposed toward their descendants. They are usually helpful for those who take the time to engage with them, although there can be exceptions. It is the duty of all heathens to have regard for their ancestors.

Earthbound ghosts or disembodied spirits, which are known as haugbúar ("mound dwellers"), are very common. In our modern society, as we become more and more removed from spirituality, such disembodied spirits seem to be rapidly increasing. It is an important duty for the spiritual workers from all cultures around the world, including völva and seiðr-workers, to help these suffering beings to cross between worlds whenever possible. If they are left unchallenged and their suffering is allowed to continue, they can cause several issues for the living.

Draugar, on the other hand, are extremely rare. A draugr is created by magic, and if you are unlucky enough to come across one, it can generally only be dealt with in the same way.

There is another slightly different category of spirits that we will also deal with in this section: the valkyries. While not technically dead themselves, the valkyries' primary functions are concerned with the dead—whether transporting the souls of dead warriors from the battlefields to the "halls of the slain" (Valhalla) or serving food and drink to the warrior spirits (called *einherjar*, "single warriors") residing within those halls. The so-called daughters of Óðinn, the valkyries are extremely complex group of wights. They have several roles in the mythology beyond just handling the dead warriors, so they are not easily compartmentalized. However, as psychopomps extraordinaire—and, arguably, your greatest allies when dealing with the dead—it seemed most logical to include them here.

Each of these aformentioned categories of wights needs to be dealt with in slightly different ways. In this chapter, we will begin to explore how we can do this using seiðr.

THE ANCESTORS

There is a prevalent misunderstanding about working with the ancestors, which is that you need to know *who they specifically are*. This leads many people to invest large amounts of time in researching their family history and genealogy. That is fine, or course, if it is an interest of yours—but it is completely unnecessary for any spiritual work. You may even come across people claiming direct descent from a famous "heathen ancestor," such as Ragnar Loðbrók, in the mistaken belief that this makes them and their practice somehow more "authentic" (and therefore more powerful) than others. There are several issues with this.

In Europe at least, no accurate birth records began to be kept until around the eighteenth century. Before that time, certain noble families may have maintained genealogies of the direct line (from father to oldest son and heir) to prove their nobility, but very few would have kept records of the wider line involving brothers and sisters, aunts and uncles, and so on. There is also considerable evidence that many of these "direct-line" genealogies were fabricated with the aim of making it appear that those recently elevated to the nobility had a much longer noble heritage than they actually did. This was certainly the case for the Anglo-Saxon royal houses of England, which had false genealogies created showing they were direct descendants of gods. This was done as a means of legitimizing their claims to rule over the people. Based on these false genealogies, I have even seen modern Americans claiming (with the "paperwork to prove it"!) that they are direct descendants of the god Baldr—even though most of the lore makes it clear that Baldr died before having any children!

The bottom line here is that it is almost impossible to prove that someone alive today is a direct descendant of any specific individual before the eleventh century, and then only from a noble house, which means that most people cannot prove any direct descendants before the eighteenth century. However, this is no deterrent for modern genealogy companies, which gladly try to sell such false genealogies as a way of encouraging people to give them money. Most modern genealogy and genetic-testing sites are a scam, part of a corporate race for profit.

Blood Ancestors: The Direct Family Line

For the past one thousand years, most all of your ancestors (if they were from Europe, at least) were Christian. There was no other choice. This means that in just about any case where you hear someone claiming to be part of a "direct line of surviving paganism"—that person is lying.*

I will freely say now I am the child of a Christian nurse and an atheist construction worker. As for my grandparents, in addition to their day jobs as miners and soldiers, some had minor functions in the local Church of England. And that is about as far back as I know my

---

*While we cannot completely rule out the possibility that some vestigial pagan line might not have survived here or there in some extremely remote backwater of Europe, this can in no way account for the huge number of Wiccan high priests and priestesses, archdruids, and others alive today who claim to be privy to arcane esoteric knowledge because they were born into an "unbroken line" of pagans!

direct ancestors. I have no knowledge of any direct descent from Ragnar Loðbrók, Eirik the Red, Brian Bloodaxe, Baldr Óðinsson, or indeed Olaf the Flatulent—though genetics dictates that there was probably some famous Viking in my ancestry somewhere, as it does for many of us. As it stands, I cannot even demonstrate a link to a minor English noble house from the Middle Ages or later. I don't know any more than this because I haven't bothered to research it. And the reason why I haven't bothered is because it really doesn't matter, and therefore it holds no interest for me.

Even though in most cases I have no knowledge of who my specific ancestors were, I still have gratitude and respect for my direct ancestral line. If it wasn't for them, I wouldn't exist. And this is why I still think it is worthwhile making the occasional blót to the ancestors to offer a general "thank you." It is *general* because they are mainly dealt with as an undifferentiated mass—hence I refer to "the ancestors" rather than any specific individual. After all, there is an unfathomable number of them. The average human brain can only cope with detailed knowledge of around two hundred separate individuals, which is why we generally think of "people" rather than specifically of, say, Mr. Chou from Chai Wan Road, Hong Kong.

When preparing to carry out a ritual to the ancestors, then, there are several scenarios to consider. Is it advisable—or even realistically possible—to remember and call upon each of the many thousands of your ancestors individually? Or should you identify and concentrate on a few known individuals—at the risk of alienating the rest? Or is it a better approach to honor all your ancestors quickly and succinctly by dealing with them as a single body, as "the ancestors" rather than as individuals.

As we can see, the collective approach has several advantages. This is especially the case for those who may have been abused or mistreated by some of their more recent individual ancestors before they passed on, or if you have a known ancestor who was involved in activities that you consider unpleasant or contrary to your own moral and ethical standards. You can honor the ancestors in general without honoring any specific individual and therefore approving of their actions.

Ancestors of Tradition

One thing that is not greatly mentioned in heathenry, but which plays an important part in other shamanic cultures around the world, as well as in several Eastern nonshamanic cultures, is the idea of "ancestors of tradition" rather than blood ancestors. These ancestors of tradition are the teachers of your teachers.

This concept is of great importance in general shamanism because no knowledge, no matter how ancient or arcane, is ever actually lost. As spirit is immortal, the holders of all human knowledge (and more) still exist somewhere in the spirit realms, and certain shamanic techniques make it possible to retrieve this knowledge. The only issue is locating these sources. While spirit is seen as immortal, it is neither omnipresent nor omniscient. Wights may know many things—often much more than the average human—but no individual wight can know everything. You should not assume that just because a guide or teacher is particularly ancient, they will necessarily be able to provide the specific nugget of knowledge you are seeking. It is still important to find the right teacher or guide for the piece of knowledge you are trying to track down.

Here we will look at engaging the ancestral first völva. This concept is not specifically taken from seiðr but from general shamanic practice, where it is known as the "ancestral first shaman." Despite some differences in the underlying myths about the origin of shamanic knowledge, the basic idea of contacting an ancestral shaman (or, in this case, ancestral völva) is easily adapted for use in a heathen context.

In the creation myths of most shamanic cultures, the special skills of the shaman were developed or discovered by a human, usually after being taught by spirit. Having mastered the skills, some of these powerful "first shamans" will often go on to become demigods for the tribe. With respect to seiðr, however, the myths make it clear that the techniques of the practice were first developed by the goddess Freyja and taught to other gods and goddesses before ever reaching humans.

While it is possible to go directly to the gods and engage with them, this is considered an advanced seiðr technique (beyond the scope of the present book) and can be dangerous. Moreover, from a general heathen point of view it is considered unwise to bother the gods unless you are in dire need, as you may anger them. Going to the gods with every little whim, question, and issue is potentially disrespectful. If at all possible, it's better to sort something out for yourself before appealing to divine aid.

The mythology further explains that the first non-god to be taught seiðr was Heiðr, but it is unclear who or what sort of being she was— human? Jötun? Trollwife? Was she perhaps an aspect of Freyja herself, or a completely different type of wight altogether? Very little information can be found in the lore about Heiðr herself, and what does appear suggests she may not have been all that friendly toward humanity. As the poem "Völuspá" (stanza 22) relates:

> Heith [Heiðr] they named her who sought their home,
> The wide-seeing witch [völva], in magic wise;
> Minds she bewitched that were moved by her magic,
> To evil women a joy she was. (Bellows 1923, 10)

It is clear from these lines that Heiðr is a relatively dangerous individual, perhaps particularly skilled in gandr magic, as bewitching minds is a particular feature of these types of techniques (see chapter 10). These sorts of techniques might appeal to some people and Heiðr could conceivably make a good, if demanding, teacher. But all power must be paid for, so the question is: Are you willing to pay the price that Heiðr may demand?

If you feel disinclined—or at least unready at this stage—to try to engage with such a powerful and potentially difficult entity as Heiðr, do not worry. There are other alternatives. After all, the fragmentary text known as "The Short Völuspá" (*Völuspá hin skamma*) also lists several other ancestors of all magic users:

> The sybils [völur] arose from Vitholf's race
> From Vilmeith all the seers are
> And the workers of charms are Svarthofthi's
> children . . . (Bellows 1923, 229)

So, there is at least some indication that the Norse honored and potentially worked with their most ancient lineal ancestors as well as their more recent blood ancestors. But there is no further information in the lore about any of the ancient figures. Nevertheless, it seems that some of them could make good candidates for you to try to contact as your own ancestral first völva.

But you might also try to work with a more personal ancestral first völva, which is what I do. This is the first person in your traditional lineage to learn seiðr, which is to say, the first in a line of teachers who taught your teachers. You might not know a name for these at first; in fact, you may never get to learn the name of the person no matter how long or how often you work with them. True names give power over a being, and therefore some ancestors may be very reluctant to reveal their true names to you, especially at first, until they come to trust you. But this really doesn't matter, and it need not prevent you from working with them.

❧ Connecting to Lineal Ancestors

In the following working we will try to connect with the ancestral first völva as a shamanic lineal ancestor.

Gather your seiðstafr and hood, and make your preparations for journeying. Using a general varðloka, begin to journey with the intention "To meet my ancestral first völva." Follow any guides that show up to direct you to where the ancestral first völva is. (Try to commit this route to memory so that in the future you can find it again quickly without enlisting any other guides.) Once you meet the ancestral first völva, introduce yourself and ask any questions you have. For example, you might want to ask if the völva is willing to share their name, how they can help you and what they would like in return, and what you need to do to honor them. Be sure that you follow any requests they have. Then ask the völva for any varðlokur that will enable you to work with lineal ancestors. At the end of the journey, thank your völva, return, and record any relevant notes in your journal.

Learning from Your Ancestral First Völva

Below I will present one way of working with the ancestral first völva to gather information from the past. There are other ways to do this, however, and over time you will likely develop your own rituals and ways of working with them. What follows is a variation of a ritual practiced by the Díne (Navajo) for working with the ancestral first shaman. The ritual is therefore not historically related to seiðr, but it is both shamanic and effective. It is specifically designed to recover lost knowledge, particularly about rituals and magical practices of the past. This recovered knowledge can then enable you to reconstruct lost rituals.

However, this comes with a strong warning: if you are able to reconstruct a procedure or ritual using this methodology, it should *never* be passed on to anyone as historically authentic unless you can find specific evidence of that practice, or something nearly identical to it, in the historic record. Any information you retrieve should be treated as UPG rather than historical fact.

Gather your equipment for journeying, but this time you will also need a strip of woven woolen fabric tied to your own ørlög (see chapter 6 for instructions on how to make this). Begin to journey with the intention "To recover information about _____," using the varðloka you obtained for working with the ancestral first völva or lineal ancestors. Merge with the ancestral first völva and, while in the middle realms and maintaining the merge, move close to the nearest wall and, when you are about an arm's length away, turn to face it. Take your strip of cloth and begin to twirl it around and around in front of you, at about chest height. Let your eyes focus on the cloth as it spins, while continuing to sing the varðloka, maintaining the merge with the ancestral first völva, and focusing on your intention. When you feel the time is right—and, trusting your own judgment, only you will know when this is—gently lower yourself to a blanket on the floor and begin to journey. Be open to whatever guides or wights you encounter and listen carefully to any information they give you. At the end of the journey, release the merge and thank the ancestral first völva before returning to ordinary reality. Make any notes you need in your journal.

While you can do this alone, it is more powerful if you perform the ceremony with other practitioners. If you do so, you can either continue to work separately on your own particular interest, or you can choose to combine your efforts (before you begin, each of you will agree to focus on retrieving the same bit of information or the same ritual). When you return to ordinary reality, you will often find that each of you has had a slightly different experience and been given some specific detail about a part of the ritual you are trying to recover. Therefore, by combining all of your notes at the end of the process, you will end up with a much more powerful ceremony. The result is thus a shared personal gnosis (SPG) rather than a UPG.

PSYCHOPOMP WORK WITH THE VALKYRIES

A psychopomp is basically a "soul midwife" or "soul escort" involved in the translocation of the spirit from one state of existence to another. At birth the psychopomp brings the spirit from wherever it was previously. If we accept the principle of the immortality of the spirit, which is broadly supported by Germanic lore, then psychopomps do not create new souls but simply fill new bodies with already existing souls. However, the most prominent job of a psychopomp occurs at death, where their role is to transport the newly released soul to its proper place in the afterlife. The true psychopomp is only involved in this transportation and transition process, and may not necessarily be engaged in caring for the spirit either before it incarnates or while it is incarnated.

Apart from certain deities like Óðinn and Freyja,* the most powerful psychopomps in Norse mythology are arguably the group of wights called the valkyries. This is evident with the valkyries: they may become involved in the birth or death of a person, but seldom in the latter's life—unless that person is one of the great heroes.

The valkyries play several major roles in the mythology and can therefore be of help to the seiðr-worker in various areas, especially that of psychopomp work, which we will cover in more detail below. But there are other, more subtle ways in which the valkyries can also become involved in people's lives. Therefore, it will be useful to begin by providing a brief introduction here to some of the mythology and associations concerning the valkyries.

Who are the valkyries? Sometimes called "shield maidens" (*skjaldmær*), they are also referred to as the "daughters of Óðinn," although none appear in lists of his children nor is there any indica-

---

*Óðinn and Freyja are both quite involved with the death process, at least when it concerns those who are slain in battle. He is responsible for choosing those who are about to die in battle, and sometimes also for releasing the soul from the body to begin its journey. Half of the souls of the battle-slain go to Óðinn's Valhalla, and the other half to Freyja's field call Fólkvangr. By contrast, although the goddess Hela is very closely associated with death, she would not technically be considered a psychopomp. She is not involved in the death process per se. It is only after having died that people's souls fall into her tender care. As a rule, she does not collect and transport the souls herself. Instead, she waits in Helheim for them to be sent to her.

tion in the lore that they are otherwise related to him. Some people even claim that the valkyries are aspects of Óðinn himself, but this is unclear. In any event, Óðinn's relationship to them is more like that of an employer than anything familial. Indeed, the name "valkyrie" itself—from Old Norse *valkyrja*, "chooser of the slain"—is best thought of as a job description.

All of the valkyries have personal names, a surprising number of which have survived in the lore. We know the specific names of at least forty different valkyries, and the sources suggest there were many more. The names are also an important source of information on the valkyries and their areas of specialization. Two examples are Mist ("Cloud"), who may have been involved in weather magic (as bad weather could affect the outcome of major battles and thus influence who lived and who died) and Rangríðr ("Shield-destroyer").

In terms of their background, the valkyries appear to be a pretty diverse group of wights, rather than a specific class of people. So, it is very difficult to generalize about the physical appearance or attributes of the valkyries and each must be treated as an individual. One thing the lore does make clear is that they were exclusively female.

The valkyries' most significant role is at the time of death, but in this case it is only for the einherjar,* the chosen heroes whom they convey to Valhalla. But the Eddas and sagas also relate several stories in which a valkyrie is persuaded to help a person during their life in Midgard. The Eddic poem "Sigrdrífumál" (The Sayings of Sigrdrífa) tells the story of Sigrdrífa, a valkyrie who is awakened by the hero Sigurd after being made unconscious by Óðinn for refusing to marry the person that Óðinn favored. In return Sigrdrífa teaches Sigurd how to use the runes and other magic. There are several overlaps between Sigrdrífa and Brunhild, the ex-valkyrie in the *The Saga of the Völsungs*

---

*For most people, however, it seems that the fylgja takes the place of the valkyrie as the preferred messenger of death (see the discussion of Germanic soul lore in chapter 8).

(*Völsunga saga*) who is also cursed by Óðinn and rescued by the great hero Sigurd. She helps Sigurd with several problems, and he later marries her. This has led several people to suggest that Sigrdrífa and Brunhild may have originally been one and the same individual. A similar story occurs in the Eddic poem "Helgakviða Hundingsbana" (The Lay of Helgi Hundingsbane) concerning the hero Helgi and the valkyrie Sigrún, which is one of the few stories in the lore that describes an instance of reincarnation.

Although the valkyries can occasionally be persuaded to help people (as they clearly do in the aforementioned examples), they should in no way be confused with the Christian or New Age concept of guardian angels. As their name suggests, a guardian angel's purpose—which appears to be entirely altruistic—is to protect the person to whom they are assigned; this is always their priority. Valkyries, on the other hand, are primarily concerned with *transporting* a person's soul from place to place. When a valkyrie is persuaded to help someone, it will be done on the valkyrie's own terms—and they will expect something in return. In most of the stories they do it for physical love and eventually marry the people they support. Nevertheless, it is still worthwhile to try to engage with your valkyrie and ask the question if they would be willing to help.

✤ Meeting Your Valkyrie

Make your preparations for journeying as you normally would. Journey with the intention "To meet my valkyrie and ask her to _____." While journeying, remember to ask for a varðloka to call and work with the valkyries, and record your varðloka in your journal.

THE GERMANIC AFTERLIFE

Before we can consider methods for dealing with the dead, it is important to gain some understanding of the concepts of the afterlife in

Germanic mythology. The Germanic peoples had several versions of the afterlife, several possible final resting places for the soul.

The early myths are vague, but there is some evidence for a belief that the soul would remain in the *grave mound*. Similar neolithic beliefs and parallels can be found in certain Celtic conceptions of the afterlife. It is clear the grave mounds and burial sites were among the first sacred places of worship. They were presumably seen as somehow connected, a series of interlinked doorways and passages that formed the world of the ancestors. It appears that during the neolithic period certain barrows were not sealed and were probably left open, or opened at specific times, so that people could go in and worship among the actual bones of their ancestors.

The dead in their burial mounds also become an intimate part of the physical landscape. In the United Kingdom where I live, one need only traverse a small section of any long-distance footpath to see how many burial mounds were placed on top of hills or other prominent places, almost like a way of putting the local people's stamp on the landscape. The effective message is: "This is our land—our ancestors have been buried here for generations." The ancestors, then, like the landvættir, become not only the guardians of the family line, but protectors of the land upon which the family lives and providers of resources through agriculture. A reflection of this belief is also evident in some legends where there is some confusion between male ancestors in their grave mound and the álfar (see Lecouteux 2018, 110–11).

In slightly later Norse beliefs, the idea of the grave mound was modified to become the *sacred mountain* where the ancestors congregated. (If a grave mound, which housed a few ancestors, can be seen as resembling a miniature hill or mountain, it would not have required a great stretch of the imagination to envision that a much vaster number of ancestors might congregate within the full-scale version.) In several Icelandic sagas there is mention of certain families' ancestors gathering at the Helgafell ("Holy Mountain"). Similarly to a grave mound, if a prominent natural hill and mountain was believed to be an abode for ancestral spirits, this would serve the function of stamping the local tribe's authority on the landscape.

In the Viking Age—probably under the influence of Christianity—these ideas begin to diversify even further, and several distinct afterlife destinations become possible. Those who die of natural causes (a "straw death"), which comprises most people, will go to Helheim. This was seen as a distant and protected place where the dead can rest in peace, thus the dead were now further removed from their former connection to the physical land of Midgard. But even here there does not seem to be any form of judgment being passed over the dead—all are accepted equally into Hela's halls. Only much later and under the influence of Christianity do we begin to see the references to Niflhel and the hall Náströnd, the place of punishment. The einherjar, the battle-slain warriors personally picked by Óðinn, go either to his great hall, Valhöll (Valhalla, the "Hall of the Slain"), or to Fólkvangr (the "Field of the Host"), which is ruled over by the goddess Freyja. Contrary to certain popularized notions today, Valhalla was not conceived of as the "heathen heaven." Valhalla had a very specific purpose: to train warriors for the final battle. (Since very few people end up in these regions, it is rarely necessary to engage with either Valhalla or Fólkvangr in the course of shamanic psychopomp work.)

Those who drowned at sea were said to go to Ægir's hall to entertain his wife Rán. Here again we see a certain category of the dead going to a specific hall, to serve a specific deity. We might then ask: Did other people who were faithful to a particular god then go to that god's hall to serve in death as they did in life? Although there may be little specific evidence about this preserved in the lore, it does appear to be a discernible pattern.

The preceding comments give some indication of just how complicated the concept of the afterlife could be—and here we are only considering the northern Germanic viewpoint! There is nothing in the lore that claims the Norse gods are the only divinities to exist in the multiverse. The Germanic peoples were relatively accepting of others' beliefs and made no claims to exclusive truth. And if the Germanic gods are not exclusive, then why should a certain set of afterlife destinations be exclusive? While the Norse soul may specifically seek out the mound, or Helheim, or some other realm that is known from the lore, an infinite multiverse should be seen as offering many potential afterlives.

There is a general shamanic belief—not necessarily Germanic—concerning the death process that is worth considering: when the soul leaves the body, it will naturally gravitate toward the afterlife it was taught to expect in life. For example, a Christian who wakes up in a bright, ethereal realm populated by angels will be more likely to accept that they are dead than if they find themself in the endless fields of Elysium or the orchards of Helheim, simply because it is what they have been taught to expect they will experience once dead. There is, however, an unfortunate secondary effect if a Christian is constantly being told that they might be unworthy to enter heaven. In this case, their expectation will be that they are going to the Christian hell, a place of eternal punishment. Chances are, then, this is where they will end up—not on account of any judgment by their God, but because of their conditioning. And who largely is responsible for this? Well, it is generally the Church. Thus, the organization whose entire purpose is to "save" their souls is also the one that condemns them to their fate.

The situation is not all bad, however. Wherever a soul ends up, it will start to come to terms with the fact of its owner's death. It then begins to recover, eventually reaching a state in which it realizes that it is not trapped in that place. The spirit realms are indeed infinite and the soul is largely free to move between them as it wills.* So, souls trapped in hell will, after a time, be able to move on. And souls that knew each other in life will be able to meet again in death, if they so

---

*The exception concerns access to places such as Valhalla, which have strict entry requirements.

wish, without having to worry about what religion they each followed.

As a result of their conditioning, many people from the Abrahamic religions are terrified of the process of death. Such fears are a kind of self-fulfilling prophecy, as there is a significant chance that upon dying, they may indeed pass into hell at least temporarily, even if it is entirely undeserved. These fears about the afterlife can also affect the soul's willingness to move on from the middle world when the time comes. But the middle world is not the soul's rightful place. If a soul becomes trapped here it will continue to suffer from fear and regret more permanently than it would have otherwise, and it can even become a burden to the living.

The bottom line is that when carrying out psychopomp work, we must learn to respect individual beliefs. Do not assume that just because *you* are a heathen all the dead whom you meet should be taken straight to Helheim. The dead have their own destinations. Abrahamic dead will expect to find their version of heaven, or the other place. Hindu dead may be looking for a doorway to reincarnation. If you take any of these people and just dump them in Helheim, they are not going to stay. You should not be surprised if, a few days after you have moved them on, they suddenly reappear in Midgard, doing exactly what they did before. Each of the dead needs to be taken to their own rightful destination.

COUNSELING THE DYING

One of the roles of the seiðr-worker is to help people with the process of dying. If people have a better understanding of the death process while they are still living, it helps to alleviate many of their fears about death. This, in turn, will make the transition much easier when their time eventually comes. More people will pass naturally into the afterlife; there will be fewer earthbound spirits, and less need for spiritual workers to spend time dealing with the dead when they could be helping the living.

Many people believe that one of the major aims of living is to achieve a good death, but nevertheless death has become taboo in our modern Western society. We seem to think that by denying death we might somehow avoid it, but all this really means is that we will be unprepared when death eventually creeps up on us. Our tendency is to shut the dying away in hospitals so that most healthy people will not have to see them. This sanitization of death does a great disservice not only to the dying but to the living as well, as it severely restricts our chances of finding our own place in the afterlife.

Make no mistake about it: as an adult from, say, your early twenties onward, you are in the process of dying. Your body is already experiencing the slow decline, disintegration, and decay that leads to one inevitable outcome. There is no need to panic, though. Hopefully for most of us this is a very slow process. And there are things you can do to slow its progress, such as by leading a healthy lifestyle. But while it is possible to delay the onset of death, it cannot be avoided altogether—and there are also a million different ways for people to accelerate the inevitable outcome as well. Humanity is quite inventive in that respect. I am not a spokesman for the General Medical Council or the Surgeon General, and this is not the place to tell you how you should be living your life. You are perfectly capable of making your own decisions in that respect. But do remember that all your choices will have consequences.

Contrary to popular thinking, what goes on in the afterlife is not a mystery—at least not for spirit workers, who have a variety of different techniques for accessing and engaging with this hidden reality. After all, if you can actively experience what your ørlög has in store, it becomes more than simply a matter of belief.

We should also make clear that trying to use seiðr to pinpoint the exact date of your death is rather pointless. As we said at the beginning of this book, time is not universal; it is both physical and local. If theoretical physics is to be believed, time has some extremely strange properties with respect to Midgard alone. And if we take the other realms beyond the middle ones into account, then all we can say about time is that it works in a wholly different way. Very few wights have any understanding of time as it affects Midgard. The one exception might be the greater Norns, but they are not going to reveal such information. None of the other wights would even be able to hazard a guess as to when "your time is up," so there is really no point in asking. If you do ask, any answer you receive will likely be wildly inaccurate. You will die when your ørlög says so.

Instead of trying to divine the actual moment of death, what you can do as a seiðr-worker is follow your own individual journey through death into the afterlife. In doing so you will certainly get confirmation that death is not the end of human existence, but simply another transitional phase to be endured. You will also see just how easy death can be, which tends to remove a lot of the fear that is otherwise associated with the process of dying. You can do this for other people, too: with their permission, you can journey to follow their path through death and describe it to them as it unrolls before you. However, it will always be more believable for the person in question if they experience it themselves. If they are open to it, it is always better to teach someone how to carry out a basic shamanic journey safely and help them through the process of journeying to their own death.

Before undertaking this process with anyone else, however, it is essential that you have experienced it for yourself. After overcoming any personal fears by exploring your own death, you will be able to convincingly explain to others that their fears surrounding death are groundless. It is also helpful for all spirit workers to be reminded every now and then that all of our efforts are headed toward the same result: one day you too will be nothing but history and memories, if you are lucky. This knowledge is a powerful corrective to prevent one's ego from becoming overly inflated. Death is the ultimate leveler—whether you were a noble jarl or a lowly thrall is of no consequence in the eyes of

Hela! It is therefore important that every spirit worker undertake this journey several times throughout their career.

❉ Journeying through Death

Gather your equipment and prepare to journey as you normally would. (You can make a prior journey to obtain a varðloka specifically for this or you may use any varðloka that you already have that you associate with death.) The intention for this journey is "To follow my personal journey into death." As we discussed earlier, in terms of Norse lore, there are several different destinations for the hugr. If you suspect your journey may entail a trip to Helheim, you should be aware that Hela does not generally welcome visitors from the living. So, if it does look like you may be entering into Helheim, it will help to change your hamr so that you more closely resemble the dead among whom you will be walking. This is achieved in the same way as any shapeshifting during journey work: try to become aware of your hamr, which appears as the external shape you "wear" during your journey work (this is distinct from your true form, which lies beneath the hamr). Once you have built a strong awareness of hamr, imagine it changing into whatever form you need—in this case, it will be a "deceased-looking" version of yourself. Remember to write down any important notes about the journey after you have returned.

HAUGBÚAR

Haugbúar (sg. haugbúi) are disembodied human spirits—ghosts, if you will. When the lík dies, the hugr or spirit only partially completes the transition to death. The hugr disengages and disconnects from the lík, but if it cannot successufully travel the *helvegr* ("Hel Path"), the road to Helheim, it becomes stuck in Midgard. Overwhelmingly, this is a situation that afflicts humans. It is not that animals lack souls or spirits, but they are much more accepting of the process of death and undergo it much more easily. They instinctively know what to do at death, and in a world of predator and prey they tend not to hold grudges with respect to the being that kills them (for most nonvegetarian people, this news should elicit a sigh of a relief). As a result, animal spirits usually pass easily out of the middle realms. Therefore, over 99 percent of the haugbúar you encounter will be of human origin.*

So why does someone become a haugbúi? There are an infinite number of variations for why people can become trapped in the middle realms, but it generally occurs due to one of these four causes:

1. Confusion/nonacceptance
2. Addictions
3. Unfinished business
4. Deliberate entrapment by the living

By far the most common cause for the creation of an earthbound spirit is the confusion and nonacceptance of the state of death. If death arrives suddenly and without warning, the hugr can become confused. This can also occur with certain forms of death by natural causes, such as heart attack, which sometimes involve violence. The hugr may not even realize that the lík has, in fact, died. Unaware of its new state, the hugr will try to carry on living as it did previously—going to its place of work, trying to interact with its family, and so on. But it will become increasingly frustrated with this situation as it discovers that all of these familiar people are completely ignoring it. Hospitals are generally places with a high concentration of these sorts of wights: people who died suddenly from natural causes or violence, but who do not realize they are dead and continue to seek treatment for whatever condition brought them to the hospital in the first place.

---

*This is not to say that animal haugbúar do not exist, but they are very rare. In these cases there are very specific extenuating circumstances why they are trapped in Midgard, which will need unpicking.

Increasingly, in the modern world, many earthbound spirits are the result of addictions. This could be an addictive craving for alcohol, drugs, food, or sex, or even for material things that are only available in Midgard. Addiction originates in the hugr and if it is not treated before death, it will carry over into the afterlife. The objects of these addictions are all found in the middle realms, so the only way a wight can satisfy such cravings is to remain in Midgard. Moreover, addictions are essentially hormonal—they require access to an intact endocrine system to get the hormone rush that will temporarily relieve the cravings. This means that an addicted earthbound spirit needs access to a living body, but not just any body—it will seek out and victimize one that is already under the influence of the same substance to which it is addicted.

Fortunately for the haugbúi—but not for the victim—people under the influence of drugs or alcohol, bloated from overeating, or blissed-out in the midst of orgasm are not usually focused on their own spiritual protection, so they are relatively easy targets. Why is that here in England, when you hear about a "haunted" pub, the paranormal activity is always centered on the toilet? Pub toilets are spiritually some of the most dangerous places on earth, because haugbúar have learned that it is easy to lurk there for their next potential victim. The only good news for the victim is that possession by an addicted haugbúi tends to be temporary—as the blood filters out the addictive substance and the symptoms of intoxication decline, the addicted spirit leaves that body in search of its next fix. But we also might also wonder: How many hangovers are partially the result of the heavy energy left behind by haugbúar?

Although relatively rare, it is possible for people with "unfinished business" to become haugbúar. For this to occur, the person must have had an overdeveloped ego and an extremely strong will, which allows them to resist the pull of the afterlife and remain in Midgard. This also means that the dead with unfinished business are some of the most complicated to handle. If you move them on before their business has been fully resolved, they will usually keep returning to Midgard.

Therefore, it is important to make sure that this business is finished to their satisfaction before you move them on.

The rarest sort of haugbúar in the modern age are those that have been deliberately trapped by the living (either by a sorcerer or a malicious seiðr-worker). In past ages they were more common, but nowadays in the "developed" West we no longer generally resort to apotropaic practices such as burying a criminal at a crossroads or taking a corpse out of a building through a wall or window. In earlier times, the aim of such actions was to confuse the wight sufficiently that it would not be able to find its way elsewhere to bother the living. However, this also often meant that the hugr could not then find its way to a realm in the afterlife and was forced to wander the world as an angry ghost.

While it is relatively easy to trap a hugr on Midgard, it is much more difficult to then control that hugr to do your will. One way to accomplish this is through soul theft, with the stolen soul parts used as "leverage" to blackmail the hugr into doing what you want. In the rare event that you come across a haugbúi under control of someone else (either another seiðr-worker or a necromantic sorcerer of some sort), this can be dealt with just like any other trapped spirit, though it may require some soul-retrieval work first. Bear in mind, however, that unless you are extremely careful, it is likely that the sorcerer will become aware of your "interference"—and may or may not choose to retaliate. This can lead to situations of shamanic warfare, which can be very unpleasant for all involved.

Dealing with Haugbúar

When you come across the spirits of the earthbound dead, it is important to remember that these are suffering beings. Trapped in the middle realms, perhaps even unaware of what has happened, they are lost, plagued by addictions, and typically afraid and alone. As a spirit worker, you have a moral obligation to try to move them on—to take them to where they need to be, which is not where they currently are stuck.

After two millennia of domination by Christianity and the suppression of spirit workers, there are very few people in Western society today who deal with the dead. But the numbers of the latter have only grown over centuries of uncontrolled population growth coupled with famine, diseases, and, more recently, wars of unprecedented proportions. Medieval people believed that it was impossible to throw a pin from the top of a tower without hitting a demon. If you substitute the restless dead for demons, that is probably an accurate claim. Frankly, in Europe where I live, the earthbound dead are reaching epidemic proportions, and this is surely true in other parts of the world as well. Therefore, it would be very surprising if you *don't* come across the dead almost daily. In fact, when you start doing psychopomp work, you will find that some of them begin to actively seek you out for your services, so you need to be prepared for this.

✤ Psychopomp Work

Gather your equipment and prepare to journey as you normally would. Using your the varðloka you obtained for working with valkyries, begin to journey with the intention "To move this suffering being along from Midgard." When you enter the spirit world, it is important that you immediately call on and merge with your wights for protection. If you fail to do this and are not fully up to power when dealing with the dead, there is a significant chance that some of them will try to possess you out of sheer desperation. It is much easier to prevent that from happening in the first place than to have to carry out a full de-possession rite for yourself later!

Once you are fully merged, call in your valkyrie. If you cannot see the dead person you are dealing with at that time, ask the valkyrie to guide you to them. Once you can see them, approach the dead with several questions:

1. Do they understand that they are dead? Be gentle with them, as up until this point they may not have realized it. Accordingly, they may react with panic, fear, and confusion.

2. If they understand they are dead, do they know why they are stuck in Midgard and have not been able to pass on?

3. Would they like you to help them pass on? At this point, many will say: "Yes." They do not want to be trapped here. But you should also expect that some spirits will be resistant, especially if they have unfinished business. Others may simply be afraid to move because they don't know who or what is waiting for them.

4. If they are resistant to your help, try to find out why. Ask if there is anything they need to do before they go, and whether there is anything you can do for them before they pass on. It is your responsibility to try to persuade them to move on, to negotiate with them, and if there is anything they need, such as soul-retrieval work because of soul theft, it is the responsibility of you and your wights to complete this work if you possibly can. You should not agree to put yourself at risk, however, trying to carry out the impossible. You always have free will in these matters—never forget that!

5. If all else fails, it is your responsibility to try to move people on, whether they agree to it or not. This may sound harsh, but remember these people are suffering from being trapped here. They should not remain stuck in Midgard and it is in everyone's best interest—including their own, though they may not realize it—for them to move on.

Once you have determined the best way to help them, call on the valkyrie to open a doorway to the appropriate place. It is important that you witness the opening of this portal. The portal itself may appear very differently to each spirit worker. If you have a background in Christianity (even if you have since converted to heathenry), you may experience the classic set of steps leading to an ornate gateway in the clouds. Or you may experience a portal such as the rainbow bridge (Bifröst), the "Hel Path" (helvegr), or a simple doorway. Be open to whatever appears—there should be some form of opening and you may be able to glimpse the landscape beyond it. I tend to experience a simple vortex in the sky, like a sci-fi representation of a black hole, only it tends to be purple and dark blue in color rather than black, and in the eye of the vortex I see the landscape beyond.

You may see figures in this opening; these are often ancestors or the spirits of close family and friends whom the deceased knew in life, coming to greet them and bring them home. If the deceased was from an Abrahamic faith, these figures may appear to be angelic. If these figures do not appear of their own accord but you think they could help, you can sometimes call on them to come forward. The deceased may try to resist, but the grip of the valkyrie, angels, or waiting figures is unbreakable: the deceased will be compelled to go with them.

Witness as the valkyrie takes the deceased through this portal to the waiting figures. (If you are curious, you can usually accompany the valkyrie through the portal and see what is on the other side, but do not stay long and be ready to return instantly if need be—the portal will not stay open long and may shut suddenly.) Sometimes you may find a guardian by the portal who will try to prevent you from entering. If so, listen to what the guardian says and do not try to ignore or push past them. There may be reasons why you are not supposed to enter here. If it is not a place you are destined to see or visit, you should respect that. (You could end up in a lot of trouble if you do not.)

Witness as the valkyrie leaves the deceased with the figures on the other side of the portal, comes back through it, and the portal closes. Thank the valkyries and any other wights involved, and return to the middle realms. In most cases, if you have done your work properly, the dead will be unable to return. Even the addicted ones seem to get some support for the addiction on the other side. However, if the dead have unfinished business that you did not deal with before you moved them on, they will make every attempt to get back—and you may encounter them again in weeks or even days.

❅ Variations on Psychopomp Work

ᛟ Delayed Work

Sometimes we are approached by the dead when we do not have time to deal with them. In this case, the haugbúi can be held in the spirit house on your staff. If you are aware of haugbúar in your area, simply extend your staff toward them and witness as they are drawn into the spirit house. After this has been accomplished, at a later point you will need to journey into the spirit house to deal with the haugbúar gathered there. Treat this like any other journey, but your intention should be "To enter the spirit house to clear it of the dead." Travel into the spirit house and deal with the psychopomp work as you would normally.

Because any haugbúar in the area will be attracted to your staff regardless of whether you have been involved in recent psychopomp work or not, it is important to periodically clear it of spirits. It is a good idea to do this on a weekly basis so that the dead do not become too frustrated if trapped here for long periods.

ᛟ Multiple Haugbúar

Occasionally it will be necessary to carry out work with concentrations of the restless dead. This can be the case at locations where a large number people passed at roughly the same time in often violent and confusing circumstances: old battle fields, sites of natural disasters, and so on. In fact, there are groups of shamans who specifically work in these places after a natural disaster has occurred, to help the victims pass over.

In these kinds of circumstances it would take too long to deal with each of the haugbúar individually. Instead, they must be dealt with en masse, as a single unit. You can call in the valkyrie as you would normally and give it free reign to deal with all the restless souls; just witness what they do and how they do it. You may have to deal with single cases if they approach you for specific help while the valkyries work.

꒦ Draugar

Draugar are extremely rare, but they do exist. It is highly unlikely that you will be called on to deal with a draugr in your work. If you should be unfortunate enough to encounter one, however, it is essential to be prepared.

Draugr are created when the önd departs from the lík at death and returns to the Allfather. The önd connectively ties the hamr and hugr to the lík, so when it departs at death this loosens the hugr enough that it can depart from the body. In the best-case scenario, the hugr will then begin the journey to the afterlife. If the hugr loses its way on the journey, it will become a haugbúi (as discussed above). In very rare cases, however, the önd can depart yet the hugr remains attached to the lík, which creates a draugr or revenant—one of the walking dead. This never occurs naturally through coincidence or accident. The creation of a draugr is always a deliberate act. It can occur in two main ways:

- Through the willpower of the hugr. This is usually because the hugr has some unfinished business. The classic example in the sagas is of a draugr that is buried with some great treasure—an extremely powerful ancestral weapon, for example. The draugr remains in the grave mound to guard the object(s). The reason to do so must be extremely powerful, and the hugr literally clings to the lík for its very existence.

- Through an act of sorcery. In this case, a third party—a myrkriða ("dark rider") or dark seiðr-worker—can tie the hugr to the lík at point of death. Usually, the myrkriðr will also bind the hugr to its will, ensuring that the resulting draugr is completely under its control. As the law of sovereignty continues after death, this is not an easy thing to achieve, and at some level the myrkriðr must get the subconscious agreement of the hugr. The creation of draugar is advanced work that goes beyond the scope of this book.

However the draugr was created, the first step in dealing with it is to break the links between the hugr and the lík. The hugr then must be taken away from the lík and contained before any psychopomp work is done to ensure that it gets to where it is supposed to go. Generally, I have recommended that seiðr work be in the direct presence of your client, but an exception should be made for cases involving draugar. In these situations, having some physical distance between yourself and the "client" is highly advisable for several reasons. First, the work itself is very involved and demands considerable time to accomplish. Second, and more importantly, trying to do the work in the same room as an enraged draugr could be dangerous.* Since most trance work functions in the spirit realms, it will be effective over a distance. Here the use of a poppet will be essential.

Taking your hood, seiðstafr, and poppet, prepare to journey as you normally would. Carry out an initial diagnostic journey using the poppet to find out where on the body the attachments are between the lík and the hugr. Then carry out a second journey with the intention "To deal with the draugr and take its hugr to where it needs to be." Using the varðloka that you obtained for working with the dead, call on the valkyries as you normally would.

It is always worthwhile to try to speak to the draugr first, before proceeding further. If you can convince the hugr that it really should not be in this realm, you might persuade it to leave the lík, at which point you can help it to move on. The draugr may ask you to perform

---

*Thankfully, I have yet to find myself in a situation where multiple "clients" needed this sort of attention at the same time. Because of the time it takes to carry out, the procedure may be of limited use in the event of a "zombie apocalypse." If you are ever faced with such a scenario, good luck!

some tasks on its behalf before it agrees; if so, make sure you do what it asks. However, given the manner by which draugar are created, this would be an exceptional outcome—most draugar are going to vehemently resist being moved on. If this is the case, the first thing you are going to need to do is to merge with the valkyries or other wights to ensure you have as much protection as possible. If you possibly can, enact a double merge.

There are several ways you can undo the attachments. Use whichever method feels most comfortable for you:

1. Using your staff, begin to work on the attachments, winding them around the head of your staff like you would any heavy energy during an extraction, and dealing with them accordingly (see the section on "Intrusions and Extractions" in chapter 8). Sometimes the attachments may be difficult to unwind. In this case, noise can help, as can singing or certain other sounds.*

2. Ask your wights to cut the attachments on your behalf.

3. Occasionally, the wights may give you a gift, which can sometimes take the form of a weapon. (Generally, gifts of this sort are first presented in the spirit realms, and later you will find a physical version that turns up in the middle realms.) These weapons often appear in the form of a Germanic sax or sword and are the equivalent of a *phurba*, a ritual dagger, in Himalayan shamanism. Such weapons are useful against any malignant wights and can certainly be used to cut the attachments holding the hugr to the lík. However, spiritual weapons of this sort are rare. If you go in search of one, it is unlikely you will find it. They must be presented spontaneously by the wights; typically, they are given as a reward for certain work. So, if you do not have one of these weapons that has been previously presented to you, and which

---

*This is another reason why I have the rings attached to the top of my staff—rattling them around the attachment can help to loosen it before you begin to wind it up.

you understand completely how to use, then you will have to rely on one of the other two methods.

Once you are sure you have removed all the attachments, ask the valkyries to remove the hugr from the lík. At this point it is likely that the hugr will resist, especially since you are technically working against the individual vili, or will, of the person involved. This could potentially be seen as a negative working in many traditions, as indeed it is. But remember, the draugr is not a natural part of Midgard and it does not belong here. This is one of the many times when it is useful for the seiðr-worker to eschew any strict ethical code. Nevertheless, the hugr can still be dangerous at this stage; it will lash out and attempt to prevent you from removing it from the lík. That is why this operation is best left to the armed spiritual shield maidens, the valkyries, who know what they are doing. Ask the valkyries to take the hugr into the spirit house at the top of your staff. This neutralizes it in certain respects, making it harder for it to do you any damage. Nevertheless, it can still be dangerous, so you should continue to treat it with some respect.

Once the hugr is inside your spirit house, its link to the lík is broken completely. Journey into the house and continue the psychopomp work as you normally would.

10
Gandr and Venom

The study of gandr is problematic for several reasons. There are differing suggestions as to what originally constituted gandr, and the meaning of the term clearly evolved over time and in different cultural contexts. Moreover, the concept becomes severely confused in later Christian sources.

In Sweden from the fourteenth century onward, *gand* is a type of wholly negative sorcery practiced by Sámi shamans that uses "elf-shot" to inflict damage and even death on people. An elf-shot is a supernatural projectile used by a sorcerer, but which may have a physical counterpart in the form of an actual object of some kind. Initially, elf-shot probably had a basis in the neolithic flint arrowheads found in flint scatters throughout northern Europe, which were often used by sorcerers. Later the term *gand* came to mean a small ball of moss or other vegetation containing nail clippings or hair of the victim, tied by a fine twine. It was created by the sorcerer and either slipped into the victim's pouch or pocket or left in their house to cause them damage in an act of sympathetic magic. This later practice appears to have been heavily influenced by Christian notions of witchcraft and the medieval use of poppets. It probably does not reflect the original sense of *gand(r)*, although there are some obvious connections.

In Old Norse the etymology of the word *gandr* seems to indicate some type of helping wight, whereas a derivative term, *göndul*, may also indicate the tool used to send that wight against an enemy. This would represent the projection of power to cause damage, whether it is achieved through sending a spirit or a ball of moss containing some of the victim's hair or nail clippings.

Parallels to this concept can be found among certain Indigenous shamanic tribes. The shamans of the Shuar (originally called the Jivaro in Spanish) of the Upper Amazon are masters par excellence of shamanic warfare. Their shamans take part in all intertribal physical conflicts against the shamans of other tribes. The Shuar spend years creating and developing *tsentsak* (spirit darts), which they fire at their enemies to cause damage. They are given these darts by the spirits of (usually highly poisonous) plants found in the rainforest after they follow a process called *dieta* for months or even years. During the dieta, the shaman eats a very restricted and extremely bland diet—no meat or fish; no alcohol; no dairy; no garlic, chilies, or other strong herbs and spices; no caffeine; no processed sugars; no citrus; and a restricted range of very bland tasting fruit and vegetables. While also cleansing the system, the dieta is designed to demonstrate to the spirits that the shaman is capable of long-term discipline and dedication.

During the dieta, the shaman lives alone in the jungle, isolated from other people for up to six months. In this time, they carry out some deep shamanic work with the plant spirit. At the end of the process, if successful, the plant spirit gives the shaman a spiritual dart or tsentsak. The tsentsak is usually stored safely in the throat of the shaman, using very specific techniques, until it is needed. The shaman understands the tsentsak is not actually physical but spiritual. If called on to remove a tsentsak from another person, in addition to the spiritual removal, through sleight of hand the shaman will often be seen to produce a physical arrowhead, which he or she has apparently pulled from the person's body during the process. This is technically not a "trick," since the tsentsak is present in the body causing damage and it is removed by spiritual means as well. While the tsentsak that did the actual damage is spiritual, the "physical evidence" often helps to convince the person being healed that the tsentsak has indeed been removed, which is psychologically comforting. It is all part of the theater of shamanism.

When needed in battle, the spiritual tsentsak is regurgitated into the mouth and spat at the opposing shaman. As a spiritual dart, the tsentsak has no maximum range and will automatically home in on the target, much like the description of the medieval gand when thrown by the Sámi shamans (noaidis).

THE CONCEPT OF VENOM IN THE GERMANIC WORLD

While the Norse never subscribed to the classical system of the four elements (earth, air, fire, and water; later a fifth element of ether or spirit was added) that was first developed and used extensively in the Hellenic and Roman worlds, the lore does talk of a few mystical substances with specific esoteric properties. Whether these constitute an actual "elemental system" used by the Norse is certainly debatable, but there can be no doubt that they believed these substances had certain spiritual associations. Depending on the source, the number of substances varies from two to around nine, and they are generally thought to have a certain hierarchy. The first pair are:

Ice—Fire

These primary substances, described in the creation myth as represented by the worlds of Muspelheim and Niflheim, are the only two that everyone agrees upon. Interactions between fire and ice create everything else in the universe: all things spiritual and physical, including the other "elements" or substances. Ice provides the structure, the stable framework for things to exist; fire provides the energy, the animating factor. As ice and fire meet and mix, they create up to seven other basic mystical substances:

1. *Water* is the result of melting ice; it is the essence of softness and flow associated with Ljósálfheim.
2. *Steam/Air* is the result of water hitting fire; it is the essence of movement associated with Asgard.
3. *Yeast* is the child of fire and air; it is the essence of growth found contained within the ice of Muspelheim, which floated through Ginunngagap, and it is associated with Vanaheim.
4. *Salt* is the product of ice and water, and it is left over when water, especially salt water, evaporates. Salt is thought to be the essence or substance of preservation, as seen in the creation myth where it becomes the only food needed to sustain Auðumbla, the primal cow who shapes the gods and giants. It is associated with Helheim.

    A combination of ice (body or framework), yeast (growth), and salt (preservation) forms rime—the original physical substance that creates and sustains life.
5. *Venom* is the heat of steam and water combined. Whereas salt is seen as the essence of preservation, venom is the opposite: the essence of dissolution, destruction, and disease. It is the essence of Jötunheim.
6. *Iron/steel* is the result of salt and fire coming together to create the essence of sharpness. The precursor of the mineral world, it is associated with Svartálfheim.
7. *Earth/land* represents all of the other substances combined into one: the essence of Midgard.

It should be noted that the above associations between the substances and the realms reflect a modern way of looking at things, suggested by the UPG of contemporary practitioners. There is no evidence that the ancient Norse themselves associated the substances with specific realms. Therefore, if you feel strongly that a certain association listed here is wrong and that salt, for example, is better associated with Vanaheim, then follow your own instincts. You may likewise choose to disregard most of these associations altogether.

Besides the well-known primordial elements of fire and ice, the exact role that many of these substances play may be unclear. The other exception to this is venom, which we will now discuss for its importance with healing. Venom plays a prominent role in the wider Germanic lore, especially that of Anglo-Saxon England. The old Anglo-Saxon herbals such as *Lacnunga* and *Bald's Leechbook* consider venom to be the root cause of much disease and suffering in the physical world, and many famous healing charms such as the "Nine Herbs Charm" are essentially intended to protect from the effects of venom.

Though many people today view venom as an agent of destruction and therefore wholly negative, from an older Germanic perspective it was considered a neutral substance. The reasons for this will become clearer if we consider the bigger picture. The physical world is a finite place; if it should become too full of physical objects, there would be no room for anything else to exist. The old and worn out, therefore, must be cleared away, broken down into their constituent components, and "recycled." This frees up the space for new things to exist at the same time as it provides the basic building blocks for their creation. The same holds true for our mental constructs—the capacity of the human mind is limited, and if we constantly hold onto old thought patterns, emotions, and behaviors that no longer serve us, then there is no room for development and new growth. Venom contains the essence of destruction, but this simultaneously enables and leads directly to ongoing creation.

In the older literature, venom is very strongly associated with serpents and wyrms. Several connections in this regard can be found in the the Norse literature. Cosmologically, it can be associated with

Níðhöggr, the dragon that gnaws at the World Tree, Yggdrasil, and may be a significant source of venom. In the poem "Lokasenna" (The Flyting of Loki), Loki is punished by the rest of the gods and tied to a rock by the entrails of one of his sons while a serpent is suspended above him to drip venom (*eitr*) into his face. In "Gylfaginning," Snorri mentions Niflheim, where Níðhöggr lives on the Náströnd ("corpse shores") in a hall that is woven out of serpents with their heads facing inward, blowing venom onto the murderers and oath-breakers below. This may be a very late source, heavily influenced by Christian thinking, but it does confirm two things: (1) the Norse, like the Saxons, knew and understood venom; and (2) venom was produced by a certain class of wights known as serpents or wyrms. A parallel can be found here with other shamanic cultures, particularly in the Amazon, where the spirits of disease are often seen as snakes or spiders ready to bite and inject venom into their victims.

Dealing with Venom

Venom is essentially one of the unconscious heavy energies that are so prevalent in the world. When accidentally picked up by someone and taken into the energetic body, venom begins to break down that body, weakening the victim and eventually leading to imbalance and disease. But because venom is non-sentient—or, at best, semi-sentient—once it is in the energetic body, venom can be dealt with and removed relatively easily by someone who knows what they are doing. Venom is handled in the same way as other heavy energies: through extraction and conversion into a lighter energy. If you have accomplished some basic healing using seiðr, the chances are that you may have already dealt with some venom without even realizing it.

In addition to being released accidentally as a kind of environmental pollutant like other heavy energies, venom has the distinction that it can also be actively created and targeted at someone. This is confirmed by the Anglo-Saxon "Nine Herbs Charm," which is designed to break up venom while in flight, before it enters the body, as well as dealing with any venom that does get through the victim's defenses. Venom, therefore, seems to be the Germanic equivalent of tsentsak, the spiritual dart used in Shuar shamanic warfare. In the Germanic context, such spiritual warfare can be equated with gandr.

BASIC GANDR

As we have noted earlier, the ancient Germanic peoples did not view things in simple black-and-white terms as good or evil. Since gandr interferes with the will (vili) of the victim, it is a technique that falls well into the dark-gray area of the moral spectrum and should be viewed with some suspicion. Nevertheless, I am including here for the sake of completeness, as gandr was an important part of seiðr in the past. Also, like the Allfather, I believe that all knowledge is important—and in the case of something like gandr, knowledge of how it works will make it easier to defend against. The good news is that the effects of gandr are relatively easy to treat by means of extraction, and this is true even in situations where the underlying cause is not self-evident.

There is one other reason why it is important to provide some information about a "shamanic warfare" technique such as gandr. From a spiritual standpoint, we are living in increasingly dangerous times. More and more people are getting involved with alternative spiritual paths and are seeking knowledge about ancient practices such as seiðr. But a little knowledge can be a very dangerous thing. There are many so-called spiritual people out there with huge egos, who very quickly and with little provocation tend to leap to the offensive as their first response to any perceived threat, no matter how slight. Unfortunately, it is likely that at some stage in your seiðr work you will come under a direct attack from a rival. Only you can determine what the appropriate response will be, but as a spiritual worker, the Germanic gods fully expect you to be prepared for anything that comes your way. Personally, because of the effects on my own ørlög, my predetermined path through life has been relatively good, which has meant that I have never had to consider initiating a preemptive strike against anyone as a prudent move. I have been forced to respond to incoming attacks by occasionally going on the offensive, however.

It is not my place to act as a gatekeeper and dictate to you what you should and should not do. That is entirely your own responsibility. I will, however, offer a warning: working within a heathen framework, we do not have the Wiccan rede "An' it harm none" or the threefold "Law of Return." But we do have the concept of Wyrd, which means that all our actions have consequences—some of these will be obvious, others much less so; some beneficial, some distinctly not. *It is only worth using gandr if you are confident that the potentially negative consequences of inaction outweigh those of action.*

❀ Gandr Workings

Gandr work is all about preparation. It is difficult to accomplish this in the heat of battle, so everything should be made ready beforehand. The first thing you must do is to prepare your gandr or göndul, which is your wand. The sources are clear that a shorter staff or wand was used for gandr work, not the full-length seiðstafr. In other traditions the perfect length for a wand is said to be the length from your elbow to your fingertips, and this works for gandr as well. You can, of course, buy a premade wand, though I would advise it is far preferable to find and craft your own. In this case, you can make use of the methodology outlined in the section of chapter 3 on the seiðstafr. The same guidelines about types of wood also apply, although I would note that in light of the particular use a gandr will be put to, blackthorn also makes an excellent choice. Just like a seiðstafr, the gandr will need seasoning before use. You can decorate your gandr as you see fit.

Once your gandr had been prepared, you will need to obtain a varðloka for use when working with serpents and wyrms. To do this, you may have to journey to the wyrm Níðhöggr and ask for his help. Once you have your varðloka, journey as you normally would, setting your intention "To prepare my gandr." Travel to the lower worlds—in this case, traveling to Jötunheim may be most appropriate for this work of finding your serpent. Try to find a serpent wight, one that will agree to come and live in your gandr with you. If a spirit is to live permanently in your gandr, you should be aware that it will need to be "fed" and honored at regular intervals, like following a dieta. Be sure to ask it what it requires, and to fulfill anything it requests. If you agree, witness as the spirit enters your gandr. You will need to adhere to any schedule if there is something that must be repeated (like "feeding" the serpent-gandr wight).

໒ Sending Venom with Gandr

When it comes time to use the gandr, sing your varðloka but while remaining in semi-trance and holding in your mind the specific intention to do damage to your enemies, watch as the wight in the gandr awakes and begins to produce venom. Using the tip of the gandr, direct the venom toward your target and witness as the venom strikes and penetrates the energetic body of the target. This is basic gandr work, which means its efficacy may be limited. If the target possesses occult or esoteric knowledge and has prepared for your attack using some form of protection, particularly shamanic protection, then the venom may not be able to penetrate. In this case, a more advanced form of offensive working may be required.

The above methodology was used in the battlefield and is most effective against warriors and other non-spirit workers who have no defenses. The venom requires a gap or weakness—caused by other intrusions or soul loss—in the energetic body to enter the latter and begin to work. However, as we pointed out in the chapter on healing, such gaps and weaknesses are very common for people in Western societies, and this is even true for other spirit workers, unless they have recently undergone shamanic healing. If the target is using any form of shamanic protection, they become "power-full," which fills in the gaps in their energetic field. In this case, the venom will simply bounce off—and if it does not dissipate quickly, it can become a hazard for the next person to come along who does have gaps in their energetic body. Gandr can be effective against other spirit workers if they are not expecting it, in which case they may be defenseless and unprepared in the face of an attack.

With a gandr attack what you are doing is essentially introducing a chronic disease into the target's system—a disease that will gradually worsen the longer it remains in the body. Because this is created from venom and delivered with the specific intention of doing harm, it tends to be more powerful than the general heavy energies that are typically created as the result of generalized anger and frustration with the world at large. The effects of venom are faster-acting and lead to more severe results than other heavy energies. Used as a battle weapon in heathen times, venom had immediate effects upon striking the target. It would induce weakness and debility, which in turn compromised the enemy's performance. Even momentary weakness is enough to make a warrior vulnerable in battle. And even if the enemy's hamingja was strong enough to ensure his immediate survival, the venom would linger in his energetic field, eroding both hamingja and health over the long term. The victim's luck would worsen and their health would deteriorate until they eventually became overwhelmed.

ꖴ Treating Venom

For anyone who knows how to recognize it and who is familiar with shamanic healing work, venom is relatively easy to deal with. It simply requires an extraction to remove it from the energetic body and then it can be converted into lighter energy. However, it is also the case that someone with this type of knowledge will be able to trace the venom back to its source—in other words, back to the sorcerer who sent it (which, depending on the circumstances, might also mean back to you!). In the worst-case scenario, the discovery of the source might lead to a shamanic flame war.

If you do use gandr and it is effective, you might subsequently decide that your victim has learnt their lesson. Here again, the good thing about venom is the relative ease with which it can be removed from the target. For the sake of your own ørlög, it is important to learn when enough is enough and when to extend the hand of reconciliation and healing.

Variants of Gandr: Glamor

In Old Norse literature there is a name that turns up, Gandálfr, which literally translates as "wand-elf." (Yes, this is where Tolkien got the name Gandalf.) The entire name may have originally referred to a spirit worker who specializes in wand magic or gandr. However, there is a particular type of wand magic mentioned in the sagas, whereby someone struck with a wand becomes very confused and potentially even loses their mind. (Needless to say, the ability to make an enemy lose their wits in the midst of battle would be a very useful skill!) The first part of the name, *gand-*, clearly refers to a "wand," the second part, *álfr*, means "elf." The elves are recognized as magic users and spirit workers, and in many cultures around the world they are particularly known for a type of magic known as "glamor" (or "glamour"). Glamor is the art of illusion—making things appear to be what they are not—and of confusing the mind.

If you have any sort of relationship with the álfar, then glamor can potentially be used to replace venom in basic gandr work. To do this, you will need to persuade the álfar to help. This is easier said than done, however, as the álfar are notoriously tricky and even more demanding to work with than serpents or wyrms. Here I can provide some pointers.

It is unwise to mix venom and glamor, so you will need to have a separate gandr that is specifically dedicated for the latter purpose. This gandr can be fashioned in exactly the same manner as any other one. While it is extremely unlikely that you will be able to persuade an álfr to take up actual residence in your wand, you may be able persuade them to create an individual glamor for you that could be stored in your wand (in the same way that the plant spirits of the Amazon create a tsentsak that is then stored in the shaman's throat). The cost of creating such a glamor is likely to far exceed that of venom, as the álfr may make high demands with respect to compensation. So, if you decide to go ahead with this, make sure you provide whatever the álfr requests—you really do not want to make an enemy of the álfar!

Glamor is directed at your target in a similar way to venom, but in this case the sagas are clear in stating that the victim must be *physically touched* by the wand. This contact should be made at a point of weakness in the target's energetic body. Therefore, you will at least need to be in a semi-trance state to see these gaps in the target.

What are the effects of such an attack? The advantage of glamor is that, unlike venom, it cannot be dealt with by a simple extraction. Once introduced, it must run its course. However, one of the disadvantages of glamor is that it is not permanent. The duration of its effects depends on the relative power of the álfr that created it. It is also possible, through your intention, to introduce psychological suggestions alongside the glamor when it enters the target. Depending on the intention, glamor can be like a heavy dose of psychedelic drugs, which causes the target to feel bombarded by enjoyable sensations. Because these feelings are pleasurable, the target subconsciously submits to them, but in reality becomes twisted according to the intention of the sender: what the target "sees" is completely under the control of the glamor. At the same time, it becomes hard for the target to resist any psychological suggestions, provided these do not completely go against the target's ingrained morals and ethics.

Epilogue

Seiðr is a very wide-ranging discipline that encompasses nearly all of the key functions of shamanism, including: (1) divination; (2) healing; (3) harming and battle magic; (4) dealing with the surrounding environment and the spirits of nature; (5) dealing with the ancestors and the dead, and (6) dealing with the gods. Contrary to popular belief, seiðr can be practiced by anyone with a basic aptitude, not just women. Seiðr is essentially based on ecstatic trance, which clearly distinguishes it from modern pagan traditions like witchcraft and Wicca. The techniques of the latter are incompatible with historical seiðr, which differs from witchcraft in its very foundations.

This book represents just a "taster" of some of the basic techniques involved in seiðr. While it is certainly not comprehensive, each technique has been specifically chosen so that the beginning practitioner will gain some experience in each of the aforementioned functions. For the prospective völva or seiðmaðr, it is my hope that the mastery of these skills will provide a basic foundation from which you will be able to go on to learn some of the advanced—and potentially riskier—techniques such as the high-seat rite (the historical precedent for which is found in *Eirik the Red's Saga*). As a more advanced practitioner, you will be able to develop your own practice, which may include (re-)discovering techniques and methods through UPG.

After all, seiðr was hardly static and unchanging when it was historically practiced. Each practitioner undoubtedly had their own specific ways of doing things within the overall framework of the tradition. The advent of Christianity in northern Europe brought about the end of seiðr in the medieval period. But even if the practice of seiðr had continued without interruption, it is ridiculous to think that its methodology would have remained static over the intervening millennia. We do not live in ninth-century Scandinavia, and as modern practitioners it is up to us to develop a living, growing tradition that is every bit as relevant to our lives today as it was to our ancestors in their own time.

The operative word here is *practice*. As my teachers used to say: *There is no such thing as an armchair shaman.* You can read as many books on the subject as you like, and you can pontificate endlessly about the finer points of theory, but you will never become a seiðr-worker unless you go out and try some of this. Experience is the key.

So, now is the time to get out of that armchair, step into the outside world, immerse yourself in nature, and really try some of the exercises. Don't worry if you only have limited success the first time around. Most of this takes a bit of practice, particularly if you are not used to working with ecstatic trance in non-ordinary reality. But if you have the basic potential, you'll get there eventually—so don't give up!

Glossary of Terms

Note: All foreign terms are Old Norse unless indicated otherwise.

Æsir: "the gods"; the primary pantheon of Norse deities, including Óðinn, Thor, Baldr, and others. *See also* Vanir.

álfr (**pl.** *álfar*): "elf"; a type of Germanic wight that inhabits the middle realm of Ljósálfheim ("Light-elf Home"). Some elves may also live in the middle realm of Svartálfheim ("Dark-elf Home").

Allfather: An epithet for Óðinn as the "father of all" and high god of the Norse pantheon. Old Norse *Alföðr*.

argr: "unmanly, effeminate, cowardly"; an Old Norse adjective used to describe male practitioners of seiðr in medieval texts.

axis mundi: The "world axis" or central column connecting the lower, middle, and upper realms in many shamanic cosmologies. In Norse shamanism it is typically the World Tree Yggdrasil.

blót: The central ceremony in heathenism in which an offering is made to one or more gods, or to other wights. Typically, a blót is led by a ritual specialist or religious leader. *See also* goði; gyðja.

bowli: A bowl in which offerings are placed on a private altar or as part of a blót ceremony.

cofgod (**pl.** **cofgodas**): "chamber god"; a domestic house spirit. Old English *cōfgod*, pl. *cōfgodas*.

dieta: A feature of some South American shamanic cultures (such as the Shipibo) whereby a shaman undergoes a period of isolation, fasting, and abstinence during which spiritual insight or knowledge is received. *See also* icaro.

dís (**pl.** *dísir*): A female ancestral spirit that helps guide the life of a descendant. *See also* Norn.

draugr (**pl.** *draugar*): A restless spirit of the dead that still has an attachment to their former body; a revenant.

dvergr (**pl.** *dvergar*): "dwarf"; a type of Germanic wight that inhabits the middle realm of Svartálfheim.

einherjar: "single warriors"; those who have died in battle and are brought by valkyries to Óðinn's hall of Valhalla, where they feast and prepare for the final battle of Ragnarok as members of his troop.

energetic body: The outer "shell" of the greater soul complex. In Norse terms, the energetic body is the hamr. *See also* hamr.

ergi: "lewdness, perversity"; an Old Norse noun used in medieval texts to describe seiðr, especially when done by male practitioners.

etin: "giant"; a type of wight such as a jötunn or troll that embodies uncontrolled forces of nature and wilderness. The term derives from Old English *eoten*.

fetch: A term from English folklore that refers to one of the major soul parts. Sometimes used in modern heathenism as equivalent to the fylgja. *See* fylgja.

fylgja: "follower"; one of the major soul parts, which is sometimes referred to as the "animal soul" of a person. At the time of death for most people, the fylgja also acts as a psychopomp.

galdr: lit. "cawing of crows"; a general term for magic that employs chanting or sound.

gandr: A type of "sending sorcery," often malefic, that has several different variants depending on when and where it was practiced. In some cases it can refer to "wand magic."

Gjallarbrú: The bridge over the river Gjöll that must be traversed by the dead to reach and enter Helheim. *See also* helvegr.

glamor (glamour): A form of gandr that uses enchantment to cause illusion and confusion. *See also* gandr.

***goði* (pl. *goðar*)**: A male heathen spiritual leader and ritual specialist.

göndul: A wand used in Germanic gandr magic. *See* gandr.

***gyðja* (pl. *gyðjur*)**: A female heathen spiritual leader and ritual specialist.

hamingja: Innate "luck" or spiritual power in a person that contributes to their personal efficacy. *See also* megin.

hamr: "shape" or "skin"; the outer "shell" of the soul complex that also determines the shape of the lík.

***hamr*-craft**: The art of shapeshifting.

***haugbúi* (pl. *haugbúar*)**: lit. "cairn dweller"; an earthbound spirit of the dead.

helvegr: "Hel Path"; the route that must be taken by the dead to reach Helheim.

high-seat rite: A larger-scale seiðr divination ceremony, a historical example of which is described in *Eirik the Red's Saga*.

hollow bone: A phrase describing the seiðr-worker as a vehicle for the wights, who are the real agents of healing.

hugr: "thought" or "mind"; one of the major soul parts, the hugr can be seen as constituting the "true" self. The hugr may, in turn, consist of further subparts. *See also* hamingja; móðr; munr; vé; vili.

Hvergelmir: One of the three wells or springs at the roots of Yggdrasil. Hvergelmir is the source of the nine rivers that flow into each of the Nine Worlds.

icaro (pl. *icaros*): Magical and medicinal healing songs used by shamanic cultures in the Amazon such as the Shipibo.

jötunn (pl. *jötnar*): "giant"; a type of wight that embodies uncontrolled forces of nature and wilderness. The jötnar inhabit the lower realm of Jötunheim ("Etin Home"). *See also* etin.

landvættr (pl. *landvættir*): "land-wight"; a land spirit tied to a specific area or geographical feature.

law of sovereignty: A recognition common to all shamanic modalities that each person is the sole ruler of their own body, mind, and spirit (soul complex), and therefore no external spirit can affect any of these without the express consent of their owner.

lich: An archaic English word (usually describing a corpse) that is sometimes used as an alternate term for *lík* (to which it is cognate). *See* lík.

lík: The soul part roughly corresponding to the physical body; it is connected to the rest of the soul complex by the animating force of the önd. *See also* önd.

lore ("the lore"): The collective body of ancient literature that concerns heathen beliefs and practices, such as the Eddas (poetic and prose), the Icelandic sagas, and other written or epigraphical sources.

megin: "might" (or, more loosely, "honor"); a non-innate form of personal power that can be accrued by an individual as a result of their actions, and which then serves to benefit their efficacy. *See also* hamingja.

Mímisbrunnr: "Mímir's Well"; one of the three wells or springs at the roots of Yggdrasil.

Mjöllnir: The name of Thor's magical hammer; also refers to small, hammer-shaped amulets worn by some heathens as a means to honor the god and display a sign of their religion.

móðr: "mood"; the seat of the emotions in the Germanic soul complex. The móðr may be a subpart of the hugr. *See also* hugr.

munr: "memory"; a minor soul part that may or may not be distinct from the hugr. *See also* hugr.

myrkriða (pl. myrkriður): "dark rider"; an epithet for a sorcerer/sorceress or "dark seiðr-worker" who works malefic magic.

noaidi: A traditional healer or shaman among the Sámi.

Norn: A goddess or wight associated with fate. The three greater Norns (Urðr, Verðandi, and Skuld) are connected to the workings of Wyrd. The lesser Norns (some of whom may be synonymous with the dísir) are supernatural figures associated with the birth, life, and ørlög of each human being. Old Norse *norn*, pl. *nornir. See also* dís; ørlög; Urðarbrunnr; Wyrd.

önd: "sacred breath"; a gift of Óðinn that ties the lík to the rest of the soul complex. At death, the önd returns to Óðinn. *See also* lík.

ongon: A spirit house in traditional Mongolian shamanism.

ørlög: "that which has been laid down"; a term for fate or destiny, either on a universal level (as part of Wyrd) or personal level (in terms of an individual's lifetime).

Ragnarok: The "twilight of the gods" or mythological final battle between the Æsir and the forces of destruction, which is then followed by a time of rebirth. Old Norse *ragnarökr* or *ragnarøkr*.

reykelsi: Old Norse term for incense (borrowed from Old English *rēcels*).

rime thurse: A frost giant. Old Norse *hrímþurs,* pl. *hrímþursar.*

runemaster: Someone skilled in the use of the runes for communication and magic.

sax: A traditional single-edged Germanic knife, used for many purposes including magic and seiðr. The Old English equivalent is *seax.*

seiðhjallr: "seiðr-platform"; a raised platform or ritual scaffold from which a seiðr-worker performs divination in more advanced ceremonies. *See also* high-seat rite.

seiðkona **(pl.** *seiðkonur***):** "seiðr woman"; a female practitioner of seiðr.

seiðmaðr **(pl.** *seiðmenn***):** "seiðr man"; a male practitioner of seiðr (although the term *maðr* could also refer to persons of either sex).

seiðstafr **(pl.** *seiðstafir***):** "seiðr staff"; an iron or wooden staff used by a seiðr-worker for divination and healing, as well as for inducing trance by tapping.

spákona **(pl.** *spákonur***):** "spae woman"; a prophetess who uses seiðr to gain a wider glimpse into the workings of Wyrd.

shared personal gnosis (SPG): Knowledge or insight gained by a group of practitioners, which may or may not correspond to the existing body of traditional lore.

sumbl: "feast"; a heathen drinking ceremony in which the participants make ritualized toasts, boasts, and oaths.

tauframaðr **(pl.** *tauframenn***):** "charms man"; a dubious enchanter or peddler of cheap amulets, false elixirs, and cures.

tiver: A red-ochre paste used for coloring runes in magical work.

tsentsak: A spirit dart used in spiritual warfare by shamans of the Shuar (Jivaro) in the Amazon.

trolldómr: A general term for magic and sorcery.

unverified personal gnosis (UPG): Knowledge or insight gained by a practitioner, which may or may not correspond to the existing body of traditional lore.

Urðarbrunnr: "Well of Urðr" or "Well of Wyrd"; one of the three wells or springs at the roots of Yggdrasil. The Urðarbrunnr is tended by the greater Norns. *See also* Norn.

valkyrie: "chooser of the slain"; a female psychopomp assigned by Óðinn to escort the souls of dead warriors to Valhalla. Old Norse *valkyrja*, pl. *valkyrjur*.

Vanir: A second family of Norse deities that includes Freyja, Frey, and Njörðr, and is associated with the realm of Vanaheim ("Vanir Home"). After losing a battle with the Æsir, the Vanir is incorporated into the latter. *See also* Æsir.

varðloka (**pl. *varðlokur*)**: "ward song"; a magical chant or song used in seiðr for inducing a trance journey for a specific purpose.

vé: "holy enclosure"; (1) a general term for a sacred enclosure or altar; (2) a minor soul part that encompasses psychic abilities. Vé is also the name of one of Óðinn's two brothers, with whom he slays the giant Ymir and then uses his corpse to create the world in the Norse cosmogony myth. *See also* hugr.

vili: "will"; a minor soul part that concerns the capacity of free will. Vili is also the name of one of Óðinn's two brothers, with whom he slays the giant Ymir and then uses his corpse to create the world in the Norse cosmogony myth. *See also* hugr.

vitka (**pl. *vitkur*)**: A sorceress who may also be specialized in rune work.

vitki (**pl. *vitkir*)**: A sorcerer who may also be specialized in rune work.

völva, **pl. *völur*:** "staff-bearer"; a female seiðr-worker.

Well of Wyrd: (1) the Urðarbrunnr; (2) a collective term for the workings of the three wells at the roots of Yggdrasil. *See also* Hvergelmir; Mímisbrunnr; Urðarbrunnr.

wight: A general term for a spirit or being. It can be used to refer to divine and lesser spirits, as well as mortal and organic creatures of all kinds. The corresponding Old Norse term is *vættr,* pl. *vættir.*

Wyrd: A term from Old English that denotes "fate" or "destiny" in a larger sense. Cognate with Old Norse *urðr,* "fate." *See also* Urðarbrunnr; Well of Wyrd.

Yggdrasil: The World Ash tree that forms the central column of the Norse cosmology, vertically traversing the three realms (lower, middle, and upper) and encompassing the Nine Worlds in its roots and branches. *See also* axis mundi; Well of Wyrd.

Works Cited

Bellows, Henry Adams, trans. 1923. *The Poetic Edda*. New York: American-Scandinavian Foundation.

Bray, Olive, trans. 1908. *Sæmund's Edda: Part I—The Mythological Poems*. London: Viking Club.

Cleasby, Richard, and Gudbrand Vigfusson. 1874. *An Icelandic-English Dictionary*. Oxford: Clarendon.

Dickins, Bruce. 1915. *Runic and Heroic Poems of the Old Teutonic Peoples*. Cambridge: Cambridge University Press.

Eliade, Mircea. 1964. *Shamanism: Archaic Techniques of Ecstasy*. New York: Pantheon.

Flowers, Stephen E., and James A. Chisholm. 2015. *A Source-Book of* Seið*: The Corpus of Old Icelandic Texts Dealing with* Seið *and Related Words*. Bastrop, TX: Lodestar.

Harner, Michael. 1980. *The Way of the Shaman*. New York: Harper and Row.

Heick, William, and Gordon Mueller. 1963. *Pomo Shaman*. Film.

———. 1963. *Sucking Doctor*. Film.

Hollander, Lee M., trans. 2011. *The Poetic Edda*. Austin: University of Texas Press.

Larrington, Carolyne, trans. 2014. *The Poetic Edda*. Revised edition. Oxford: Oxford University Press.

Lecouteux, Claude. 2013. *The Tradition of Household Spirits: Ancestral Lore and Practices*. Translated by Jon E. Graham. Rochester, VT: Inner Traditions.

———. 2015. *Demons and Spirits of the Land: Ancestral Lore and Practices*. Translated by Jon E. Graham. Rochester, VT: Inner Traditions.

———. 2018. *The Hidden History of Elves and Dwarves: Avatars of Invisible Realms*. Rochester, VT: Inner Traditions.

Magnússon, Finnur. 1824. *Eddalæren og dens Oprindelse*. Copenhagen: Gyldendal.

Price, Neil. 2019. *The Viking Way: Magic and Mind in Late Iron Age Scandinavia*. Oxford: Oxbow.

Rysdyk, Evelyn C. 2016. *The Norse Shaman: Ancient Spiritual Practices of the Northern Tradition*. Rochester, VT: Destiny.

Sammarco, Francesco. "Icaros: Magical Songs of the Amazon." *Sacred Hoop* 68 (2010) : 20–24.

Sephton, John, trans. 1880. *Eirik the Red's Saga*. Liverpool: Marples.

Smiley, Jane, ed. 2005. *The Sagas of Icelanders*. London: Penguin Classics.

Sturluson, Snorri. 1916. *The Prose Edda*. Translated by Arthur Gilchrist Brodeur. New York: American-Scandinavian Foundation.

Thorsson, Edred. 2016. *The Nine Doors of Midgard: A Curriculum of Rune-work*. Fifth revised and expanded edition. South Burlington, VT: Rune-Gild.

———. 2021. *Rune-Song: A Guide to Galdor*. North Augusta, SC: Arcana Europa.

Index